Harry Potter
for Nerds

Essays For Fans,
Academics, and Lit Geeks

Edited by

Travis Prinzi

This book has not been prepared, approved, or licensed by any person or entity that created, published, or produced the *Harry Potter* books or related properties. Harry Potter, characters, names, and related indicia are trademarks of Warner Bros. and **Harry Potter** Publishing Rights © J. K. Rowling

Harry Potter for Nerds
Copyright © 2011 Travis Prinzi

All rights reserved. Except in the case of quotations embodied in critical articles or reviews, no part of this book may be reproduced or transmitted in any form or by any means, electronic or mechanical, including photo-copying, recording, or by any information storage or retrieval system, without written permission of the publisher.

For information, contact Unlocking Press
www.UnlockingPress.com

Unlocking Press titles may be purchased for business or promotional use or special sales.

Cover Design by Aaron J. Smith
10 - 9 - 8 - 7 - 6 - 5 - 4 - 3 - 2 - 1

www.UnlockingPress.com

97809829633-2-6

For Jack William,
future nerd

Table of Contents

Harry Potter for Nerds:
Why Elvendork Magic is Cool

Travis Prinzi

T HE COOLEST KID IN the entire world is a wizard with dorky, spello-taped glasses. He believes in dragons, unicorns and spells, dark arts and good magic, phoenixes and hippogriffs. And he takes all these things seriously.

In short, the coolest kid in the entire world is a complete nerd.

I remember the first time I was at a Harry Potter conference. Somehow, the nerdiness of it all didn't strike me until partway through. I remember thinking, perhaps two days in, "Oh no...I'm at a Star Trek Convention!" In other words, it occurred to me that I had become a part of the newest group of nerds, uniting around a fictional world, even going so far as to dress up in costumes and get together by the thousands to talk about our beloved fantasy series. I realized at Prophecy 2007 (HPEF) that just as Star Trek fans still gather together decades after the series originally aired, 30 or 40 years from now, there very well may be Harry Potter conventions.

Jim Dale, reader of the U.S. versions of the audiobooks, made a very astute observation at our press conference with him at Portus 2008 (HPEF) in Dallas. He said that the conference was just amazing, because there were people walking around the hotel in wizards robes and all kinds of costumes, and then there were all the people who were not there for the conference, just regular travelers, who were paying no attention to the robed witches and wizards at all. It was just like a Harry Potter book, he said![1]

I'm throwing that word "nerd" around, and you're probably wondering what I mean by it. Or more likely, you're probably having visions of nerds yourself: Screech from *Saved by the Bell*, for example, or maybe the *Revenge of the Nerds* films. Nerds are generally thought of as socially awkward or isolated, primarily due to their obsession with either academics in general or one particular subject, e.g. computer nerds. Nerds are not the cool and popular ones in school. They're the ones you cheat off of in math or physics. While most of the school is out drinking after the football game, nerds are gathered in a basement somewhere playing Dungeons and Dragons.

Or reading *Harry Potter*.

Perhaps a more recent nerd will help us get a handle on the perception of nerdiness: Dwight K. Schrute, from *The Office*. Dwight is painfully socially awkward, has a nerdy haircut, big glasses, and he loves *Battlestar Galactica* and, you guessed it, *Harry Potter*. When Jim and Pam agree to a getaway at Dwight's Bed and Breakfast on his beet farm, one of their amenities is a bedtime reading of *Harry Potter and the Goblet of Fire*.

Return to that word "obsession" - nerds are involved in some kind of obsession, and what comes to mind most often are things like computers, fantasy, science fiction, and other

---

1. To hear our entire press conference with Jim Dale, listen to Hog's Head PubCast #56, which can be found at http://thehogshead.org/hogs-head-pubcast-56-jim-dale-press-conference-814/

technical-type stuff. J.K. Rowling told Stephen Fry that *Harry Potter* is "a book for obsessives."

> The funny thing is that I did always think that, if it ever did get published, it was a book for obsessives. I'm quite an obsessive person. I think you can probably tell.[2]

In other words, *Harry Potter* is a book by a nerd, for nerds.

So if *Harry Potter* fits into the world of nerds, and nerds are generally awkward, isolated, and unpopular, why, Mr. Prinzi, are you associating yourself with it, and writing books about it?

A fantastic question. Thank you for asking. Because nerd is the new cool.

Not that I've ever cared that much about being cool. In high school, plenty of the popular kids were nice to me and included me in their conversations; I chose to grow ugly, awkward facial hair, don beat-up flannel, and hang with the Nirvana fans instead. But I'm noticing, with many others, a cultural shift in the perception of nerds, geeks and dorks. J.K. Rowling followed up her comment about "obsessives" with this:

> And I did think if people liked it they would probably like it obsessively. I just never.... but I thought that it would be an obsessive few – I never guessed it would be an obsessive many, as has happened.

The "obsessive many." What a great phrase. Notice the set-up: "it would be an obsessive few"; in other words, a small gathering of nerds. It turns out there are a lot of us. And much like Harry discovered his wizard status from Hagrid, many of us have discovered our nerd status from Harry.

As I've already argued above, the coolest kid in the world is a nerd. A few weeks ago, sitting in a doctor's office, I noticed a copy of *Entertainment Weekly* with the stars of the fantastic movie, <u>The Social Network</u> on the cover, and the words: "The

2 http://www.accio-quote.org/articles/2000/0700-bloomsbury-fry.html

Sexiest Geeks Alive." Sexy geeks? Really? Nerds and geeks are finding a regular and influential place in society, and Rowling even gives a nod to dorks: "Elvendork - it's unisex!" Don't worry if you're not the popular kid: nerds, geeks and dorks are taking over the world, it appears.[3]

We are the obsessive many, the Harry Potter nerds, the lit geeks, the elvendorks.

If you're not already aware of them, look up the Nerd Fighters. John Green called Nerd Fighters, "nerds who tackle the scourge of popular people." With that in mind, let's rejoin Harry (this is an essay about Harry) at the beginning of his fifth year at Hogwarts.

Our young hero has spent several years alternating between being the Wizarding World's most popular kid and being a social outcast. In his first year, he arrives as hero of the world, and he ends up being a big sports star, too. In his second year, people decide he's the heir of Slytherin. (Huge turnaround, that.) In the third year, he's essentially back to hero status, but in the fourth, the whole school thinks he's a cheater and he has a very awkward and nerd-like experience at the high school dance (Yule Ball). When we hit the fifth year, we're hoping the poor kid gets a break again, especially since Voldemort had just lured him to a graveyard where he stole his blood and almost killed him.

This is not what we get. Harry gets on the train for his fifth year of Hogwarts and, after being kept out of the loop for months, would like nothing more than to have a moment to impress the popular, pretty girl, Cho Chang. It backfires, and you remember how: he finds himself in a compartment filled with nerds. By the time Cho finds him, he's covered in stink sap from Neville's magical plant. While he does manage to "get the girl" in this book, two important considerations come into play: (1) He gets her in the first place by being a nerd, and (2) he loses her

3. http://www.youtube.com/watch?v=tuvCb5eBbjE&feature=channel

because he's a nerd.

How does he get her by being a nerd? Think about it: he leads a study group. About a school subject. It even has an immensely nerdy name: Dumbledore's Army. Now, this might seem even more nerdy if not for the fact that their teacher was an awful, oppressive toad, and learning this school subject was literally life or death. But that's a big part of being a nerd, really: believing that learning the academic stuff really matters.

So Harry hooks up with Cho as a result of a study group where they practice magic, and he loses her because he's as socially awkward and clueless as it gets. Cho wants to do all the expected things that popular kids do, like getting all romantic and Madam Puddifoot's. One can easily imagine Cedric Diggory navigating Cho's expectations with smooth, easy confidence. Harry is socially awkward and doesn't have the first idea what one would do in Madam Puddifoot's tea shop.

The nerds continue their meetings, and all the study pays off when they find themselves in a real-life battle with Death Eaters. After this, Harry's status as social outcast ends, and he becomes the "chosen one" and the most popular kid in the world.

Then he rejects it. On the train to school his sixth year, he chooses deliberately to sit with the nerds. When the popular kids explain to him that he doesn't have to associate with them anymore, he calls them his friends. Harry has embraced his inner nerd, and being the most popular kid in the world, he has affirmed and vindicated all of nerddom.

I mentioned earlier the "sexiest geeks in the world." The reference is to Mark Zuckerberg, founder of Facebook, and his friends and enemies. It's precisely this kind of social networking - Facebook and the more Potter-specific sites and discussions groups like HPforGrownUps, HPEF, The Leaky Cauldron and Mugglenet - that have created a space for nerds to come together. Having found each other online, we couldn't leave it there, so visionaries began putting together conferences. The most recent one, as of my writing of this essay, saw about 2500 fans descend upon the new Wizarding World of Harry Potter for a few straight days of academic nerdiness and frivolity.

Out of these conferences comes not only a good deal of creativity and fun, but serious academic discussion - sort of a group of extreme nerds within a group of nerds. The book you're holding in your hand is a book written by nerds, for nerds. At the end of this book, you can "meet the nerds" by reading their biographies. I want to tell you a little bit about their essays and why I included them.

The lead essay in this volume is Sandra Miesel's "Is There Hope for Slytherin House? or Can the Serpent Change Its Skin?" I remember standing in the registration line at Prophecy 2007, my first HP conference, and being asked what house I wanted to be in. I replied, "Oh, Gryffinder, like everyone else probably." "Oh no," came back the shocking response. "Most people want to be in Slytherin." I was taken aback by this, but I've found it pretty consistently true: Slytherin is pretty popular. But then, Slytherin actually fits the "popular" category at Hogwarts. These are the rich kids, the ones with influence in society. So as a fully-credentialed nerd, we have to ask the question, "Is there any hope for them?"

We then dive into nerdiness at its best and most potent: Two essays on literary chiasmus.

On what?

Literary chiasmus. Can't you read? The first essay of these two essays, by Steve Lee, will lay out nicely the concept of chiasmus, some important thoughts on why it's used, and how Rowling created the entire series on a chiastic structure. The essay provides 3 helpful charts for seeing the important parallels between books 1 and 7, 2 and 6, 3 and 5.

John Granger, then, my good friend, fellow Potter Pundit, and "The Dean of Harry Potter Scholars,"[4] delves into the meaning of literary chiasmus and shows us how the entire series turns on *Harry Potter and the Goblet of Fire*. At this point, you'll realize at least two things: This series provides endless fascination, and Rowling is a genius. And let's face it: You just can't go wrong with a John Granger essay. Over the past 6 years, nothing has increased my appreciation for Potter more than my discussions with John.

James W. Thomas, our other esteemed Pundit, gives us a course in Muggle Studies that is not to be missed. What is the real meaning of the magic in *Harry Potter*, and what do we find when we compare magic to technology? James always delivers, clearly and powerfully, the heart of the *Harry Potter* stories.

Joel Hunter continues this theme with "Technology Anarchy," an essay that explores the moral and ethical implications of the use technological advances. I first met Joel at the Barrett Honors College at Arizona State University, where he was serving as the faculty representative for a Harry Potter Society. In a Saturday morning discussion with the society, we got onto the subjects of magic, science and technology, and Joel challenged the group with a poignant question: As we continue to advance technology, we need to ask ourselves - just because we can do something, does that mean we should?

Speaking of that Barrett Honors Society, Kathleen Langr was one of its officers, and she's also brilliant with languages. So when I discovered she was presenting a paper on swearing in *Harry Potter* at Infinitus 2010, I knew it needed to be in a book about *Harry Potter* and nerds. Does it get any nerdier than that?

Speaking of Infinitus 2010, about 2,500 nerds attended this conference at Universal Studios and got their first look at

---

4. http://techland.com/2009/08/28/john-granger-dean-of-harry-potter-scholars-the-nerd-world-interview/ - Note the title: It's a "Nerd World Interview."

the Wizarding World of Harry Potter. Priscilla Hobbs's essay explores this theme park and evaluates whether or not it works as a magical space that embodies the Harry Potter experience.

Then, it's time for astronomy class with two essays on planetary imagery in *Harry Potter*. It turns out, according to Erin Sweeney and Lancelot Schaubert, that the centaurs are onto something when they read meaning in the stars. These two authors serve as your astronomy professors and teach what Rowling was doing with the night skies in the series.

J.K. Rowling stands in a tradition of fantasy literature, so no collection of *Harry Potter* essays would be complete without pointers to the past. Elizabeth Baird Hardy looks at Spenser's *The Faerie Queen* and finds some fascinating connections to Voldemort's Horcruxes, with thematic tie-ins. Even if you've not read Spenser, you'll find this essay intriguing and will probably want to read Spenser when you're done. John Patrick Pazdziora then points us to George MacDonald's handling of the theme of death, which is obviously central to Rowling's stories. It's a common misconception that nerds are interested in things that aren't all that important, and perhaps even immature (like video games). Quite the contrary - our stories, obsessions, and even our video games touch upon some of the most important subjects, like death.

And love. Which leads us to Jenna St. Hilaire's essay on the greatest of all virtues. Just as Rowling gathered together all her ideas and story lines and details and drove us to the power of love, so this book culminates in a reflection on that most important of all subjects - as Dumbledore would say, the most powerful form of magic.

So, my fellow nerds, geeks, and elvendorks, I hope you find this collection of essays both entertaining and instructive, and I cordially invite you to The Hog's Head (http://thehogshead.org) to discuss them when you're done reading.

Is There Hope for Slytherin House?
Can the Serpent Change Its Skin?

Sandra Miesel

But they're not all bad. They literally are not all bad. Well, the deeper answer, the non-flippant answer, would be that you have to embrace all of a person, you have to take them with their flaws, and everybody's got them.

--J. K. Rowling on Slytherins
The Leaky Cauldron, 16 July 2005[1]

C AN SLYTHERIN HOUSE BE saved? *Should* it be? What does the lair of the silver snake contribute to Hogwarts and the wider wizarding world? Wouldn't the ancient school be better off organizing its students as a nice harmonious triad of Mind (Ravenclaw), Body (Hufflepuff) and Spirit (Gryffindor)? Why did J. K. Rowling choose a four-fold structure for Hogwarts, with the houses corresponding to the Four Elements? She assigns Fire to Gryffindor, Air to Ravenclaw, Earth to Hufflepuff and Water to Slytherin.[2]

This symbolic division is far more than a decorative flourish, for nearly every human culture divides the totality of creation into four parts: four directions, four phases of the moon, four seasons, four limbs in a human body and so forth. Associations multiply in Western and Biblical lore, from the four temperaments and the four cardinal virtues to the four living creatures and the four Gospels. (See chart 1) Because four is the number of cosmic ordering, the micro-cosmos of Hogwarts properly has four Houses, just as an ancient city had four quarters springing from a central crossing. The whole cannot exist without all four components—including Slytherin.

But necessity alone cannot make Slytherin House attractive. It seems tainted from the beginning by the sinister character of its fen-born Founder, Salazar Slytherin. Bearing the name of a modern Portuguese dictator, Salazar's withered simian appearance, his rare talent for speaking to snakes, and his bias against Muggles are less than appealing qualities. Yet he was a pre-eminent wizard of his day and—initially—the best friend of his polar opposite, Godric Gryffindor. Then Salazar's growing obsession with purity of blood veered into genocidal hatred that broke the Founders' fellowship. After hiding a basilisk beneath Hogwarts to kill Muggle-born students, Salazar left the school forever. His departure left a permanent imbalance in the system. It was, in effect, the Primal Sin of the wizarding world in Britain. As the Sorting Hat explains:

> And never since the founders four
> Were whittled down to three
> Have the Houses been united
> As they were meant to be.[3]

Afterwards, Slytherin House produced more than its share of Dark Arts adepts, including Tom Riddle/Voldemort. In Harry Potter's time, the House enrolls a clutch of Death Eaters' children. Although they are only a small minority among Slytherins, plot necessity magnifies their prominence. Nevertheless, Slytherin students fail to join the resistance and make themselves scarce during the Battle of Hogwarts.

J. K. Rowling admits that Slytherin "does not encapsulate the most generous and noble qualities,"[4] yet she defends its continuing presence at Hogwarts. She even professes to see "spooky beauty"[5] in its ghoulish cavern of a common room. Most significantly, she holds out hope for Slytherin's future prospects in a re-harmonized tetrad of Houses.

How can this be, given the revulsion snakes stir in most people and the many negative connotations they carry in Western cultures?

The conundrum can be resolved through the language of symbols. Symbolism transcends the boundaries of logic to move in a realm where opposites can coincide and be transformed into a new unity. Symbols connote as well as denote. They are not allegories or signs to be mechanically decoded. "There is no such thing as a symbol, emblem or power with only one kind of meaning," says Mircea Eliade. "Everything hangs together, everything is connected, and makes up a cosmic whole."[6] Only arbitrary man-made labels such as mathematical designations have a 1:1 relationship between signifier and signified. We do not "read" a dollar sign and a rose the same way. Above all, symbols are fluid. They vary within cultures and among cultures,[7] perceived by the imagination more than analyzed by the mind. Labile and polyvalent, altered by time and recast by human effort, symbols evade easy understanding.

Arthurian legends illustrate this evolutionary process: Chrétien de Troyes would be unlikely to recognize his *graal* in the cauldron of the Irish god Dagda or in Dan Brown's Grail. The history of the Tarot offers an even more concentrated example of re-purposed symbols. Two centuries of occultists have imposed their own conflicting interpretations and design modifications on what had originated as an innocent Renaissance card game.[8]

Returning to the Potterverse, each of the Four Elements defining Hogwarts' Houses encompasses positive and negative properties. Earth is womb or tomb for living things. Air in its palpable form as wind refreshes or demolishes. Fire warms or incinerates. Water cleanses or drowns. They may even do both at once: baptismal water combines both spiritual cleansing and drowning to bring forth a new creature reborn in Christ. The

Elements are, of course, far richer in significance than these basic capacities indicate. They are "not the material earth, air, fire and water which we know, but subtle abstract principles emanating from the source of all creation (and are obviously present in the familiar material elements)."[9]

Though all Four Elements matter, Rowling focuses on the conflict between fiery Gryffindor and watery Slytherin: solar gold and red against lunar silver and green. From the novels' Harry-centric viewpoint, readers familiar with the Bible will readily see Gryffindor as the Lion of Judah and Slytherin as the serpent of Eden. Fewer will recall "be wise as serpents (Mt 10:16) or "the devil as a roaring lion" (1 Pet 5:8). Far fewer will remember that lions and snakes are liked together as threats to the Chosen People (Is 30:6) and dangers that the Messiah will trample underfoot (Ps 90/91: 13). Only the truly obsessive will notice that the Bible contains more negative references to lions than to all serpentine beasts combined. Psalm 148 even foresees dragons praising the Lord along with his other creatures (Ps 148: 7, 10).

At the risk of over-proof, this discussion has been necessary to establish the polyvalency of symbols. A fundamental error in many Christian attacks on Harry Potter has been a narrow, simplistic reading of symbolism. To these "Vigilants,"[10] anything serpentine is Satanic and any positive presentation of reptiles confuses essential concepts of right and wrong. Catholic writer Michael O'Brien was a trailbreaker here, years before he turned his attention to Harry Potter. After identifying dragons as universal symbols found throughout the world, "uniformly depicted as malicious and sly," O'Brien says: "In the West, dragons have always been regarded as powerful agents of evil, guardians of stolen treasure hoards, destroyers of the good and the weak (children, maidens, small idyllic kingdoms), and on the spiritual level, a personification of Satan."[11] Furthermore, "the imagination fed on truth knows that the serpent is a symbol of hatred and deceit, of evil knowledge and power without conscience."[12] Cuddly dragons and helpful snakes are abominations in the eyes of Vigilant critics. "To them," said C. S. Lewis, "criticism is a form of social and ethical hygiene."[13] Ambiguity deserves no quarter. "A work, or a single passage, cannot for them be good in any sense unless it is good simply, unless it reveals attitudes which are essential elements in the good life."[14]

Leaving such critics to their Vigilance, what does the language of symbolism really say about Slytherin House? Many aspects of Slytherin are communicated through its Element (Water), its colors (silver and green), and its emblem (the snake). Keying the Houses to the Elements gave Rowling a suitable armature for her story in the form of alchemy, as John Granger has discovered and explained.[15] "To invent this wizarding world," Rowling admitted, "I've learned a ridiculous amount about alchemy."[16] Outwardly, alchemy is the art of transmuting base metal into gold but inwardly, its symbolic operations perfect the alchemist's soul. Rowling's alchemical framework supports layer after layer of mystic lore, including modular subunits of astrology. But the artistry of her execution is her own. (See chart 2 for astrological symbolism. Planetary conflicts and complementarities among Houses of Hogwarts fit their historic experience.)

In alchemy, everything in creation is composed in varying proportions of the Four Elements, abstract qualities that emerged from an amorphous first substance (*prima material*). They are capable of being transformed into each other via shared descriptive properties (cold or hot, moist or dry). Water is cold and moist, holding the seed of all things within it. The mastery of water "brings peace."[17] Slyerthin's Element Water is opposed to Gryffindor's hot, dry Fire. Appropriately, the Slytherin common room is beneath the lake at Hogwarts but Gryffindor's home is in a tower.

Water is closest to the primal chaos. In the beginning, the Spirit of God moves over the watery void (Gen 1:2). It gives life, cleanses, and regenerates but can also destroy. Although Water sometimes stands for sin and death, it is also a passage to rebirth, a blessing and a sign of grace. It is the Element of possibilities, fertile and ever changing, a model of feminine receptivity.[18]

Astrologically, the cardinal sign of Water is Cancer, the sole house of the Moon, a feminine planet of mutability and mystery[19]. It measures, weaves, and binds the endless rhythmic cycle of existence from birth to death to rebirth. Lunar influence waxes and wanes over that which grows or is fluid. It can over-stimulate emotions to the extremes of hysteria and insanity. The sublunary world is imperfect, a place of suffering and history. The Moon cannot shine of itself; it only reflects the light of the self-luminous Sun. The metal of the moon is silver and its color green, just like Slytherin. Though silver is precious, it can tarnish, unlike Griffindor's solar gold.[20]

Green is a secondary hue on the color wheel while red, its opposite, is a primary. Red is the "ripe" phase of green. Green can symbolize envy, poison, death, and decay but also tranquility, hope, life, and growth. Note another crossover: Harry's eyes are emerald green, like his heroic mother's, while Voldemort's are red like those ascribed to dragons. Emerald green eyes—famously seen in Dante's Beatrice—signify joy and chastity, Like the gem, they also treat eye disease, including Dante's bedazzlement in Paradise.

The serpent, of course, is the troublesome element in Slytherin's repertoire of symbols. As discussed above, it carries many negative associations—not the least because venomous species actually exist—but these do not exhaust its meaning. The serpent is primarily a lunar animal, linked to water and femininity. It manifests the ever-changing nature of the Moon by shedding its skin to renew itself and shares its planet's attributes. Thus, the snake emblem of Slytherin is appropriately lunar silver.

In Near Eastern mythology, serpent-like monsters represent watery chaos that must be subdued by sky deities so that creation can proceed, for instance in the ancient Babylonian epic, the *Enuma Elish*. Although the Lord slaying the crooked sea-serpent Leviathan with his sword (Is 27:1) is a remote echo of the Cannanite god Baal's annual combat with Lotan, it refers to a definitive day of reckoning. Then, in the future Messianic Age, children will safely play near formerly deadly snakes (Is 11:8). From the successful Tempter in Eden (Gen 3) to the Evil

One who will be cast into the fiery lake forever (Rev 20: 2, 10), the Bible brackets human history between visitations by Satan in serpent form.

Classical myths also have their share of gods and heroes who destroy snaky monstrosities: Jupiter over Typhon, Apollo over Python, Perseus over Medusa, and Hercules over Hydra. Subduing did not always require killing. The caduceus (staff) of Mercury entwined with two serpents that he reconciled has been the logo of the medical profession since antiquity. The staff of the god's son Asculapius, which carries a single serpent, represents pharmacy. Real snakes lived in the temples of Asculapius where devotees went for cures. Hygeia, daughter of Asculapius and goddess of health, is depicted feeding snakes.

As frequent companions of Mesopotamian and Mediterranean "great goddesses," snakes are connected with sexuality, fertility, death, and cults commemorating ancestors. They are protectors and healers, transmitters of prophetic power and givers of wisdom. The snake's periodic rejuvenation by sloughing off its skin connects it with endless life.[21] In the epic of *Gilgamesh*, a serpent steals an herb that would have rendered the hero immortal. Other snake-like creatures guard the Tree of Life and the Fountain of Youth against the intrusions of men— not always successfully. The cosmos itself is encompassed by a serpent called Uroborus. Like a nut screwed into a bolt, it functions simultaneously as male and female by swallowing its own tail, continually begetting itself. The closed circle formed by the beast's body signifies the eternally revolving cycle of existence or simply, eternity.

Despite many evil roles played by Biblical serpents, the staff that Aaron uses to smite Egypt with plagues had previously been turned into a snake to devour snakes conjured by Pharaoh's magicians (Ex 7:8-8:19). Later, the brazen serpent that Moses mounts on a pole to heal victims of fiery poisonous snakes sent as punishments for sin (Num 24:4ff) is a sign of Christ crucified (Jn 3:14-15). What kills can cure.[22] Symbols scarcely get more ambivalent than that.

In alchemy, the serpent or dragon represents the raw material with which the transmutation starts, the "mercurial water" that transforms it, and the *prima materia* that is ultimately transmuted into the object of the procedure—the elixir or Philosopher's Stone. Rowling's seven novels trace the course of the alchemical process through the experiences of various characters, especially Harry's journey from despised orphan to victorious hero. But while Harry, a true lion of Gryffindor, is being ripened into gold, snake-loving Voldemort is finishing his own transmutation into dross. Not for Voldemort is the slow process of nature or the humble one of alchemy. His ravening ego must exercise total control over the process.

In remarkable display of virtuosity handling symbols, Rowling shows Voldemort and his two scaly tools as "manufactured" menaces. The hungry green basilisk beneath Hogwarts, Salazar Slytherin's parting gift, is unnatural both in conception and gestation, for it was laid by a chicken and incubated by a toad. (Tradition specifies an elderly cock and adds a dunghill for the nest to create the "royal snake.") Voldemort's pet and horcrux the serpent Nagini reached her giant size through his sorcery and the diet of human flesh he provided. Voldemort's use of the Dark Arts, culminating in his monstrous rebirth, has molded him as close to the semblance of a serpent as a humanoid body can be. He emerges from the cauldron "tall and skeletally thin" with a nightmarish face "whiter than a skull, with wide, livid scarlet eyes and a nose that was flat as a snake's with slits for nostrils. . ." (*GoF*, 32) His glorification is self-mutilation.

By contrast, the natural snakes in the books are harmless victims--the sad boa constrictor that Harry frees from a zoo, the local snake that Voldemort's Uncle Morfin Gaunt nails alive to a door, and the forest snakes who die soon after Voldemort possesses them. The same is true of Rowling's fiery dragons. Hagrid's pet, Charlie Weasley's research subjects, the first peril in the Triwizard tournament, and the Gringotts' guardian are merely dangerous animals, no more sapient than dinosaurs. A stubborn Vigilant might still argue that arousing pity for the captive watch-dragon subtly undermines readers' proper fear of demons, but sometimes a reptile is just a reptile and not a manifestation of metaphysical evil. Hogwarts' school motto,

Draco dormiens nunquam titillandus ("Let Sleeping Dragons Lie") offers sage, not sinister advice.

The horrors perpetrated by Salazar Slytherin and Voldemort rebound on them, not the symbols they employed. On a cosmic scale, serpentine beings, the metal silver, the color green, and the element Water still endure with their inherent ambiguities intact. Locally, the darkest products of Slytherin House have been cleansed by instruments of fire, not only by the hands of Gryffindors (Dumbledore, Harry, Ron, and Neville) but by its own brutish member Crabbe (like Cancer, its cardinal zodiac sign).[23] Two of Voldemort's horcruxes are destroyed by the fangs of Salazar's basilisk and Voldemort himself by the recoil of his own lethal spell. As in *The Lord of the Rings*, evil is the worst enemy of evil.

Harry's calm surrender and willingness to die overcomes Voldemort's frantic craving for endless life and universal dominion. This is the Christian solution, not the typical pattern of Indo-European mythology where the Hero must kill the Triple Monster.[24] Although the "true Gryffindors" Harry and his double Neville dispatch the basilisk and the cobra with their Founder's sword, Voldemort dooms himself. After years of baleful strokes against them and their families, he has shaped them into the heroes they are. Voldemort with his two monsters recalls wicked King Zahhak in the *Shah Nameh*, the Persian *Book of the Kings*. After Zahhak murdered his father, twin serpents grew from his shoulders and had to be fed on human brains. He was overthrown—not directly slain--by a prophesied young hero whose father he had killed trying to forestall fate.

Draco with his two bullying sidekicks is—literally—a pale imitation of the Dark Lord. By not killing him, Harry unwittingly sets up his own survival and victory over Voldemort. He and a chastened Draco manage to exchange a civil nod in the epilogue of *Deathly Hallows*: the passive dragon is not molested.

By staying alive, Draco has the opportunity to marry fellow Slytherin and pureblood Asteria[25] Greengrass and beget Scorpius Hyperion Malfoy. Mythologically, the constellation for which Draco is named was a dragon seized by Minerva during the war between the gods and the giants and flung into the sky. Astronomically, it connects the signs Cancer and Scorpio. It was the polar constellation 4,000 years ago, but celestial bodies shift position.

Draco's son Scorpius is Rowling's only character directly named after a sign of the zodiac. In astrology, Scorpio was the Great Beast whose sting killed Orion[26] and nearly stampeded the horses of the Sun.[27] Its influence is baleful, connected with discord and the groin. As a Water sign in the dying year, it also signifies a return to primal chaos, a precondition for rebirth. Alchemists regarded Scorpio's month as the most propitious time for transmuting iron into gold. A hint as to whether Scorpius Malfoy will be a force for good or ill lies in his second name, Hyperion, which comes from a son of Heaven and Earth in classical mythology who fathered the Sun, Moon, and Dawn. Will Scorpius be his generation's subject of the alchemical Great Work? The answer lies not in his stars but in himself.

Names in Draco's family[28] reflect where Slytherin House has been and where it may be going. Draco bears an astral name like many of his maternal relatives, descendants of Phineas Nigellus Black, once a notably strict headmaster at Hogwarts. Phineas[29] is taken from Greek mythology, referring to a jealous uncle of Andromeda who was turned to stone by viewing the snaky head of Medusa. Nigellus would be the masculine form of Nigella, a plant that produces the pungent, bitter black spice kalonji. Seven "white sheep in a Black family" have been disowned for failing to live up to familial standards, for instance by marrying or even sympathizing with Muggles. By the end of the series, the Blacks are extinct in the direct male line. Draco is the nearest remaining heir, although Arthur and Molly Weasley are cousins of the Blacks.

The Weasleys demonstrate that it is possible for an ancient pureblood family carrying a few Black genes to be Muggle-friendly, despite drawing bigots' contempt as "blood traitors." Arthur survives an attack by Nagini but Molly took the offensive.[30] To save her child, this slightly frumpy hausfrau duels and kills Voldemort's would-be consort Bellatrix— another resounding victory for mother love in the series. Less dramatically, highly domestic Molly restores cleanliness and order to the dilapidated Black family mansion. What impact will her twelve grandchildren have on Hogwarts? Some already unite differences of nationality, race, and blood-status. Will they play a part in harmonizing the Houses and even the wider world?[31]

Blood prejudice has been defanged. Slytherin House has been purged of its Founder's baleful legacy; Voldemort and his Death Eater minions are gone. But expelling evil is not enough. Something good must take its place. Can Slytherin House apply its traits of "resourcefulness—determination—a certain disregard for the rules" (*CoS*, 18) to positive ends? Can it renew itself like the snake? Grow green as a meadow? Recover the memory, intelligence, and foresight of its cardinal virtue, Prudence? Manifest the life-giving essence of Water, its Element? Progress will depend on the choices its members make.

Earth, Air, Fire, and Water comprise one cosmos. Each and every one is necessary for the existence of the whole. A united Hogwarts would be like the tetramorphs of Ezechiel's vision (Ez 1) who combine traits of Man, Lion, Ox, and Eagle in one glorious being. Although it is impossible—even in fiction—to fully "immanetize the eschaton," Rowling is an optimistic writer. Her Harry Potter novels relate improvements in the mortal condition that have happened to suggest what may happen in the future. She proclaims that green is the color of Hope and that the Serpent can indeed change its skin.

Endnotes

1   Melissa Anelli and Emerson Spartz, "The Leaky Cauldron and Mugglenet interview Joanne Kathleen Rowling: Part Three," 16 July, 2005. accessed at http://www.accio-quote.org/articles/2005/0705-tlc_mugglenet-anelli-3.htm November 9, 2009.

2   *Ibid.*

3   OP, 11

4   Anelli and Spartz, Rowling interview

5   *Ibid.*

6   Mircea Eliade, *Patterns in Comparative Religion.* Trans. Rosemary Sheed (Meridian Books, Cleveland, 1963) 156.

7   Consider the varying grammatical and mythological gender of Sun and Moon across the world. The masculine Sun and feminine Moon are by no means universal.

8   Tarot imagery in Harry Potter would be an interesting subject for research, although the suits were not traditionally matched with the Elements until the later eighteenth century and remain inconsistent. But major arcana motifs such as the Fool, the Hanged Man, the Tower, the Moon, and the World do appear in Rowling's text and the Houses of Hogwarts. Even Salazar's withdrawal from the school has a parallel in the loss of Prudence from the set of four cardinal virtues in the major arcana.

9   Lyndy Abraham, *A Dictionary of Alchemical Imagery* (Cambridge University Press: New York, 1998, 2001) 68.

10   C. S. Lewis, *An Experiment in Criticism.* (Cambridge University Press: London, 1961) 124-129. Lewis acknowledges their sincerity but not their attitude. "They see all clear thinking, all sense of reality, and all fineness of living, threatened on every side. . . ."

11   Michael D. O'Brien, *A Landscape with Dragons: Christian and Pagan Imagination in Children's Literature.* (North River Press: Quyon, Quebec, 1994) 25. The larger argument is developed 24-37 and 45-47. O'Brien's most recent critical effort is *Harry Potter and the Paganization of Culture* (Fides et Traditio Press: Rzeszdw, Poland, 2010). The component essays can be read at his website www.studiobrien.com.

12   *Landscape*, 26.

13   Lewis, 124.

14   *Ibid.*, 126-127.

15   John Granger, *The Hidden Key to Harry Potter* (Zossima

Press: Port Haddock WA, 2002) 92-102. In Rowling's novels, elemental lore generally trumps astrological, but characters' natal signs may or may not be more significant than their house Element. e.g.: Snape and Voldemort are both Capricorns, an Earth sign ruled by Saturn.

16   Anne Simpson, "Face-to-Face with J. K Rowling: Casting a spell Over Young Minds," *The Herald*, December 7, 1998. accessed at <http://www.accio-quote.org/articles/1998/1298-herald-simpson.html> September 13, 2010.

17   Abraham, 213.

18   Salazar Slytherin's maleness is not an astrological inconsistency—sex and gender are separate concepts in astrology. If the "rules" had been followed mechanically, Rowena Ravenclaw would have had to have been male, but Rowling is too creative for that.

19   The celestial Moon (Luna) is important in Harry Potter. Neither her terrestrial aspect (Diana, goddess of hunting, chastity, and childbirth) nor her subterranean one (Hecate, goddess of necromancy and fertility) appear, although the dangerous transformations of Remus and Sirius in PoA take place under moonlight.

20   Ironically, Godric Gryffindor's sword is silver, although set with huge leonine rubies. It not only escapes Voldemort's foul designs, but destroys Salazar Slytherin's locket, which is a horcrux. The latter is decorated with green stones outlining a snake. Perhaps the treasured sword and locket go back to a time when the founders were still friends.

21   Voldemort's Dark Mark, an undying serpent darting from a skull's mouth, is a ghastly twist on this idea.

22   According to medieval alchemist Nicholas Flamel, a crucified snake represents the final perfect elixir created in the *rubeo* (reddening) stage of the alchemical work. Abraham, 181.

23   Crabbe's foolhardy use of magic fire—a rival Element--costs him his life. Similarly, Dumbledore is mortally injured by Slytherin's ring and tormented by enchanted green water in Voldemort's seaside cave.

24   In ancient India and Iran, the beast is a three-headed dragon; in Rome, it is the Curiatii triplets killed by Horatius.

25   Her name has also been given as "Astoria" <http://www.time.com/time/specials/2007/personoftheyear/article/0,28804,1690753_1695388_1695569,00.html> but certainly looks like "Asteria" in Rowling's handwritten family tree: <http://www.hplex.info/images/jkr/weasleyfamilytree-website.jpg> and has more appropriate connotations. Asteria is any gem that shows a star (ruby, sapphire, topaz,

moonstone). One Asteria in mythology was a titaness and the mother of Hecate who was an underworld goddess, crowned with snakes and associated with plant potions. Astoria would imply wealth and luxury as in the Waldorf-Astoria hotel. "Greengrass" combines the Slytherin color with the qualities of submission and service.

    26   Our constellation Orion the Hunter was called the Snake or the Madman by Arab astronomers. It includes the star Bellatrix, "the Female Warrior" for which Draco's aunt, Bellatrix Black Lestrange, was named.

    27   Yet *Genista scorpius* or "Scorpion's thorn" is a shrubby, yellow-flowered Mediterranean plant used to cure scorpion stings.

    28   There is no need to repeat all the names and connotations of the Black family here when these are available at www.hp-lexicon.org.

    29   Given the Blacks' obsession with their pureblood status, is it only a coincidence that in the Bible Phinehas was a zealous priest who killed both an Israelite man and his foreign lover with a single spear thrust? (Num 25:7-11)

    30   Molly is the only character identified as born under Scorpio, a Water sign ruled by Mars. Will she interact with Scorpius Malfoy?

    31   Harmony needs to be established among the Houses, between wizards with other magical races, and between all of these and the Muggle world. Georges Dúmezil's work on Indo-European mythologies could provide some interesting tools for exploring the Potterverse.

ADDITIONAL BIBLIOGRAPHY

Allen, Richard Hinkley. *Star Names: Their Lore and Meaning.* Dover Publication, Inc. New York. 1963.

Battistini, Matilde. *Astrology, Magic, and Alchemy in Art.* Trans. Rosanna M. Giammanco Frongia. J. Paul Getty Museum, Los Angeles, 2007.

Biedermann, Hans. *Dictionary of Symbolism: Cultural Icons and the Meanings behind Them.* Trans. James Hulbert. Penguin Meridian. New York, 1994.

Burckhardt, Titus. *Alchemy: Science of the Cosmos, Science of the*

Soul. Fons Vitae. Louisville KY, 1997.

Chevalier, Jean and Alain Gheerbrant, *The Penguin Dictionary of Symbols.* Trans. John Buchanan-Brown.   Penguin Books. New York, 1996.

Decker, Ronald and Michael Dummett. *A History of the Occult Tarot 1970-1970.* Gerald Duckworth & Co., Ltd. London, 1988.

Lyons, Albert S. *Predicting the Future: An Illustrated History and Guide to the Techniques.* Harry N. Abrams. New York, 1990.

McKenzie, John L. *Dictionary of the Bible.* Macmillan Co. New York, 1965.

CHART 1. ALCHEMICAL SYMBOLS

House	Element	Virtue	Gospel	Temperment	Alchemical Stage
Sign	Qualities		Symbol	Humour	Color
Seasons			Zodiac sign		
Hufflepuff - fall	Earth cold & dry	Justice	Luke Ox Taurus	melancholic black bile	*nigredo* black
Slytherin + winter	Water cold & dry	Prudence	Matthew Man Scorpio	phlegmatic phlegm	*albedo* white
Ravenclaw - spring	Air hot & moist	Temperence	John Eagle Aquarius	sanguine blood	*citrinitas* (obsolete) yellow
Gryffindor + summer	Fire hot & dry	Fortitude	Mark Lion Leo	choleric yellow bile	*rubedo* red

CHART 2 ASTROLOGICAL SYMBOLS

House	Cardinal Sign (Divides Year)	Fixed Sign	Mutable Sign
Element	Planet	Planet	Planet
Hufflepuff Earth	Capricorn diurnal Saturn	Taurus nocturnal Venus	Virgo diurnal Mercury
Slytherin Water	Cancer Moon	Scorpio nocturnal Mars	Pisces nocturnal Jupiter
Ravenclaw Air	Libra diurnal Venus	Aquarius nocturnal Saturn	Gemini nocturnal Mercury
Gryffindor Fire	Aries diurnal Mars	Leo Sun	Sagittarius diurnal Jupiter

There and Back Again
The Chiastic Structure of J.K. Rowling's Harry Potter Series

J. Steve Lee

J. K. ROWLING, THE author of the resoundingly successful Harry Potter series, is simultaneously praised and reviled. Having been compared to C. S. Lewis and J. R. R. Tolkien, Rowling has won the Nestle Smarties Book Prize, British Book Awards, Sheffield Children's Book Award, Booklist Editors Choice, Whitaker's Platinum Book Award, Publishers Weekly Best Book, Scottish Arts Council Children's Book Award, Whitbread Children's Book of the Year, and the Hugo Award amongst others.

Harry Potter is now a global brand worth an estimated £7 billion ($15 billion), and the last four Harry Potter books have consecutively set records as the fastest-selling books in history. The series, totaling 4,195 pages, has been translated, in whole or in part, into 65 languages.[1]

Not all remarks concerning Potter have been of such high praise. In fact, some have been downright spiteful. Harold

---

1. "J. K. Rowling." *Wikipedia.* http://en.wikipedia.org/wiki/J._K._Rowling#Harry_Potter_books Accessed May 17, 2010.

Bloom, the Sterling professor of Humanities and English at Yale University, revels in his disdain for the Harry Potter series. Early in the Potter series life Bloom comments in a piece in the Wall Street Journal entitled "Can 35 Million Book Buyers Be Wrong? Yes." He begins berating Rowling's by declaring that "[h]er prose style, heavy on cliché, makes no demands upon her readers."[2] Not ending there he continues the scolding: "Can more than 35 million book buyers, and their offspring, be wrong? Yes, they have been, and will continue to be for as long as they persevere with Potter."[3] And to add insult to injury: "Why read it? Presumably, if you cannot be persuaded to read anything better, Rowling will have to do."[4] After naming his choices of the five most important books (Shakespeare's *Works, Canterbury Tales, Comedia, Don Quixote,* and *The Iliad*) in a piece titled, "A Life in Books" Bloom turns to children's literature and declares Lewis Carroll's *Alice in Wonderland* books as the finest fantasies ever written but then goes on to insult Rowling by declaring that ". . . the Harry Potter books are going to wind up in the rubbish bin. The first six volumes have sold, I am told, 350 million copies. I know of no larger indictment of the world's descent into sub-literacy."[5]

Contrastingly, while the *Harry Potter* series is not Homer or Chaucer, much less Shakespeare (no one is claiming that it is), there is a value beyond the impressive storytelling that Rowling has mastered as a children's author. Just as Lewis' *Narnia* chronicles had been derided by J. R. R. Tolkien as incoherent and a hodgepodge, Rowling's *Potter* series has been scoffed as cliché and amateur. But Lewis has been vindicated by Michael Ward in *Planet Narnia.*[6]:

For over half a century, scholars have laboured to show that C. S.

2. Bloom, Harold. "Can 35 Million Book Buyers Be Wrong? Yes." *Wall Street Journal,* July 11, 2000.

3. Ibid.

4. Ibid.

5. Bloom, Harold. "A Life in Books." *Newsweek* March 12, 2007.

6. Michael Ward, *Planet Narnia: The Seven Heavens in the Imagination of C. S. Lewis* (New York: Oxford University Press, 2008).

Lewis's famed but apparently disorganised *Chronicles of Narnia* have an underlying symbolic coherence, pointing to such possible unifying themes as the seven sacraments, the seven deadly sins, and the seven books of Spenser's *Faerie Queene*. None of these explanations has won general acceptance and the structure of Narnia's symbolism has remained a mystery. Michael Ward has finally solved the enigma. In *Planet Narnia* he demonstrates that medieval cosmology, a subject which fascinated Lewis throughout his life, provides the imaginative key to the seven novels. Drawing on the whole range of Lewis's writings (including previously unpublished drafts of the *Chronicles*), Ward reveals how the Narnia stories were designed to express the characteristics of the seven medieval planets - - Jupiter, Mars, Sol, Luna, Mercury, Venus, and Saturn - - planets which Lewis described as 'spiritual symbols of permanent value' and 'especially worthwhile in our own generation'. Using these seven symbols, Lewis secretly constructed the *Chronicles* so that in each book the plot-line, the ornamental details, and, most important, the portrayal of the Christ-figure of Aslan, all serve to communicate the governing planetary personality. The cosmological theme of each Chronicle is what Lewis called 'the kappa element in romance,' the atmospheric essence of a story, everywhere present but nowhere explicit. The reader inhabits this atmosphere and thus imaginatively gains connaître knowledge of the spiritual character which the tale was created to embody.[7]

Ward has seemingly uncovered the secret code behind the books that was intentionally placed there by Lewis. Likewise, Rowling has secretly imbedded the *Potter* series with a structure that is "everywhere present but nowhere explicit." John Granger has revealed this "kappa" element[8] of the *Potter* series with the

7. From product description of *Planet Narnia* Oxford University Press website: http://www.oup.com/us/catalog/general/subject/ReligionTheology/HistoryofChristianity/Modern/?view=usa&ci=9780195313871.   Accessed June 1, 2010.

8. The "kappa" element is a reference to a term coined by Lewis in a presentation he delivered to a literary society in Oxford. In a paper entitled "The Kappa Element in Romance" Lewis revealed that stories are most valuable for the quality or atmosphere. "Kappa" is the first letter of the Greek word meaning "cryptic" or "hidden."

use of "literary alchemy."[9] Not only this, a close examination of the novels reveals that Rowling has carefully used a literary arrangement that has made so many of Harold Bloom's favorite books "great" in the first place: Literary chiasmus.

CHIASTIC STRUCTURE

Chiasmus is a literary structure which mirrors key ideas or phrases in the reverse order of presentation. Sometimes called "reverse parallelism," "ring structure," "palistrophes," "symmetric structure," or "concentric structures," chiasmus has been a part of ancient literature such as the *Iliad* and the *Odyssey* as well as *Beowulf, Paradise Lost,* and the *Bible.*

I was personally introduced to chiasmus when enrolled in an Old Testament survey course in seminary. Hebrew poetry is structured by mirroring thoughts and ideas rather than by meter and rhyme. Pre-literate societies passed down culture forming stories orally and apparently developed a structure of storytelling and didactic instruction in chiasmus for easy memorization. As people groups developed written languages and began to record their stories, the structural use of chiasm was obviously brought over with the transition.

Arthur G. Patzia, senior professor of New Testament at Fuller Theological Seminary, and Anthony J. Petrotta, professor of Old Testament at Fuller Theological Seminary, define chiasm as such:

> Derived from the Greek letter chi (which is shaped like a letter X), a rhetorical device whereby parallel lines of a text correspond in an X pattern, such as A-B-C-B'-A' (in this case the center of the chiasm is C, and on either side line A will correspond to line A' and so forth). For example, a chiastic pattern (without a C element) may be observed in Mark 2:27 and set out in the following fashion:
>
> A: The sabbath was made
>   B: for humankind,
>   B': and not humankind

---

9. See John Granger, *Unlocking Harry Potter: Five Keys for the Serious Reader* (Wayne, PA: Zossima Press, 2007), p. 47-118.

A´: for the sabbath

> The pattern can be as simple as a verse in Mark or as elaborate as a whole poem, a parable or a book. In using this device, an author can show both progression of thought and intensification of meaning. Chiasm is a way of "layering" words and themes.[10]

A simple, and probably the most well-known, chiasm in modern speech is the antimetabole[11] of John F. Kennedy's: "Ask not what your country can do for you, but what you can do for your country," "What your country can do for you," is mirrored by the same words "what you can do for your country." All antimetaboles are a type of chiasm, but not all chiasms are antimetaboles.

Chiastic structure can be simple as:

A

B'

B'

A'

A more complex or lengthy structure can be modeled as:

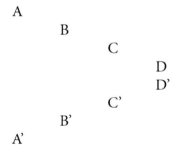

At times, chiastic structure can contain a turn phrase

---

10. Arthur G. Patzia and Anthony J. Petrotta, *Pocket Dictionary of Biblical Studies* (Downers Grove, Ill.: InterVarsity Press, 2002), 24.

11. A figure of speech, used in written work, speeches, poetry and advertisements. It is a form of chiasmus, and the word comes from the Latin *anti*, which means "against" or "opposite," and *metabole*, which translates to "turn around" or "about." In antimetabole, a person uses the same words in two independent clauses but in reverse or changed order. The second clause shifts emphasis or the meaning of the first clause, by reversing the words.

such as:

```
      A
          B
              C
                  X
              C'
          B'
      A'
```

As mentioned, biblical literature is replete with chiastic structure. Amos 5:4-6 is fine example:

Seek me and **live**;   A
  but do not seek **Bethel**,   B
  and do not enter into **Gilgal**   C
  or cross over to Beer-sheba;   X
  Gilgal will surely go into exile,   C'
  and **Bethel** shall come to naught." B'
Seek the LORD and **live**,   A'

Notice line A contains the words 'seek' and 'live' which is repeated or paralleled in line A'. 'Bethel' is in lines B and B', while 'Gilgal' is symmetrical in lines C and C'. While this example of chiasm in Amos is more complex than antimetaboles, even more complex chiastic structure can be found in biblical literature. Craig Blomberg in his *Jesus and the Gospels* reveals the chiastic structure of the gospel of Luke with the Acts of the Apostles.[12] Luke opens his gospel with a global perspective by dating the birth of Christ in reign of the Roman emperors (Luke 2:1, 3:1). Jesus' ministry moves from Galilee (Luke 4-9), to Samaria and Judea (Luke 10-19), settling in Jerusalem (Luke 19-24). The Acts of the Apostles follows in the opposite direction. Opening were the gospel left off in Jerusalem (Acts 1-5), to Judea and Samaria (Acts 6-9), traveling through Syria, Asia Minor, and settling in Rome (Acts 9-28). The chiastic structure of Luke/

---

12   Craig L. Blomberg. *Jesus and the Gospels.* (Nashville TN: Broadman & Holman. 1997), 140-145.

Acts is found in the geography and is indicated in Acts 1:8 when Jesus says "you shall be my witnesses both in Jerusalem, and in all Judea and Samaria and even to the remotest part of the earth." The structure can be diagramed as such:

Rome, the ends of the earth (Lke2:1,3:1)   A
   Samaria and **Judea** (Lk 10-19)   B
      Jerusalem (Lk 19-34)   C
      Jerusalem (Acts 1-5)   C'
   Judea and **Samaria**, (Acts 6-9)   B'
Rome, the ends of the earth (Acts 9-28)   A'

A huge amount of literature in the Bible has chiastic structure. From simple passages, to whole books, the Bible is one of the premiere examples of the use of chiasmus.[13]

Other literature has contained chiastic structure. The overall structure of John Milton's *Paradise Lost* is evident as chiastic[14]:

Satan's **sinful actions** (Books 1-3)   A
   Entry into **Paradise** (Book 4)   B
      War in heaven (**destruction**) (Books 5-6) C
      Creation of the world (Books 7-8)   C'
   Loss of **paradise** (Book 9)   B'
Humankind's **sinful actions** (Books 10-12)   A'

---

13   See Nils W. Lund *Chiasmus in the New Testament: A Study in the Form and Function of Chiastic Structures* (Hendrickson Publishers, 1992) and David A. Dorsey *The Literary Structure of the Old Testament: A Commentary on Genesis-Malachi* (Baker Books, 2004).

14   Leland Ryken, "Paradise Lost by John Milton (1608-1674)," edited by Kelly M Kapic and Randall C. Gleason. *The Devoted Life: An Invitation to the Puritan Classics.* (Downers Grove, Ill.: InterVarsity, 2004).

Other literary works containing examples of chiasm include Beowulf,[15] the Book of Mormon,[16] and Homer's work.[17]

Chiastic structure was developed to aid in memorization especially in oral cultures and traditions that carried it over into written works. Rowling has silently but deliberately utilized this literary technique so often incorporated by Homer, Milton, and others.

CHIASTIC STRUCTURE IN THE HARRY POTTER SERIES

M. Brett Kendall broke significant ground on this subject in early 2006[18], although many blogs, websites, and fan postings came to realize the structure of chiasmus in Rowling's work independently.[19] On a lengthy post dated January 30, 2006 on his blogspot titled "Muggle Matters," Mr. Kendall wrote a piece entitled " 'X' Marks the Spot: The Goblet of Fire and Chiasm."[20] He followed up with even lengthier posts in June 7 and 14 of 2007.[21] But as early as 2005 the chiastic structure was being utilized to predict the coming plot and events to take place in yet-to-be published Potter works. Meredith Warren at veritaserum.com encouraged further investigation of books

15   John D. Niles "Ring Composition and the Structure of *Beowulf*" PMLA (Modern Language Association) 94 (5): 924-35.

16   An example is Mosiah 3:18-19. See also H. Clay Gorton *A New Witness for Christ: Chiastic Structures in the Book of Mormon* (Horizon Publishers, 1997)

17   Cedric M. Whitman, *Homer and the Heroic Tradition* (Cambridge, Harvard University Press), 1958.

18   Thanks to John Granger and Travis Prinzi for this insight, via personal email.

19   See: http://jathacker.xanga.com/604423028/the-chiastic-structure-of-harry-potter/;   http://virtueofpotter.wordpress.com/2007/08/01/chiastic-structure-in-harry-potter/;   and   http://wc6.worldcrossing.com/webx?14@@.1de67edc/13.

20   http://www.mugglematters.com/2006/01/x-marks-spot-goblet-of-fire-and-chiasm.html - accessed August 16, 2010.

21   http://mugglematters.blogspot.com/2007_06_01_archive.html - accessed August 15, 2010.

one and two in order to speculate on the happenings of then-to-be published books six and seven.[22] The parallel structure of the books has been no secret to many serious readers.

It is now obvious that J. K. Rowling has taken the method of chiasmus and applied it to her work as a whole. The seven volume series has a chiastic structure of A-B-C-X-C'-B'-A'. The first volume, *The Sorcerer's Stone* parallels or mirrors the seventh volume, *The Deathly Hallows*. *The Chamber of Secrets* (book two) parallels *The Half-Blood Prince* (book six), while *The Prisoner of Azkaban* mirrors *The Order of the Phoenix* (books three and five respectively). *The Goblet of Fire* is the turn book. It can be diagramed as follows:

The Sorcerer's Stone	A		
Chamber of Secrets	B		
Prisoner of Azkaban		C	
Goblet of Fire			X
Order of the Phoenix		C'	
Half-Blood Prince	B'		
Deathly Hallows	A'		

The method of parallel that Rowling employs to develop a chiastic structure is the use of key plot points, physical items, characters, events, and even dedications that are utilized in the first three books and then completed, brought back up, or mirrored in some fashion in the last three books. For example, Harry Potter is brought as a baby to the Dursley's home on Privet Drive by Hagrid riding on a flying motorcycle that belonged to Sirius Black in the first book, *The Sorcerer's Stone*. Rowling mirrors this event in *The Deathly Hallows* by opening the book with Harry departing the Dursley's home by means of Hagrid driving Sirius Black's flying motorcycle. *The Chamber of Secrets* contains a flamboyant teacher who threw a Valentine's party and starts a dueling club in Gilderoy Lockhart; the *Half Blood Prince* also contains an odd teacher who threw a Christmas party and starts the Slug Club in Horace Slughorn.

22   http://www.veritaserum.com/editorials/?view=41. – accessed August 16, 2010.

The Knight Bus appears in only the *Prisoner of Azkaban* and the *Order of the Phoenix*. Harry stumbles across the Knight Bus after abruptly leaving Privet Drive in the former work, while in the later work, the Knight Bus escorts Harry, Ron, and Hermione to 12 Grimmauld Place for the winter holiday.

The series is replete with chiasmus. Rowling has carefully structured plot elements, character development, and several items to reflect this parallel structure. Provided below is a simple list of mirrored or paralleled elements set up by book connection.

Sorcerer's Stone and the *Deathly Hallows*

The Sorcerer's Stone	The Deathly Hallows
Mention of dragon in Gringott's Wizarding Bank	Appearance of dragon in Gringott's Wizarding Bank
Bathilda Bagshot mentioned	Significance of Bathilda Bagshot
Snape is expected to be evil, but turns out to be a savior	Snape expected to be a Death Eater, but turns out to be a sacrificial person
Harry gets his wand	Harry breaks his wand
Start of story doesn't start with Harry's point of view (it is the Dursley's)	Start of story doesn't start with Harry's point of view (it's Snape's)
Ginny is begging to go to Hogwarts at King's Cross train station	Little Lily (Ginny's daughter) is begging to go to Hogwarts at King's Cross in epilogue
Griphook takes Harry down to vault in Gringotts bank	Griphook sneaks Harry into Gringott's bank
Quirell has two faces (a vessel for Voldemort)	Snape has two faces on both sides of war

Harry arrives as a baby to Dursely's on Sirius Black's motorcycle driven by Hagrid	Harry departs Dursley's on Sirius Black's motorcycle driven by Hagrid
Neville's courage wins the House Cup for Gryffindor beating Slytherin house	Neville's courage wins battle of Hogwarts by destroying last Horcrux of the heir of Slytherin
Sorcerer's Stone	Resurrection Stone
Five challenges placed by professors of Hogwarts to be overcome to reach the Sorcerer's Stone	Five Horcruxes to be destroyed to defeat Voldemort
Snape looked at as evil, but ends up good helping Harry at Quidditch match	Snape looked at as evil, but ends up good protecting Harry
Gringott's broken into	Gringott's broken into
Dumbledore uses Deluminator (aka – Put-Outer)	Dumbledore gives Deluminator to Ron
Mirror of Erised saves the day	Two-way mirror saves the day
Harry's first encounter with Snape they look at one another straight into the eyes	Harry's last encounter with Snape they look at one another straight into the eyes
Ollivander introduced and helps Harry with wand	Ollivander tries to repair Harry's wand
Dumbledore gives Harry tools (cloak) and clues (mirror) to fight Voldemort	Dumbledore gives the trio tools (put-outer, sword, snitch/ring) and clues (*Tales of Beedle the Bard*) to finish Voldemort
Ron and Hermione hate each other in the beginning	Ron and Hermione end up married

Harry receives Invisibility Cloak from Dumbledore	Harry learns of the significance of Invisibility Cloak as a Deathly Hallow
Harry's "resurrection" after three days of unconsciousness	Harry's literal resurrection after King's Cross
Ron yell's at Hermione at Devil's Snare "ARE YOU A WITCH OR NOT!?"	Hermione asks Ron at the Whomping Willow, "Are you a wizard, or what!?"
Hagrid carries Harry after Harry is attacked as infant by Voldemort	Hagrid carries Harry after Harry is attacked by Voldemort
Ollivander teaches Harry about wand choice when buying first wand	Ollivander teaches Harry about wand choice
Ron uses "Wingardium Leviosa" spell on a club	Ron uses "Wingardium Leviosa" spell on a stick
Firenze (a centaur) breaks custom of non-involvement with Centaurs by helping Harry escape from Voldemort	The Centaurs break their custom to fight Voldemort
Voldemort kills a professor of Hogwarts	Voldemort kills several professors of Howarts

The Chamber of Secrets and *The Half-Blood Prince*

The Chamber of Secrets	The Half-Blood Prince
Harry mistakenly Floo powders to Knockturn Alley	Follows Draco to Knockturn Alley
Harry spies on Malfoy throughout the novel	Harry spies on Malfoy at Borgin and Burkes and on train

Hand of Glory in Borgin and Burkes	Hand of Glory used by Draco in invasion of Hogwarts
Harry hides in vanishing cabinet in Borgin and Burkes	Vanishing cabinet used to sneak Death Eaters into Hogwarts
Peeves smashes vanishing cabinet	Vanishing cabinet fixed by Malfoy to allow entry into Hogwarts for Death Eaters
Harry stays at the Weasleys' home	Harry stays at the Weasleys' home
Missed start-of-term feast crashing into Whomping Willow	Late to start-of-term feast because of Full Body Bind placed on him by Malfoy
Snape meets Harry on way to castle to berate him for being late	Snape meets Harry on way to castle to berate him for being late
Harry can't get on the Hogwarts Express in time	Harry can't get off the Hogwarts Express in time
Lockhart a flamboyant/odd teacher	Slughorn a flamboyant/odd teacher
Lockhart organizes a Valentine Day party	Slughorn hosts a Christmas party
Lockhart starts a dueling club	Slughorn organizes the Slug Club
Harry hit by rogue bludger during a Quidditch match	Harry cracked skull due to a bludger hit by Cormac McLaggen
Harry hospitalized when arm incompetently de-boned by Lockhart	Harry hospitalized when hit by bludger playing Quidditch

Visited by Dobby in hospital wing of Hogwarts	Visited by Dobby in hospital wing of Hogwarts
Moaning Myrtle introduced	Moaning Myrtle appears to comfort Draco, who is worried about the task given to him by Voldemort. After Harry injures Malfoy using Sectumsempra, Myrtle is not hesitant to spread the news throughout the school, screaming that Harry has murdered him
Climax of story a mysterious underground chamber of secrets connected to Voldemort	The climax of novel is a mysterious underground Horcrux cave containing a part of the soul of Voldemort
Colin Creevey is an annoying young Gryffindor student always trying to capture Harry Potter on camera	Romilda Vane is a pushy, annoying student in Gryffindor always trying to capture Harry' heart
Harry and Ron use Polyjuice Potion to turn into Crabbe and Goyle	Crabbe and Goyle turn into girls by Polyjuice Potion to guard the Room of Requirement while Malfoy repairing the Vanishing Cabinet
Hermione develops a complex potion of Polyjuice	Felix Felicis potion, another complex brew, is developed
Love potions mentioned	Love potions used
Dedicated to a single person instead of multiple people (as all other books are): Sean Harris (JKR childhood friend)	Dedicated to a single person instead of multiple people (as all other books are): Mackenzie (JKR daughter)

Ginny attached to a book: Tom Riddle's diary	Harry attached to a book: potions text
Harry helps Ginny get rid of Riddle's diary	Ginny helps Harry get rid of potions book
Fawkes the phoenix introduced	Fawkes' single last song at Dumbledore's death then leaves forever, being a wild phoenix
Lockhart has a secret-he is a phony who never actually did any of the heroic acts he claimed to have done	Slughorn has a secret-he gave Tom Riddle information on Horcruxes
Tom Riddle is in the diary	Tom Riddle is in the Pensieve
Harry's romantic interest in Ginny is introduced	Harry's romantic interest in Ginny is developed
Harry protects Ginny from Basilisk	Harry protects Ginny by breaking up with her
Harry hardly gives Ginny a thought, until the Chamber. He is embarrassed by her affections	Harry desires her affections and is jealous of the other boys she dates
Ron's wand backfires on him and he ends up spitting up slugs	New professor "Slug" horn is introduced
Horcrux is (unknowingly) introduced in Tom Riddle's diary	Horcrux is developed in chapter twenty three
First Horcrux is destroyed (diary of Tom Riddle)	Second Horcrux is destroyed (Marvolo Gaunt's ring)
Aragog, the giant Acromantula, introduced	Aragog dies

The cursed opal necklace seen by Harry at Borgin and Burkes	Opal necklace afflicts Katie Bell as she accidentally touches it
Story revolves around the Horcrux (diary) and end up at a deadly location designed by a Slytherin	Story revolves around explaining Horcruxes and ends up at a deadly location designed by a Slytherin

Prisoner of Azkaban and the _Order of the Phoenix_

The Prisoner of Azkaban	The Order of the Phoenix
Cornelius Fudge introduced	Fudge fired as Minister of Magic
Sirius Black introduced	Sirius Black killed
Trelawney introduced	Trelawney fired
Time Turner used by Hermione to double up on classes and to rescue Buckbeak and Sirius Black	A large supply of Time-Turners is kept at the Ministry of Magic in a glass-fronted cabinet which is destroyed
Before school starts, Harry encounters Dementors on Hogwarts Express	Before school starts, Harry encounters Dementors in an alley near his home on Privet Drive
Harry trained to produce a Patronus charm	Harry trains D.A. to produce a Patronus charm
Snape wants Lupin out of Hogwarts for being a werewolf	Snape wants Sirius Black out of Order of the Phoenix because he can turn into a dog
Ministry attempts to take Buckbeak and fails	Ministry attempts to take Dumbledore and fails

Gryffindor wins Quidditch cup	Gryffindor wins Quidditch cup
Fred and George are troublemakers with Marauders' Map	Fred and George cause trouble and end up escaping Hogwarts with a bang
Hagrid teaches about Hippogriff, a flying creature	Hagrid teaches about the Thestral, a flying creature
Boggart in Defense of Against the Dark Arts room when training with Lupin	Boggart found in 12 Grimmauld Place
Divinization offered as an elective with Trelawney	Firenze begins teaching Divinization adter Trelawney fired by Umbridge
In 1993, Harry Potter stumbles across the Knight Bus after leaving 4 Privet Drive following the inadvertent inflation of his Aunt Marge	The Knight Bus is seen once again in 1996 when Harry, Ron, and Hermione travel back to Hogwarts from 12 Grimmauld Place after the winter holiday
Sirius Black breaks out of Azkaban	Mass breakout of ten prisoners out of Azkaban
Harry receives special Patronus lessons from Lupin	Harry receives special occlumency lessons from Snape
Aunt Marge is blown up	Uncle Vernon mentions the Aunt Marge incident
Harry is threatened with expulsion from Hogwarts for underage wizardry for blowing up Aunt Marge	Harry threatened with expulsion for fighting off Dementors from Dudley
Harry has to save Sirius from Dementor's kiss in Hogwarts tower	Harry has to save Sirius from Voldemort in Ministry of Magic

Harry wants to kill Sirius after going down the Whomping Willow	Harry wants to save Sirius after going down to the depths of the Ministry of Magic

THE NATURE OF THE CHIASTIC STRUCTURE IN POTTER

While it is definite that Rowling has constructed a chiastic pattern in the series, there is an added element that gives the literary mechanism its own tone and purpose in the books. So far we have focused on the parallels found in books one through three and five through seven respectively. Book four, *Goblet of Fire* serves as the "turn" book. Given that the series has an odd number of books instead of an even amount, *Goblet of Fire* serves as the turn to a more dark and serious tone with the rise of Voldemort in the rebirthing mass in the graveyard after Harry and Cedric were transported by the Cup serving as a Portkey. In support of the theory that *Goblet of Fire* is the turn book, remember that Harry receives his wand in *Sorcerer's Stone,* breaks it in *Deathly Hallows,* but actually learns of the connection of his wand to Voldemort's wand as "brothers" in *Goblet of Fire.* From *Goblet of Fire* the books take on a seriousness not found in the first three volumes. Harry sees death first hand with the loss of Cedric in *Goblet of Fire.* We find that many of the second listings of the parallels are much more dark and sinister than when they are first introduced. For example, the appearance of Sirius Black in *Prisoner of Azkaban,* seemingly sinister and frightening to Harry, turns out to be a wondrous reunion of Harry with his lost godfather. At the end of *Order of the Phoenix,* Black's life is lost and Harry is alone and separated from what was one of his only connections to his parents. After the death of Cedric in *Goblet of Fire,* Harry begins to experience death at a much more rapid rate in each subsequent book: Sirius (OP), Dumbledore (HBP), and Mad-eye Moody, Dobby, Lupin, Tonks, Colin Creevey, Fred, Severus Snape and finally Lord Voldemort (DH) all find death in the last three books of the series.

Rowling stays consistent with chiastic structure not only in developing a dark and grisly second half to the series, but in maintaining this coherence with elements that are seemingly irrelevant to the plotline. His owl Hedwig that he received in *Sorcerer's Stone* is lost in *Deathly Hallows*. Buckbeak, a flying creature, is mirrored by the Thestrals, flying creatures, which can only be seen by those who have seen death. Even the foolish and odd teacher of Lockhart is paralleled by Slughorn, himself an odd bird, but much more complex a character with a secret ever more sinister than Lockhart's.

This fascinating use of chiastic structure is not only used for mere parallelism, but to advance the storyline and plot in a much deeper and compelling way. It causes us to return to the books again and again because of the delicate and elaborate story scaffolding that provides continuous rewards for the attentive reader.

CONCLUSION

Joanne Rowling has masterfully constructed, on multiple levels, a novel series that is not merely children's fiction (which it is and is great at this level). Without obstructing the surface plot line, she has built into the story the ancient element of chiastic structure. This level of complexity and knowledge of literature is hardly evidence of the world's descent into sub-literacy as some have claimed. Whatever else might be said of Rowling's work, it touches all the elements of literary genius. Peeling back layers of meaning and structure with a deliberate pattern, the intelligent reader will walk away satisfied with many readings of Potter. Anyone who begs to differ must be blooming deceived.[23]

---

23   Thanks is necessary to many of the students of Prestonwood Christian Academy, especially Courtney Stevens and Grant Tucker, who provided insightful pointers to the many parallels found in the series..

On Turtleback Tales and Asterisks:
Picturing the Harry Potter Novels and their Many Interrelationships

John Granger

T HIS IS A BOOK for nerds, right? And, specifically, for nerds who have read *Harry Potter* more than once or twice, correct? That means, I hope, that I can skip the stuff everyone who has seen the movies knows and, more important, that I needn't apologize for focusing on a subject which casual readers might think of as trivial or arcane. Great!

What I want to talk about here is the *shape* of the Hogwarts Saga, something I couldn't include in my latest book, the revised *Unlocking Harry Potter,* because the chapter into which it belonged already threatened to become a book of its own. The shape or form of the seven book series, though, is a subject that Potter Pundits and *Goblet* geeks will eat up because you folks understand both how elusive and difficult seeing the series as one picture is and how rewarding thinking about this over-arching structure is for grasping both the books' meaning as well as the cause of their popularity.

Let's look at possible shapes for visualizing the series as a whole, moving from simplest to most involved, always with an eye on the mirror (!) and on picturing relationships between the seven books as accurately as possible.

Simple Sequence: The Straight Line

The easiest mental picture is the one everyone has or at least anyone who owns the books or has seen them on library shelves. The seven books line up one to seven quite literally as a line, *Philosopher's Stone* to *Deathly Hallows,* and I've never seen a private collection, bookstore display, or library shelf that doesn't keep the books in that sequence. Considering they probably *should* be shelved alphabetically or by Dewey Decimal number in libraries, that's saying something. The public understanding of the books and films is that they form a straight line, 1 -2 -3 -4 -5 -6 -7 (or 7a -7b with respect to the films).

Which makes sense, of course. Each of the books follows almost immediately after the action of the previous work and chronicles Harry's Hogwarts education in year-to-year sequence. This is so much of a commonplace among serious Potter readers that the almost universally accepted shorthand for book titles is the letters 'HP' followed by the numbers 1 to 7, e.g., HP1 for *Philosopher's Stone,* an abbreviation that leaves no one scratching his or head and asking, "What is 'HP3'?"

No matter what shape we ultimately arrive at, then, that shape will have to show the books in sequence without a break as well as whatever other relationships we discover. Those remarkable relationships do, alas, make the Straight Line figure inadequate as a picture of the series, but depicting these other connections cannot displace the 'base line' figure of sequential connection linking the seven books as a series.

The Circle: Meeting of Beginning and End

After the sequence idea we all have, the next most compelling mental picture of how the books relate is a circle in which the series beginning and end overlap. The number and out-in-the-open quality of the connections between *Philosopher's Stone* and *Deathly Hallows* make this re-drawing of our line so its ends meet a natural next step.

I drew up a chart of these connections – of which I'm sure there are more than I picked up back in 2007! – for my book on the series finale, *The Deathly Hallows Lectures* (Zossima, 2008). I reproduce it here rather than write them out or explore them at length:

Deathly Hallows	Philosopher's Stone
Hagrid with Harry on Sirius' Bike	Hagrid with Harry on Sirius' Bike
Hagrid carries Voldemort-attacked Harry	Hagrid carries Voldemort-attacked Harry
Harry, Ron, and Hermione rescue dragon	Harry and Hermione rescue Norbert(a)
Harry's resurrection after King's Cross	Harry's resurrection after three days
Neville out of nowhere is Gryffindor Champion defeating Slytherin serpent	Neville's surprise points cause Gryffindor victory over Slytherin House
Dumbledore's Deluminator key to Ron's return	Dumbledore's Deluminator on Privet Drive
Stoppered Death potion revealed	Snape mentions ability to "stopper death"
Harry rides the rails at Gringotts with Griphook	Harry rides the rails at Gringotts with Griphook
Hermione to Ron at Whomping Willow: "*Are you a wizard, or what!?*"	Ron to Hermione at Devil's Snare: "ARE YOU A WITCH OR NOT!?"

Driving Mystery: The Deathly Hallows and, specifically, the Resurrection Stone	Driving Mystery: Finding the Philosopher's Stone and keeping it from Snape
Harry found worthy of Hallows and Mastery of Death because he doesn't want to use them	Harry able to "find" Stone and take it from Mirror because he doesn't want to use it
Harry abandons magical objects giving him faux immortality with Dumby's approval	Dumbledore explains why he and Flamel agreed to destroy the Philosopher's Stone
Ollivander teaches Harry about wand-choice	Ollivander teaches Harry about wand-choice
Draco and Harry are united on a broom	Harry and Draco have it out at their first flying lesson
Ron uses "Wingardium Leviosa" on a stick	Ron uses "Wingardium Leviosa" on a club
Harry learns origin of Invisibility Cloak and receives Resurrection Stone from Dumby	Harry receives Invisibility Cloak as gift from Dumbledore at Christmas
Harry learns his family story at Christmas in Godric's Hollow	Harry sees his family for the first time in the Mirror of Erised on Christmas Day
Harry hates Severus but learns in the end that Snape was Dumbledore's closest ally	Harry hates Severus but learns in the end that Snape protected him from Quirrelldemort
The Centaurs break their rule of non-involvement to fight Lord Voldemort	The Centaur Firenze breaks Centaur custom by rescuing Harry from Quirrelldemort

Harry in obedience goes into Forbidden Forest to confront Lord Voldemort	Harry serves a detention in Forbidden Forest and has near-death experience with Voldy
Harry goes underground seven times in trials and opens Resurrection Stone	Harry overcomes seven obstacles underground to reach Philosopher's Stone
Harry decides he must seek Horcruxes and tries to convince R&H to stay behind	Harry decides he must protect the Stone and tries to convince R&H to stay behind
Neville is left behind and misses adventure	Neville is left behind and misses adventure
Order of Phoenix parents die in battle leaving orphan boy named "Gift from God" *Theodore	Order of Phoenix parents die in battle leaving orphan boy named "Heir of Father" (Pater)
Voldemort kills Hogwarts Professors (2)	Voldemort kills Hogwarts Professor
Harry's victory is won and celebrated in Hogwarts' Great Hall	Harry's victory is revealed and celebrated in Hogwarts' Great Hall

Ms. Rowling in these story echoes was clearly asking the reader to see Harry's final journey in *Hallows* as a return to his story's origins in *Stone*. A circle reflects this conjunction of beginning to end without violating the base-line sequence of the novels, one to seven.

What is curious is that more than a few readers *predicted* that Deathly Hallows would have this overlapping or story-echo relationship with *Philosopher's Stone* years before the last book was published. Other relationships that the circle figure reveals were sufficiently clear as far back as 2003 that the chiasmus theory, a traditional story circle that would align the stories as A-B-C-D-C'-B'-A', was already being discussed as a strong possibility on thoughtful Hogwarts Saga websites like 'Harry

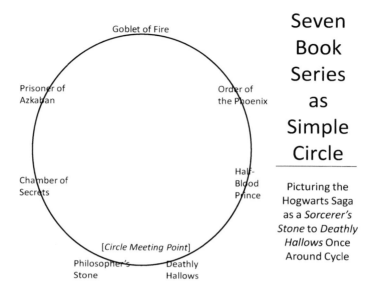

Seven
Book
Series
as
Simple
Circle
_____

Picturing the
Hogwarts Saga
as a *Sorcerer's
Stone* to *Deathly
Hallows* Once
Around Cycle

The Ladder Relationships: Books 2 and 6, 3 and 5

This idea would change the circle figure by drawing in lines between the books that are opposite one another, i.e., connecting *Chamber of Secrets* and *Half-Blood Prince* as well as joining *Prisoner of Azkaban* with *Order of the Phoenix*. Joyce Odell, writing as 'The Red Hen,' was a leading voice in Potter Fandom whose website posts were read and discussed by millions of readers in the run-up to *Deathly Hallows*. She nailed down the *Chambers-Prince* connection with a mind-boggling 50 links in 2005:

> 1. In both Book 2 *and* Book 6 it is beginning to look very much as if the whole central issue was precipitated by Lucius Malfoy's foolish and self-serving decision to deploy the Riddle Diary, without permission.
>
> 2. A House Elf who despises his Master shows up and pitches a fit in #4 Privet Drive.

3. Harry is removed from Privet Drive in the middle of the night, to an unfamiliar destination. He ends up spending the rest of the summer with the Weasleys.

4. Harry meets this year's new teacher before the school year starts. New teacher is determined to strike up an association with Harry.

5. New teacher is a celebrity hound with a flair for the dramatic, an ostentatious wardrobe, a weakness for boasting, and keeps drawing attention to Harry in his class throughout the year.

6. Hagrid meets Harry in Diagon Alley.

7. Malfoy is in Diagon Alley the same day as the trio, in company with one of his parents.

8. An altercation with the Malfoys occurs in a Diagon Alley shop. One of the Malfoys provokes it by making nasty, uncalled-for comments related to Hermione's parentage. Ill-breeding is displayed by all parties in the confrontation.

9. We pay another visit to Borgin & Burke's. The same black lacquer cabinet is a centerpiece. The same cursed opal necklace is again pointed out to our attention.

10. We spy on the Slytherins in their own territory. Malfoy drops heavy hints about helping the Dark Lord.

11. Harry is prevented from getting into Hogwarts on his own. This time we *know* Malfoy is responsible.

12. Harry arrives at Hogwarts late, and the first staff member to meet him is Snape, who is characteristically unpleasant.

13. One of the first new student characters we meet is a member of the "upper crust," with comments regarding the new teacher.

14. Someone is presented with a used book, and develops an emotional attachment to the previous owner. ("A friend that I can carry in my pocket!") Neither the book nor the previous owner are what anyone could call *harmless*.

15. The book dates from something in the neighborhood of 50 years ago. This is the aforementioned "ringer." We are supposed to recognize the echo. But the book's date doesn't actually relate to anything actively deployed in the text and certainly does not relate to Riddle, or the Riddle era at Hogwarts. (Close, but no cigar!)

16. Someone spends the whole year pulling a Lockhart (taking credit for someone else's work).

17. Hermione blatantly breaks rules to advance a personal agenda.

18. Hermione attracts the attention of the new teacher. She is very pleased to have it.

19. The new teacher sets up a club. Everyone in Gryffindor seems to be interested in it.

20. Much attention gets focused upon a complex Potion. This Potion is later used to acquire crucial information.

21. How many people remember that our very first introduction to how a Pensieve works was in CoS? Yes, that's right. Riddle incorporated the function of a Pensieve into the Diary.

22. Harry accesses some valuable information through the unconscious use of Parseltongue.

23. Partway through the first term of the year we are introduced to a complete sad sack of a girl who is bullied, put-upon, and fundamental to the underlying problem du jure. This "born victim's" own conduct is anything but exemplary.

24. A member of the Slytherin family is described as elderly and "monkey-like". (His son spends his spare time in trees. Query: are we supposed to now be wondering whether "Slytherin" is some high-falutin attempt at a variant on "simian"? ["We are DEVO!"])

25. Mysterious attacks are made upon students. With more good luck than good management these attacks are non-fatal, but the victims spend a variously extended time out of commission. (The earlier the attack, the longer the time out of commission.)

26. Molly and Arthur Weasley rush to the school in response to an attack on one of their children.

27. We first encounter Tom Riddle himself in chapter 13. The two chapter titles are deliberate echoes of one another.

28. We spend quality time in Herbology wrangling with dangerous plants.

29. The newest teacher on Staff throws a Holiday party.

30. A correctly brewed Potion goes badly wrong, leading to long-term adverse effects upon one of the trio.

31. Harry is injured at Quidditch and spends the night in the Hospital Wing. Dobby shows up in the night, unexpectedly.

32. Somewhere in the Castle there is a room that no one can find. Or, if find, open. In the climax of the story a monster gains access to the school through this uncharted space.

33. Polyjuice espionage with Crabbe and Goyle. 'Nuff said.

34. We finally acquire the key to the mystery *du jure* immediately following an encounter involving Aragog.

This key leads us directly to information concerning pivotal actions of young Tom Riddle when he was still a student at the school.

35. A significant discovery takes place in a bathroom. Myrtle is present.

36. Harry and Draco get into a duel which is brought to a shattering end by one of them using a spell which originally came from Severus Snape. There are publicly unpleasant consequences from this conflict for Harry.

37. We first encountered the Vanishing Cabinet in CoS. Peeves broke it at that point, at Nearly Headless Nick's urging, in order to keep Harry from getting a detention from Filch for tracking mud into the Castle. Someone had put it physically back together again, although it seems to have taken Malfoy some months to repair the spells on it.

38. Snape himself gets surprisingly little page time during most of the year. We see him at the beginning and the end of the book, but only get a glimpse or two in the middle, mostly through report.

39. He does contribute his efforts to at least one medical crisis, however.

40. Dumbledore leaves the school before the climax of the story; this absence is connected with the actions of one of the Malfoys. He returns only when the final confrontation is upon everyone.

41. ... leading to a confrontation between the Malfoy involved and Albus.

42. The climax of the tale involves a visit to a grand, perilous, ancient chamber, underground, which cannot be accessed except by complying to specific conditions, and is associated with a Slytherin.

43. Someone significant to Harry nearly dies there. [In CoS, Harry is forced to *kill* something there.]

44. An artifact of some significance is brought out of this chamber. Upon examination, there turns out to be either something *more*, or something *different* to the artifact than was first assumed.

45. A decent person is discovered to have been acting under an enemy's control over the past year.

46. A Malfoy's close connection with the school is brought to an end.

47. Somebody gets thrown off a staircase.

48. The climax and/or its aftermath is accompanied by Phoenix Song.

49. The school Governers are invoked.

50. Exams are cancelled.[1]

Pretty exhaustive and exhausting echoing there, no? Here's an easier way to think of the *Chamber-Prince* connection that these 50 links make undeniable: Chamber and Prince are the two Harry Potter novels that are largely about the Dark Lord. We meet him in *Chamber* and learn a good deal of his back story. Prince is largely a story wrapped around Harry and Dumbledore's repeated trips into the Pensieve to learn Voldy's secret past.

Books 3 and 5, *Azkaban* and *Phoenix*, have a similar connection via a character, namely, Sirius Black. He's prisoner in *Prisoner of Azkaban* and the story is the slow reveal and lead-up to Harry's understanding of his godfather's history. Harry gets the rest of this history during his summer sojourn at The House of Black in *Phoenix*, the book that closes with Sirius' heroic death. The alchemical stage that is depicted in Phoenix is the nigredo or 'Black Stage,' and that label is a match with the

---

1   http://www.redhen-publications.com/2ndGuessing.html

novel's second subject and with Harry's experiences that year.

Here are twenty internal reflections, some straight up, many "reverse echoes" or story inversions, between Prisoner and Phoenix to help anyone struggling to see this connection:

Prisoner of Azkaban	Order of the Phoenix
Book opens with Harry furious with Dursley near relation, Aunt Marge.	Book opens with Harry furious with Dursley near relation, Dudley.
The Dementors assigned by the Ministry attack Harry on the Hogwarts Express and during a Quidditch match.	Ministry deployed Dementors attack Harry on Privet Drive
Harry hears about Sirius Black several times before leaving for Hogwarts and learns about him throughout the year	Harry stays at the House of Black before leaving for Hogwarts and communicates with him throughout the year.
There's a boggart in the Staff Room wardrobe that Lupin uses in a Defense Against the Dark Arts class.	There's a boggart in the writing desk at the House of Black and Lupin consoles and instructs Mrs. Weasley after she is frightened by it.
Sirius fights with the Fat Lady painting at the Gryffindor Tower entrance.	Sirius does daily battle with the painting of his mother at the House of Black entrance.
Cornelius Fudge is personally involved with the aftermath of Harry's blowing up Aunt Marge, something he addresses before Harry leaves for Hogwarts	The Minister of Magic does everything in his power to expel Harry from Hogwarts after his fighting off the Dementors, to include a full court trial before Harry leaves for Hogwarts

Harry attends tutorial lessons to learn high-powered magic none of his contemporaries need, i.e., the ability to create a Patronus	Harry attends tutorial lessons to learn high-powered magic none of his contemporaries need, i.e., the ability to practice Occlumency
His ability to conjure a Patronus saves his life at story's end.	His ability to conjure a Patronus saves his life at story's beginning.
The Ministry's intrusion into Hogwarts life, the detailing of Dementors at the school supposedly for the students' protection, makes life relatively miserable and restricted for them	The Ministry's intrusion into Hogwarts life, the assignment of Dolores Umbridge supposedly for the school's reformation, makes life relatively miserable and restricted for everyone there
Harry's father is revealed to him as a great wizard and cool dude, "Prongs"	Harry's father is revealed to him as something of a self-important jerk, "Snape's Worst Memory"
We see the visceral and unforgiving hatred Sirius and Severus feel for one another in the Shrieking Shack	We witness the visceral and unforgiving hatred Sirius and Severus feel for one another in the House of Black
Harry believes for a short time at the end of the bok that he will be able to leave the Dursleys and live with his godfather Sirius	Harry leaves the Dursleys at the beginning of the book to spend a short time with his godfather Sirius
We witness an authentic Prophecy from Professor Trelawney	We see the memory of an authentic Prophecy from Professor Trelawney

Hagrid shows his students flying magical creatures who are misunderstood by Witches and Wizards, i.e., Hippogriffs	Hagrid shows his students flying magical creatures who are misunderstood by Witches and Wizards, i.e., Thestrals
Hagrid begs Harry, Ron, and Hermione for help with Buckbeak's defense	Hagrid begs Harry, Ron, and Hermione for help with Grawp's education
Severus is furious with Harry at story's end; he seems borderline unhinged because Sirius escaped death and holds Harry responsible	Harry is furious with Snape at story's end; he is borderline irrational because of Sirius' death for which he thinks Severus is largely responsible
Harry saves Sirius from certain death at risk of his own life by flying in at the last moment to provide him with the opportunity to escape, i.e. Buckbeak at the Astronomy Tower top	Sirius saves Harry from near-certain death at the cost of his own life by arriving at the last moment and creating the opportunity for him to escape; i.e., Apparating into the Department of Mysteries
Harry outscores Hermione on a Defense Against the Dark Arts final exam	Harry outscores Hermione on the Defense Against the Dark Arts O.W.L.
Voldemort mysteriously absent from everything but Harry's dreams and thoughts	Voldemort mysteriously quiet, an invisible presence except in Harry's mind until the very end
Harry has his first serious feelings for Cho Chang	Harry's crush on Cho Chang becomes a kiss in the Room of Requirement and a few dates before ending when her friend betrays the DA

Are there more? Sure there are. Does any one of these story reflections in itself nail down the *Prisoner-Phoenix* connection? I don't think so. Taken collectively, though, it seems more than plausible that the author intentionally wanted to us to draw a mental line at least between the third and fifth books. Drawing in the *Chamber-Prince* connection in our story circle as well, we have the image of a ladder with rounded sides:

Goblet of Fire: 'Hiccup' in Pattern or Story Heart?

Looking at this story picture, every book except *Goblet of Fire*, HP4, has a partner in the circle. An advocate of a chiasmus interpretation, M. Brett Kendall, a graduate student in theology at Fordham in 2005 and 2006, argued that this conception was faulty because the tradition of literary chiasm requires that the center point or turn in any A-B-A' sequence be the kernel or

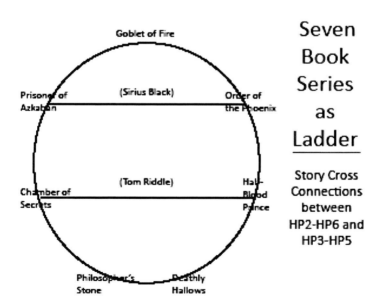

hidden treasure that unlocks the meaning of the other parts. Kendall joked that the circle parallels in isolating *Goblet* made it more of a "hiccup" than story heart and labeled its fandom advocates "Tripping Billies" after a popular song because *Goblet* was left as something to trip over on the walk from story start to finish.[2]

And he has an excellent point. *Goblet* is not a work in isolation or just a book in which we transition from front half to back half. It seems, believe it or not, to be tied into the connections between the first and last book of the series, *Stone and Hallows*, whose point of conjunction is opposite in our story circle. Here is a chart detailing a bunch of these *Stone-Goblet-Hallows* story links:

Stone-Goblet-Hallows Reflections and Echoes

Philosopher's Stone	Goblet of Fire	Deathly Hallows
Opening Deaths: The day Lord Voldemort murdered Potters	Opening Death: Lord Voldemort murders Frank Bryce	Opening Death: Lord Voldemort murders Charity Burbage
Harry's first appearance: in 'bedroom' thinking about scar	Harry's first appearance: in bedroom thinking about scar	Harry's first appearance: in bedroom thinking about scar
'Letter from No One' Hogwarts letter that causes Dursley departure from Privet Drive to escape witches and wizards		'Dursleys Departing' Magical escorts taking Dursleys from Privet Drive to escape evil witches and wizards

---

2 http://mugglematters.blogspot.com/2007/06/merlins-manifesto-further-support-of.html

'Letter from No One' floods through fireplace into living room	'Invitation' The next letter Harry receives by stamp post precedes Weasleys flooding into fireplace	
Hagrid knocks down door of Hut on the Rock and has difficulties with Dursleys	Mr. Weasley, Fred and George, blow through blocked fireplace and meet with angry Dursleys	
Dudley transfigured (pigtail)	Dudley transfigured (tongue)	Dudley transformed (wishes Harry well at departure)
Harry catches a Remembrall while on broomstick in conflict with a flying Draco	Harry snatches a Golden Egg away from the a flying dragon, mama Hungarian Horntail	Harry steals the Horcrux Cup from Gringotts and escapes on a flying dragon
Harry catches Snitch in first Quidditch match as Gryffindor Seeker with his mouth		Dumbledore leaves Snitch from first match to Harry in his will – as cover for Resurrection Stone
	Harry at Burrow before year's adventure begins	Harry at Burrow before year's adventure begins

	The Terrific Trio travel together to the site of the Quidditch World Cup and set up Perkins' tent that is really a house	Hermione Side-Along Apparates Ron and Harry to the Quidditch World Cup glade and they set up Perkins' tent again
In Leaky Cauldron Harry meets Quirinus Quirrell who is murdered by Dark Lord	Harry meets Barty Crouch, Sr., at World Cup and he is murdered by a Death Eater soon after	Harry meets with Rufus Scrimgeour and he is murdered by Death Eaters soon after
Ron ashamed of being poor boy on Hogwarts Express	Ron ashamed of being poor boy at QWC, on Hogwarts Express, and in pajamas before first trial	Ron ashamed of being "third man out" in Harry-Ron-Hermione trio
Defense Against the Dark Arts teacher is Lord Voldemort stooge in disguise	Defense Against the Dark Arts teacher is Lord Voldemort stooge in disguise	Hogwarts Textbook author is human wrapping for Lord Voldemort familiar
Ollivander appears – Diagon Alley	Ollivander appears – Weighing of the Wands	Ollivander appears – Malfoy Manor, Shell Cottage
Norbert the Dragon (baby)	Hungarian Horntail (mother and egg)	Gringotts Dragon (ancient of days)

Harry faces Cerebrus ("Fluffy"), a mythological monster, in the series of trials that conclude his year's adventures	Harry meets the Sphinx, a mythological monster, in the Maze's collection of tests that conclude the official Tri Wizard Tournament	Harry survives Fiend Fyre in the Room of Requirement, which "welcome back" to Hogwarts horror in the Battle's series of tests takes the shape of chimaeras, a mythological monster
Vanishing Glass/ Mirror of Erised: Explained by Dumbledore	Foe Glass: Reflects Fiery Dumbledore in confrontation with Faux-Moody	Gilded Mirror at Malfoys,' Sirius' Mirror Fragment: Eye of Dumbledore responds to Harry's call for help
Harry confronted by Lord Voldemort's murderous henchman in Forbidden Forest	Lord Voldemort's henchman murders Barty Crouch, Sr., at edge of Forbidden Forest	Harry confronts Lord Voldemort and henchman in Forbidden Forest – and is murdered
Battle with Lord Voldemort: no wands, sacrificial love of mother decisive	Battle with Lord Voldemort: wand cores decisive	Beginning and End Battles with Lord Voldemort: Wand Cores decisive in each
Appearance of parents in Mirror of Erised	Appearance of parents within Phoenix Song Sphere	Appearance of parents via Resurrection Stone

Albus Dumbledore Denouement post three day resurrection	Albus Dumbledore denouement after Harry returns from graveyard	Albus Dumbledore denouement after Harry rises from sacrificial death and defeats Dark Lord
Story Pivot: 'Midnight Duel' first out-of-bounds adventure with Ron, Hermione, and Neville to meet Fluffy	Story Pivot: Midnight meeting with Hagrid to see Dragons, talk with Sirius	Story Pivot: Christmas Eve Midnight nightmare meeting with Nagini, witnessing first murders
Hagrid welcomes Harry to Wizarding World at story's start in Hut on the Rock at midnight	Hagrid reveals dragons of first task at midnight to Harry at story's center in pivotal novel	Hagrid's creatures and friends from the Forest, having shamed Bane, lead the decisive attack on Voldemort and the Death Eaters
Good Guy Harry thinks is a Bad Guy turns out to be a Good Guy (Severus Snape). Bad Guy Harry thinks is a Good Guy turns out to be a Bad Guy – who dies (Quirinus Quirrell)	Frightening Guy Harry thinks is a Good Guy turns out to be a Bad Guy -- who dies (Barty Crouch, Jr./Faux Alastor Moody). Good Guy Harry found out was a bad guy turns out to be a Good Guy (the real Alastor Moody)	Good Guy Harry thinks is a Bad Guy turns out to be a Good Guy who dies (Severus Snape); Dead Good Guy Harry changes his mind about turns out to be a Good Guy (Albus Dumbledore)

Harry has two adventures his first year that he plans and a third against a variety of obstacles that he has to wing: his midnight meeting with Fluffy, his dragon rescue mission, and the faculty-set hurdles that protect the Stone. Then he meets Lord Voldemort	Harry has three Tri-Wizard tasks, two of which are set pieces he is given time to prepare for and the third being a series of tests he has to wing: taking an egg from a dragon, the underwater rescue mission, and the Great Maze with its magical plants, creatures, and a mythic beast. Then he fights the Dark Lord.	Harry has two big adventures he plans in the finale – the invasion of the Ministry (and Cattermole rescue mission), the Great Gringotts Bank Robbery – and then a series of obstacles and skirmishes in the Battle of Hogwarts leading up to his two meetings with Lord Voldemort
Firenze tells Harry about the effects of drinking Unicorn blood unworthily and story turns on the value of the Stone's 'Elixir of Life.'	The Goblet of Fire is a Grail symbol, the Communion Cup of the Last Supper, and the Dark Lord returns to a human body via a Black Mass featuring Harry Potter's blood	Harry Potter survives the Death Curse again because of the Bond of Blood and the choice of a sacrificial death in love for his friends

Enough? I think so. The simple, undeniable link is that Harry fights the Dark Lord man to man only in these three books and each time the story turns on the bond of blood and their phoenix feather wand cores. Drawing in the line connecting *Goblet* and *Stone/Hallows* changes our ladder-shape into something like the back of a turtle shell.

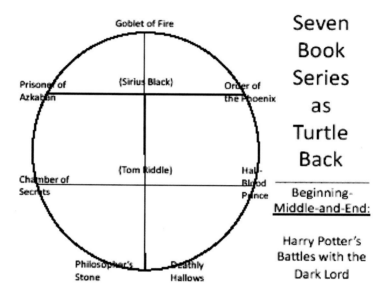

The Hogwarts Saga as Ring Composition

The "turtleback" story shape simultaneously displays the seven books in sequence, the meaningful correspondences between books, and *Goblet* less as a hiccup than the story pivot connecting the beginning and end. *Goblet* here, though it isn't obvious in its position at the circle summit, has become the axis rather than a peripheral point of the saga.

This is in keeping with Ms. Rowling's comments about *Goblet* at the time of its publication:

> *And how vital is book four in the whole seven book series to Harry?*

JKR: Crucial. The fourth is a very, very important book. Well you know because you read it, something incredibly important happens in book four and also it's literally a central book, it's almost the heart of the series, and it's pivotal. It's very difficult to talk about and I can't wait for the day someone's read all seven and I can talk completely freely about it. But it's a very, very important book.[3]

The word "central" of course can be understood as just the middle term in a sequential series but "pivotal" suggests a change of direction, which, with her pointing to a *Goblet* event as "something incredibly important," seemed to mean that Voldemort's rebirth and presence would mean a change in the series. Her saying that we would have to wait until the end of the series, *Deathly Hallows*, to appreciate its importance all but draws the vertical line down the turtle's back. And saying that it is "crucial," literally, "like the cross," is just a hoot as we'll see in a moment.

What's fascinating to me about this turtleback diagram is that it shows how Ms. Rowling's seven Hogwarts Saga novels are what Mary Douglas, renowned anthropologist, calls a "ring composition." In her *Thinking in Circles: An Essay on Ring Composition* (Yale, 2007), she details how stories from Homer's *Iliad* to Laurence Sterne's *The Life and Opinions of Tristam Shandy, Gentleman,* to include key passages and books of the Old and New Testaments and epics from every aural culture living and dead are configured as rings with specific characteristics. She explains that this "macro-structure" is invisible to the analytic modern readers focused on plot, language, and theme but that its internal echoing on top of its beginning and end conjunction mark a ring as deliberate artistry.

> Closure is not the only, or even the principal, condition for a ring. Essentially, ring composition is a double sequence of analogies. First a sequence is laid down, then at a certain point the sequence stops and the

---

3   "JK Rowling talks about Book Four," *cBBC Newsround*, July 8, 2000; http://www.accio-quote.org/articles/2000/0700-cbbc-mzimba.htm

series turns around and a new sequence works its way
backward, step by step toward the beginning. This puts
each member of the new series parallel to its opposite
number in the first series, so the return journey reverses
the order of the outgoing journey. The longer ring
forms tend to embellish the mid-turn with an elaborate
commentary. A well-marked turning point is a sign of
a well-designed ring composition. Sometimes, it takes
the form of a minor ring. Sometimes it is so long as to
mislead the reader about its place in a larger structure.[4]

The best way to picture a "double series of analogies,"
stories that parallel one another as they ascend to and descend
from a turning point opposite the closure of beginning and end
is our turtleback loop. Ms. Douglas has "abstracted seven rules
or conventions from long ring compositions" whose "meaning
is in the middle" that help identify this story scaffolding and
reveal its principle message.[5] These seven "rules" are not "hard
and fast" but indicators reflecting the technical problems to
be overcome in telling a successfully rounded tale. For our
purposes I think they can be distilled even further down to four
characteristics:

1. The Beginning and End Meet: No closure, no ring.
Duh.

2. The Big Turn: Prof. Douglas explains it this way --

*If the end is going to join the beginning the composition
will at some point need to make a turn toward the start.
The convention draws an imaginary line between the
middle and the beginning, which divides the work into
two halves, the first, outgoing, the second, returning. In
a long text it is important to accentuate the turn lest the
hasty reader miss it, in which case the rest of the carefully*

---

4   Mary Douglas, *Thinking in Circles: An Essay on Ring Composition*,
Yale University Press, New Haven CT: 2007; p. 34
5   *Thinking*, op. cit, pp. 35-38

balanced correspondences will also be missed.[6]

3: Parallel Front and Back Halves: Prof. Douglas –

After the mid-turn the next challenge for the composer of a ring is to arrange the two sides in parallel. This is done by making separate sections that are placed in parallel across the central dividing line. Each section on one side has to be matched by its corresponding pair on the other side. In practice the matching of sections often contains surprises; items are put into concordance that had not previously been seen to be similar. Parallelism gives the artist opportunities of taking the text to deeper levels of analogy. When the reader finds two pages set in parallel that seem quite disparate, the challenge is to ask what they may have in common, not to surmise that the editor got muddled.[7]

4: Rings Within Rings: a curious trait of Ring Writers, not to be confused with Ring Wraiths, is that they insert ring compositions within larger ring stories (cf., Prof. Douglas' explanation of the Sacrifice of Isaac inside the larger biblical narrative[8]).

I think we've established how the seven books pass the first three ring litmus strip tests. But where are those "rings within the ring"?

This is probably the most fascinating thing about Ms. Rowling's circular artistry – *every single book in the series is a detailed ring composition or turtleback tale.* Prof. Douglas cites W. A. von Otterlo, the Dutch classicist who wrote the first work on Ring Composition (*De Ringcompositie als opboawprincipie in de Epische Geschicten van Homerus,* 1948), as pointing out that "the major ring may be internally structured by little rings."[9]

---

6   *Thinking,* op. cit, pp. 36
7   *Thinking,* op. cit, pp. 36
8   *Thinking,* op. cit, pp. 18-27
9   *Thinking,* op. cit, p 37

Incredibly, this is the case with the Hogwarts Saga. The larger ring is made up of books each of which is an independent turtleback tale itself.

I cannot demonstrate that here in detail, of course, but the necessary charts and graphs are in the Ring Composition chapter of *Harry Potter Unlocked* along with the explanation of *why* Ms. Rowling does this and *how* it fuels Potter-mania that I cannot get into at any depth in this essay. As a sample of this artistry, though, here is the chart detailing the parallels between opposite chapters along with a turtleback diagram for *Goblet of Fire*, the series axis.

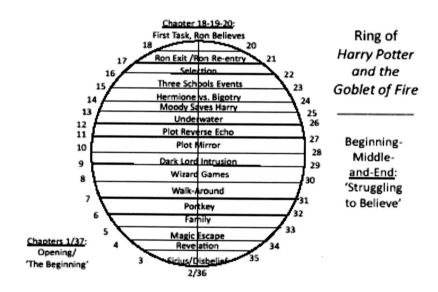

Harry Potter and the Goblet of Fire

Chapter Number and Chapter Title	Reflection or Reverse Echo	Chapter Number and Chapter Title
1: The Riddle House	***The Dark Lord's Murders*** The first chapter is set in the house destroyed by Tom Riddle's first murders and the caretaker whose life was taken from him figuratively by gossip and literally at last by Voldemort; "The Beginning" at story's end features Dumbledore's open speech about the murder of Cedric Diggory, that the Dark Lord did it, and our best response to it. The finish is the antidote to the wreckage seen in the opening.	37: The Beginning
2: The Scar	***Talking with Sirius about the Dark Lord*** Harry wakes up from his vision of the Bryce murder with a scar-ache and writes Sirius to ask if it is possible that the Dark Lord is returning; Harry tells Sirius and Dumbledore about Voldemort's resurrection and Fudge refuses to accept the signs.	36: The Parting of the Ways

3: The Invitation	***Not What You Thought*** Harry is invited to the Quidditch World Cup and eats cake while Dudley starves; he is surprised and elated that his world isn't what he thought. Barty Crouch, Sr., reveals the back story to the Dark Lord's return and Harry is shattered to learn Moody isn't who he thought he was.	35: Veritaserum
4: Back to the Burrow	***Unexpected Visitors' Entrance and Magical Escape*** The Weasleys come for Harry through a blocked fireplace and rescue him from the Dursleys; Harry's parents arrive out of Voldemort's wand and help him escape from the Little Hangleton graveyard.	34: Priori Incantatem
5: Weasleys' Wizard Wheezes	***Good Family; Evil Family*** Harry goes to the Burrow, meets the happy Wizarding family, and sees at last what a positive family life is like. In the reverse echo chapter, Lord Voldemort tells Harry the Riddle "family history" as his "true family returns," the Death Eaters.	33: The Death Eaters

6: The Portkey	***Portkey Destinations*** Harry travels at dawn with Weasleys and Diggorys to Quidditch World Cup via Portkey. In the dark reflection chapter, he travels via Portkey again with a Diggory, this time to a graveyard and the dawn of the new Lord Voldemort	32: Flesh, Blood, and Bone
7: Bagman and Crouch	***Walk Around and Friend's Deal*** Harry walks around QWC campgrounds meeting old friends and learning new things. He makes a deal with Ron to get past how much each owes the other. In 'Task' he walks around the maze fighting magical creatures – and makes a deal with Cedric so they are "even," no debts, at the Maze center.	31: The Third Task

8: The Quidditch World Cup	**The Gang's All Here** In a stadium of passionate wizards and witches, Harry sits in the Top Box with Barty Crouch, Jr., Ludo Bagman, Bulgarian officials, top Ministry officials, and the Malfoys at the Quidditch World Cup. In Dumbledore's Pensieve on the far side of Goblet, he steps into a spectator-full courtroom of angry wizards and witches to watch the trials of Barty Crouch, Jr., Ludo Bagman, and other former Death Eaters by top Ministry officials.	30: The Pensieve
9: The Dark Mark	**Dark Lord Intrusion** The sign of the Dark Lord appears above the World Cup campgrounds; Harry on the far side sees Lord Voldemort 'forgiving' and torturing Wormtail. Crouch unhinged in field is near parallel with 'Madness of Mr. Crouch' (chapter 28)	29: The Dream
10: Mayhem at the Ministry	**Plot Mirror** Two chapters both featuring a recap of Quidditch World Cup events, Percy's defense of Mr. Crouch, Ron's poverty concerns, SPEW notes from Hermione, and troubles via Rita Skeeter.	28: The Madness of Mr. Crouch

11: Aboard the Hogwarts Express	***Plot Reverse Echo*** Clueless kids getting bad dope transformed into insiders hearing the secret real history. Amos Diggory tells Mad-Eye Moody story about a paranoid loser named Moody and trio hear hints of Tournament in the front half; Sirius explains that Mad-Eye was a great Auror and tells Crouch and Karkaroff stories in the parallel chapter.	27: Padfoot Returns
12: The Triwizard Tournament	***Underwater*** Arriving students soaked by curtain rain and Peeves' water bombs while first years cross lake in storm. Dennis Creevey goes underwater. Harry's second task is the underwater trip into the lake to save his Wheezy.	26: The Second Task
13: Mad-Eye Moody	***Moody Saves Harry*** Mad-Eye intervenes in Potter-Malfoy skirmish to turn Draco into a bouncing ferret. In second half, he jumps in between Snape and Potter on staircase to protect the invisible Harry and the Map.	25: The Egg and the Eye

14: The Unforgivable Curses	***Hermione vs. Bigotry*** Hermione rolls out S.P.E.W. organization to take action against wizard discrimination and bigotry in re house-elves. She takes direct action in parallel chapter by scolding Skeeter publicly and confronting Hagrid about half-giant prejudice.	24: Rita Skeeter's Scoop
15: Beauxbatons and Durmstrang	***Three Schools Events*** We meet the students from Durmstrang and Beauxbatons; we party with our guests at the Yule Ball. These chapters are the principal two three-school events in the novel.	23: The Yule Ball
16: The Goblet of Fire	***Selection*** The first chapter is about the Goblet of Fire choosing Harry to his great discomfort; the parallel is Harry's experience trying to select a date for the ball, to his equally great discomfort.	22: The Unexpected Task
17: The Four Champions	***Ron Exit/Ron Re-Entry*** Ron flies off the handle at Harry's being chosen as Hogwarts' second champion and the trio is dissolved; on the other side of the center, Ron has just seen the error of his ways and the trio are back in action again.	21: The House-Elf Liberation Front

18: The Weighing of the Wands	***Four Champions: Before, During, and After*** The four champions go through preliminary ceremony and publicity meeting with Skeeter vignette; the four champions endure wait in tent and dragon task with Skeeter vignette.	20: The First Task
	19: The Hungarian Horntail Dead Center of series finds Harry under Invisibility Cloak visiting Hagrid at midnight (see Stone pivot) to see four dragons. Story nadir: Harry confesses woes to Sirius and has bitter exchange with Ron.	

And y'know what is really great about *Goblet?* The story climax – Harry battling with the Dark Lord in the graveyard at Little Hangleton – turns on the *Priori Incantem* effect of two wands with a shared wand core substance being forced to do battle. Not only is this a big link between *Stone-Goblet-and-Hallows,* Dumbledore describes this rare effect as "echoes" appearing in "reverse" sequence (*Goblet,* chapter 36, p. 697-698).

Forgive me, but this note, sounded as it is at the end of the turning point novel, just as the series is about to begin its "reverse echo" of the first three books in the last three novels, is too accurate a description of Ms. Rowling's Ring artistry to have been accidental. I'm beginning to think that she had Dumbledore die consequent to a cursed ring because his death was required by her obligations to the traditional ring story formula.

But that would be a stretch, right?

Whoops! Four Reasons the Simple Circle Ring and Turtle-Back Won't Work as Pictures of the Hogwarts Saga

Here's the funny thing, though. The turtleback image that works for all the interior rings of each book turns out not to work so well for the series as a whole. We've already seen that *Goblet* should be the center between the beginning and end rather than the top of the circle opposite *Stone/Hallows*. That reflects a bigger problem than aesthetics. There are four inter-book relationships that the '*Goblet* on Top' model won't reflect accurately.

The first two are inter-book pairs, *Philosopher's Stone* with *Order of the Phoenix* and *Prisoner of Azkaban* with *Deathly Hallows*. We could draw lines on the turtleback figure to represent these relationships but it's going to mess up the beautiful symmetry of the drawing.

And there's no denying substantive links between HP3 and HP7 and between HP1 and HP5. The entire Severus Snape sub-plot that threatened at several points to almost take over the series (who cares about Harry and Voldemort? More Snape-Rickman!) is resolved in *Hallows* as an intentional echo of the revelations in *Prisoner's* Shrieking Shack and Harry's "world turned upside down." In *Prisoner*, Sirius, Lupin, Pettigrew, and Snape together and separately (sep-*a-rat*-ley?) reveal that the big "bad guy" of the whole book, a man living with a death sentence over him and whom Harry hates, is actually a *very* good guy determined to do everything possible to save and protect him. Sirius, of course, in the parallel book opposite *Prisoner*, does wind up sacrificing himself when protecting Harry.

In *Hallows,* Snape is revealed to be Sirius' *Doppelganger* in his Shrieking Shack scene and the memories Harry collects from him there after Nagini's attack. Harry had sworn to kill Severus Snape, a man that he and the entire Wizarding World believed committed a murder that turns out *not* to have been a murder, just as Harry vowed to kill Sirius in *Prisoner* and just as Sirius was misunderstood to have murdered Pettigrew. Severus is killed after begging the Dark Lord for permission to "find the boy" which Harry learns in the Pensieve was his mission for more than fifteen years, i.e., protect Harry from harm in order to keep him alive and to do penance for his part in Lily Potter's death (think "Bloody Baron"). This HP3-HP7 connection, the Tao of Sirius and Severus, sworn contraries meeting near identical ends as resolution like yin and yang, is no small thing.

Similarly, the connections between *Stone* and the fifth book, *Order of the Phoenix*, are impossible to overlook. They're essentially the same story written twice, and, as *Phoenix* is close to twice as long as *Philosopher's Stone*, maybe that's reflected in their lengths (not). Joyce Odell detailed the many parallels between the two books soon after *Phoenix* was published in this story outline that describes the events of both books simultaneously:

1. There is a memorable incident concerning magic that involves Dudley.

2. Soon afterward the Dursleys are being inundated with owls. Harry ends up locked in his room.

3. Harry is removed from the Dursleys' custody in the middle of the night. They apparently have nothing to say about the matter. Harry is ultimately introduced to a "whole new world" for which nothing he knows has really prepared him. Some weeks later he boards the Hogwarts Express.

4. The DADA teacher is utterly useless. No one is ever stated as having learnt anything in the class.

5. Off in the background, Dumbledore is running an elaborate scam trying to lure Voldemort out of hiding.

6. The scam is wrapped around an artifact of great significance (or at least of great significance to Voldemort).

7. The artifact, under guard, has been carefully placed below ground in a maze/puzzle/labyrinth. There is a trick to getting hold of it. Harry ends up being about the only person who qualifies to do so.

8. Harry and his friends have no idea what is really going on regarding Dumbledore's scam, apart from the fact that *something* is going on. They are being purposely kept in the dark and repeatedly told to *leave it alone.*

9. Snape gets into a heavy confrontation with a person who dies in the final showdown.

10. Harry is inadvertently given a piece of critical information a bit before Christmas.

11. Around Christmas Harry makes a crucial discovery (Ron is also involved in this) and Dumbledore, who to this point has been rather a distant figure, steps forward and he and Harry have a significant encounter in which vital information is transmitted.

12. Hagrid turns up with a dangerous creature that he can't really control, and which puts him, personally, in an unnecessary state of risk.

13. He dumps the final dealing with the creature on Harry and his friends. This entails the breaking of school rules.

14. At the last moment, at the end of the year, Harry, who has hold of the wrong end of the stick, is convinced that he has to mount a rescue effort.

15. He doesn't do it alone. His friends accompany him.

16. The artifact that Dumbledore's current scam is wrapped around is at the destination point of this effort.

17. Obstacles which Harry must traverse before he can get to the "rescue" site include monsters from Greek mythology, tangled plant life, flying, a dangerously oversized humanoid (who is not actually a threat by that point), and problems requiring strategy and logic.

18. Ron is taken out of the equation in an attack involving the head/brain.

19. Hermione performs well to a point and after that point is simply unavailable.

20. When Harry gets to the "rescue" rendezvous, he comes face to face with Voldemort's agent.

21. Harry gets possession of the artifact anyway, right under the enemy's nose, and refuses to give it up. The whole exercise was probably a mistake, since it was safer where it was.

22. Voldemort reveals himself, reads Harry's mind.

23. Harry is attacked. Somebody *is* killed in the fracas, Harry has reason to feel some responsibility for the death, although he did not do the killing.

24. Dumbledore manages to rescue Harry, Voldemort escapes.

25. General debriefing between Dumbledore and Harry. The question of why Voldemort wants Harry dead is raised.[10]

That's at least as strong as any relationship between books other than the *Stone-Goblet-Hallows* axis. If that weren't enough along with HP3-HP7 to sink our turtle, M. Brett Kendall points out two more relationships our turtleback-drawing doesn't illustrate. These are *chiasmus* relationships connecting books 3-4-5 and books 2-4-6.

Chiasmus you recall is understanding a text as a series with echoes reflected after a pivot, which in a straight line series of seven would look like A-B-C-D-C'-B'-A', with D being the point of greatest meaning, through which the other points connect. Kendall points out that many of the 2-6 and 3-5 correspondences we graphed above have story echoes in *Goblet* that highlight how the fourth book is the crossing point for these correspondences.[11]

10   http://www.redhen-publications.com/2ndGuessing.html
11   M. Brett Kendall, 'X Marks the Spot: The Goblet of Fire and Literary

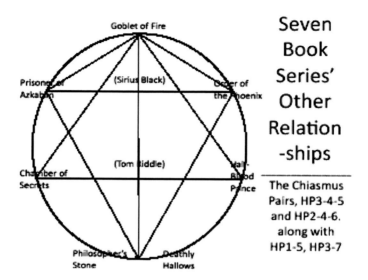

Seven Book Series' Other Relation -ships

The Chiasmus Pairs, HP3-4-5 and HP2-4-6. along with HP1-5, HP3-7

Go ahead and draw in those lines, too. I see a Star of David in there, which is interesting because of its alchemical meaning of resolving contraries, but I think it's fair to say these four lines obscure rather than clarify the core book correspondences and relationships in the series.

Fortunately, we don't have to live with the scratched-up turtleback as our mental picture of the series. There's a better, simpler way.

The Asterisk: A Picture of Every Book Relationship

Here are the specifications that our best-possible-image has to meet. Every book relationship and correspondence has to be shown by having the books in question adjacent to or directly opposite one another in the illustration. The relationships identified as most important are:

Chiasm,' http://www.mugglematters.com/2006/01/x-marks-spot-goblet-of-fire-and-chiasm.html and 'Merlin's Manifesto: Further Support of Chiasm in the Harry Potter series,' http://mugglematters.blogspot.com/2007/06/merlins-manifesto-further-support-of.html

- The Books in chronological order and by order of publication
- *Philosopher's Stone* with *Deathly Hallows*, preferably with *Goblet of Fire* between the two
- *Chamber of Secrets* with *Half-Blood Prince*, preferably with *Goblet of Fire* between the two (chiasmus)
- *Prisoner of Azkaban* with *Order of the Phoenix*, preferably with *Goblet of Fire* between the two (chiasmus)
- *Philosopher's Stone* with *Order of the Phoenix*
- *Prisoner of Azkaban* with *Deathly Hallows*

As improbable as it may seem, it's not that hard to do. Draw an asterisk or six pointed star inscribed by a circle. Put *Stone* at the circle and star top, *Goblet* at the asterisk and circle center or hub, and *Hallows* at the bottom opposite *Stone*. Put *Chamber* at the left of *Stone* and down a bit, say, 10:00 on the clock face, and *Prisoner* at 8:00. *Phoenix* goes to the right of *Stone*, a little down, say 2:00, opposite *Prisoner*, and *Prince* at the remaining star point in the Southeast corner.

Go ahead and try to draw that in the space provided here. Give it a shot before turning the page.

If you're struggling with that bit of drawing, here's a quick sketch:

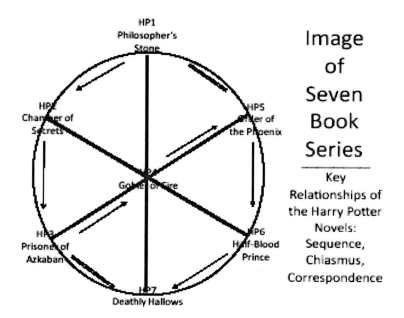

Conclusion: A Christogram in the Star?

Prof. Douglas tells us that recognizing the Ring Composition of a book – and the series is still clearly a ring if not of the turtleback variety – "usually changes prior interpretations of a book." I can think of several ways that acceptance of Ms. Rowling's work as a ring and specifically the asterisk above will change the way *Harry Potter* is understood by Potter fans and by literary critics.

Most obviously, the meme that survives among many academics that Ms. Rowling is a hack writer who got lucky with a cleverly told tale has been effectively shattered. Her success, as she has always claimed, is due to meticulous story planning, and has had very little to do with luck.

About the planning, we know she planned the seven books in detail for five years before even finishing the first book. From the archives of the invaluable *Accio Quote!* website:

KING: Do you know, J.K., where you're going?

ROWLING: Yes.

KING: You do? You plot it out?

ROWLING: Yes, I spent five years – it was five years before – between having that idea and finishing the first book and during those five years I was planning the whole seven book series, so it's already written in stone. That's how it's going to happen.[12]

We know, too, that she spent at least two months re-planning the new novel she was working on before she began writing it:

AjXTee: How long does it take you to plan a book before you even start writing? Or do you just plan as you go along?

JK Rowling replies: It's hard to say; book six has been planned for years, but before I started writing seriously I spent two months revisiting the plan and making absolutely sure I knew what I was doing.[13]

Planning, too, is one essential difference between good writers and bad.

ALEXANDRA LE COURTEUR WILLIAMSON for the South Australian Advertiser: When you start, do you do a complete plan before you start writing, or do you just have an idea from the start and then just keep writing?

JK ROWLING: I do a plan. I plan, I really plan quite meticulously. I know it is sometimes quite boring because when people say to me, "I write stories at school and what advice would you give me to make my stories better?" And I always say and people's faces often fall when I say, "You have to plan," and they say, "Oh, I prefer just writing and seeing where it takes me". Sometimes writing and seeing where it takes you will lead you to some really good ideas but I would say nearly always it won't be as good as if you sat down first and thought: Where do I want to go, what end am I working towards, what would be good, a good start? Sorry, very dull.[14]

At last we know what she was planning. I've always thought the "lucky lady" Cinderella story was preposterous and borderline misogynist; common sense dictates that anyone this successful over an extended period of time is doing something right that others are not. Literary alchemy and the other "keys" we have discussed the last ten years are, no doubt, a big part of that. Ring Composition, though, may be the most important single key.

I think that because it opens up so much of the others. Literary alchemy, most notably, is story meaning and artistry that this scaffolding and organization only buttress. The resolution of contraries in love and the elision of reader and story as subject and object as in a mirror are the transcendent experience that ring composition delivers in its mirrored halves and conjunction of beginning and end.

Which is another critical "prior interpretation" that this Ring Composition structure changes. Otherwise thoughtful folks I meet scoff as often as not when I tell them that the *Harry Potter* books deserve critical attention and that they open up the better books of the English tradition and Western Canon for contemporary readers. I think especially of the principal of a Great Books 'Great Hearts' School in Arizona who, when I pushed back on his intentionally elitist but in fact bass-ackwards policy that *Harry Potter* could never be mentioned in his school's classrooms, all but had a coronary event at my audacity and, to his mind, ignorance. That a professor in the University of Arizona's Honors College and Great Books

14   www.accio-quote.org/articles/2005/0705-edinburgh-ITVcubreporters.htm

program has an article in this book speaks to the fact, perhaps, that the corner has been turned on what has been a truism, namely, the idea embedded in William Safire's dismissal of the stories as "unworthy of adult attention."

And the last and greatest obstacle? The Christian content of the stories. When a reader like Prof. Alan Jacobs at Wheaton College writes after *Deathly Hallows* that Harry Potter is not a Christ-figure we have reason to scratch our heads and marvel.[15] An English professor, C. S. Lewis scholar, and fan of Rowling at a Christian college doesn't get this, even after *Christianity Today* proclaimed the obvious in an article entitled 'Harry Potter 7 is Matthew 6'?[16] Maybe the Ring Composition, and especially the asterisk, will help.

The asterisk, especially one with a nearly closed loop in the Northeast quadrant (where Books 1 and 5 are adjacent), is a traditional symbol of Christ, the Chi Rho of orthodox Christian tradition. Constantine, as answer to his prayers before the Battle at the Milvian Bridge, was told in the sky and in a dream that "in this sign you will conquer" (*touto nika;* in hoc signo vinces). The sign was the Greek letter rho, which looks like an English 'p,' superimposed over a Greek chi, our 'x,' to form an asterisk or star. The Chi Rho as the first two letters of 'Christos' in Greek has been considered a Christogram ever since.

Coincidence? Maybe. But as I say to audiences who question that the resurrection Harry experiences in every book in the presence of a symbol of Christ or *as* a symbol of Christ was *intentional*, the obligation at this point in the critical venture for skeptics of Ms. Rowling's Christian artistry to demonstrate the negative. The positive assertion that the books are filled with "obvious" Christian symbolism has not only been

---

15   'The Youngest Brother's Tale,' Alan Jacobs, *Books and Culture,* August 2007, http://www.booksandculture.com/articles/2007/sepoct/1.47. html; see also http://www.hogwartsprofessor.com/alan-jacobs-harry-potter-is-not-a-christ-figure/

16   'Harry Potter 7 is Matthew 6,' Dave Bruno, *Christianity Today,* 2 August 2007, http://www.christianitytoday.com/ct/2007/augustweb-only/131-43.0.html

confirmed by the author[17] but by the experience of millions of readers. The shape or figure of the stories turning out to be a Ring Composition that supports the transcendent meanings of the series and a Ring Composition, no less, in the shape of a traditional Christogram makes her Christian meaning only that much more up-front.

I don't think this is much of a reach because of the central place in this composition of *Goblet of Fire*. As I wrote in *How Harry Cast His Spell*, the goblet that chooses the worthy champions, the "pure of heart" in Harry's case, is an allusion to the Holy Grail or Communion Cup of Christ, that only the worthiest Arthurian knights were privileged to see. Rowling compounds this image making the Goblet a wooden cup containing non-consuming fire, a reference both to the Burning Bush and, again, to the Eucharist, which Christians refer to as "fire burning the unworthy." Here is what Jean Cirlot writes about the Goblet symbol in his *Dictionary of Symbols*:

> In Romanesque times, and especially when, as a chalice, it was furnished with a lid, [the goblet] was a symbol of the human heart. In a broader sense it is, like the coffer and the chest, a notable symbol of containing. To a certain extent, it may be seen as a material expression of the surrounds of "wrapping" around the mystic Centre.[18]

At the heart of the books, we have a Grail symbol representing the human heart, the blood of Christ, and "the mystic Centre." This Grail chooses Harry over his personal wishes and brings him eventually to a Black Mass in the Little Hangleton graveyard, by which liturgical sorcery Voldemort creates a new body with Harry's blood.

This blasphemous magic turns out to be Voldemort's <u>downfall in the</u> final conflict when this Bond of Blood is

17   Adler, Shawn. "'Harry Potter' Author J.K. Rowling Opens Up About Books' Christian Imagery." *MTV.com*, 17 October, 2007. http://www. accio-quote.org/articles/2007/1017-mtv-adler.html

18   Jean Cirlot, *A Dictionary of Symbols*, Dorset Press, New York, 1971: p. 119

revealed to mean in Harry's sacrifice that Harry cannot die as long as Voldemort lives. But the Dark Lord was "cursed" in *Philosopher's Stone* as well.

The Stone's "elixir of life" is a traditional symbol of the blood of Christ both in its color and its salvific effects, promising immortality. Voldemort longs for this but proves incapable of creating a Stone himself or worthy even to steal another's. This is due not only to Harry's greater worthiness but to the time in the Forbidden Forest when the Dark Lord through Quirrell drinks the blood of a unicorn. The unicorn's blood, because the unicorn is a traditional transparency for Christ, has the story equivalent of the blood of Christ: saving those even at the brink of death but condemning those who drink it unworthily to a "cursed life" (see 1 Corinthians 11:23-29, Firenze in *Philosopher's Stone*, chapter 15, *How Harry Cast His Spell,* Chapter 11).

What the Ring Composition of the Series clarifies about the books' meaning is the central place of the *Stone-Goblet-Hallows* axis, a link that is clear from the title of the books to the most powerful, haunting events in each, is about the Blood of Christ, its salvific power for the pure of heart, and how the abuse of this hallowing sacrament means death to the ungodly.

I look forward as always to your comments and correction, which you can send to me at 'John@HogwartsProfessor.com.'

Muggle Studies 101:
Metaphorical Possibilities of Being Magic or Muggle

James W. Thomas

W HEN RON DISCOVERS THAT Hermione is taking Muggle Studies in their third year at Hogwarts, he is incredulous. Why, Ron wonders aloud, is she taking Muggle Studies since she is Muggle-born and, as he tells Hermione, "You already know all about Muggles!" (PA 57).[1] Her response is that it will be "fascinating to study them from the wizarding point of view." This, it seems to me, is exactly what Rowling would have us do throughout the forty-one hundred pages of Harry's saga: we Muggles must, in a sense, study Muggles from a magical point of view—with those magical views ranging from those who hate us, like Lucius Malfoy and You-Know-Who, to those, like Arthur Weasley, who find us fascinating with our "escapators," plugs, and post offices. Rowling has enrolled us in Muggle Studies 101.

I am reminded of Robert Burns's often-quoted lines near the end of "To a Louse" (in modernized English): "O <u>would some P</u>ower the gift give us/ To see ourselves as others

---

[1] Page references to the Potter books are to the American editions and will be cited parenthetically throughout.

see us." For hundreds of pages and in countless scenes involving magic folk and their relations with Muggles and the Muggle world, we are the "others." The British Prime Minister is the "Other Minister." Our skyscrapers ascend into the sky with ever higher numbered floors from bottom to top; the Ministry of Magic is essentially an underground high rise, mirror imaging Muggle skyscrapers, with Ministry floors numbered in ascending order from top to bottom. Our doctors are "Muggle nutters that cut people up" (*OP* 484), and our guns are "a kind of metal wand that Muggles use to kill each other" (*PA* 38).

Tracing through some of the references to Hermione's first and last year to study Muggles at Hogwarts yields some interesting results. Initially, her stated reason for a Muggle-born studying Muggles from a magical perspective is reminiscent of an American taking an American literature course at the Sorbonne. Practically speaking, I suspect that another of Hermione's reasons to take Muggle Studies could be the "easy A" or, in this case, the "easy O" she hopes to achieve. I appreciate the humor in little Muggle-Studies-related details, like Hermione's textbook having "diagrams of Muggles lifting heavy objects" (*PA* 244). How amusing it would be for witches and wizards to see someone carrying a marble-top table up a flight of steps instead of saying *Mobilitable* or *Accio marble*.

Another reference to Hermione's course comes as virtually all the Gryffindors are celebrating a Quidditch victory while the overworked Hermione tries to read her "enormous" textbook: *Home Life and Social Habits of British Muggles* (*PA* 264). Eventually in *Prisoner of Azkaban*, Rowling puts Hermione out of her misery, having her drop the course (430). By the end of Book 3, the ever-practical Hermione has dropped Muggle Studies and Divination. The former subject involves matters she already knows; and the latter, in Hermione's view, involves matters that cannot be known. Ron informs us, by the way, that Hermione did make three hundred and twenty percent on her final exam in Muggle Studies, which might imply that this Muggle-born young witch knows about three-and-a-quarter times more about us than we know about ourselves—which may be about what gifted, insightful, Muggle-born authors like Rowling seem to know about the human race.

Rowling gives us several other reasons to smile at the ineptitude, inferiority, naiveté, and Muggle-o-centricity of Muggles when compared to magic folk. In *Order of the Phoenix* when Ron, Hermione, and Harry are looking through leaflets on various wizarding career opportunities, they discover that some fields are very demanding: Healing, for example, requires an E or above at N.E.W.T. level in five different subjects (*OP* 656). Working in Muggle Relations, however, requires only one O.W.L.—and that is in Muggle Studies—along with "*enthusiasm, patience, and a good sense of fun*" (657). To magic folk, it is tempting to say, Muggles may not be all that interesting or, dare I say, not all that bright. You might recall that when the de-gnoming of the Weasley garden is in progress, the gnomes leave their holes and come up to see what is going on, which gets them yanked and swung and flung by the boys. As George says to Harry, "See, they're not too bright" (*CS* 37). Draw your own parallels between working with Muggles and de-gnoming a garden.

The range of reactions to Muggles in the Potter books is vast: as I have pointed out, some in the wizarding world see Muggle-borns, Mudbloods, as not fit to live. Muggles to them would be virtually subhuman. At the other extreme, there is Arthur, who, in *Chamber of Secrets*, wants Harry to sit near him at dinner so he can ask about "life with Muggles," including, predictably, "plugs and the postal service" (*CS* 42-43). Once Harry has explained telephone usage, Arthur exclaims, "*Fascinating . . . Ingenious*, really, how many ways Muggles have found of getting along without magic" (43). A few pages later, catching sight of the Doctors Granger, an excited Arthur says, "But, you're *Muggles!*" (57). And you may recall in *Order of the Phoenix* when Harry and Arthur are on the way to the Ministry for Harry's hearing, Arthur finds even the broken automatic ticket machines in the Underground "[s]imply fabulous" and "[w]onderfully ingenious" (*OP* 124). A middle view of Muggles might be that of Hagrid in *Sorcerer's Stone*; having difficulty negotiating the London Underground, Hagrid simply says, "I don't know how the Muggles manage without magic" (*SS* 67). The Dark Lord would not deem

Muggles fit to live; Arthur's comments clearly indicate that he is amazed at Muggle ingenuity; and Hagrid's words may imply that he is simply exasperated at our relative ineptitude.

With the varied views of magic folk on the subject of Muggle life in mind, let us now consider some parallels between the two worlds, and I would like to begin with Muggle technology and how it compares with magic. Consider first the negative implications of parallels between magic and Muggle science and technology. Benjamin Lipscomb and Christopher Stewart, in an article entitled "Magic, Science, and the Ethics of Technology," have addressed this subject thusly: ". . . the indiscriminate use of magic in Harry's world creates problems closely analogous to the problems created by the improper use of applied science in our world" (in *Harry Potter and Philosophy* 81).

The ultimate example of the use, or abuse, of magical power is the willful taking of the life of another by the *Avada Kedavra* curse, comparable in our world to first-degree murder. Whether killing a wizard by magic with a wand or murdering others on a small or a grand scale with a "metal wand," murder is murder—magical or non-magical, imaginary or real. What Voldemort has begun by Book 7, and what would have ensued if Harry had not vanquished him, plays out in reality in much of twentieth-century history. Trace the events just prior to and during World War II, for example. On April 26, 1937, the peaceful Basque town of Guernica was bombed by German aircraft in cooperation with the Spanish forces of Franco; it was the first non-strategic, civilian target for a bombardment from aircraft. Think of the science behind all this: the still relatively new phenomenon of a heavier-than-air craft flew through the air and dropped explosives which detonated upon falling to the earth. The bombing of Guernica resulted in a few hundred casualties and was comparatively primitive, but the principle, the science, this application of the killing curse, is the thing to consider here. For only eight years separate Guernica from Hiroshima, and the bomb that exploded over Hiroshima in 1945 was approximately 1/800 as powerful as state-of-the-art nuclear weapons developed during the Cold War by both the U.S. and the U.S.S.R.

Back to the Muggles' metal wand metaphor for a
moment: it is not difficult to find estimates of how many
guns there are in the U.S. which vary by two hundred million
or so. Some estimate that we have one-hundred million guns
among us, and others contend that we have over three-hundred
million. The point is we do not even remotely know how many
potentially deadly wands are among us, though every bullet
is a potential killing curse. I feel that Rowling draws subtle
parallels between Voldemort's one-on-one killing of another
and his plans, presumably, to kill all inferior beings and our
own proclivity to kill an individual or an entire race of humans.
What a momentous cautionary tale this aspect of Harry's saga
is, for all weaponry—imagined or real, magic or Muggle—
which is used to kill innocents is an unforgivable curse indeed.
As hostilities escalate in Rowling's world from the rampaging
wizards who toss the Muggle family in the air at the Quidditch
World Cup to the collapsing bridges and increasing disasters
that lead us into Book 7, I can only imagine the Armageddon
that could have been in the Potterverse if Voldemort
attempted some kind of military conquest of Muggles: eye
for eye, tooth for tooth, wooden wand for metal wand.

Now, to bring us back from the brink of Armageddon,
back to Oz in a way, I would like to point out some parallels
between magic and Muggle science and technology which have
positive implications, which enrich our lives daily, and which
have changed our lives profoundly in a few brief years. First,
what I find extraordinary when I compare magic elements and
devices in Rowling's world with Muggle science and technology
are some striking similarities. McGonagall (and also Toothless
Tom the innkeeper) can start a roaring fire with their wands;
so can we if we have a gas fireplace with a remote. In fact, any
remote control is a wand, a kind of plastic wand that Muggles
use to change channels; we just point to the TV, punch the right
numbers, and perform a wordless *Accio ESPN*. In the early
twentieth century people were so amazed at the magic of films,
they called them moving pictures. And recall what Robert
Zemeckis does with moving the reality of moving pictures as he
inserts Forrest Gump into major filmed events of the twentieth

century; it is not just the Fat Lady who goes in and out of her frame.

There are more parallels between magic and Muggle worlds involving devices and inventions. Omnioculars essentially exist among Muggles; check out a 2007 invention called the Binocular Digital Camera. Consider Harry and Hermione's time travel (an old sci fi standard) in light of real Muggle technology as we see ourselves on video a few seconds or several years after the actual time of the event, or we DVR our shows and watch them at our whim—manipulating time itself and, maybe most wonderful of all, eliminating commercials. Or we use our GPS to get from point A to point B, and the magic of that device is almost like Apparating. We say or punch in our destination, and though getting there is not instantaneous, getting there almost automatically at seventy-five miles an hour is not too bad, is it? Never has the interrelationship between magic and science been more succinctly and, in my view, more aptly described than when Arthur C. Clark wrote way back in 1961: "Any sufficiently advanced technology is indistinguishable from magic."[2]

As we continue our focus on this aspect of Muggle Studies 101, how about some examples of science in our world that would have been viewed as magic in the world of a generation or two ago? Readers who are fifty-ish or older can recall some of the following with me. Those who are twenty to forty or so will remember some of these innovations. But those under twenty I would encourage to have a long talk with their grandparents because only those of us of *that* generation can fully appreciate the magic of Googling something, the magic of taking pictures and videos and of talking in a variety of voiced and silent ways on our cell phones. I would cite more examples here, but I certainly do not know what all today's cell phone can do since I have no idea what all my cell phone can do. Yet I know but a few years separate us from the days of those cordless phones you see the *Seinfeld* characters talking on (they look more like Korean War walkie-talkies than they do the phones of today). And just a few years B.S. (Before *Seinfeld*),

2   This and my later Clarke quotation are two of his often-published "laws of prediction."

we could not talk to anyone from more than eight or ten feet removed from our phone plug and only dreamed of the day a cordless phone could free us to talk anywhere ("cordless phone anywhere" for the first few years we had them was within eight or ten feet of the base of the phone, which was plugged in).

Here are three more examples of magic/Muggle science that someone of an older generation can personally appreciate; I will begin with television. I have watched a flickering, snowy twelve-inch diagonal black-and-white TV, and so think how magical my HDTV seems to me. Consider how I have heard music in my lifetime. I have listened to music on scratchy and warped and breakable 78 rpm platters, on scratchy and warped but less breakable 45s and LPs, on cassettes, on 8-Track tapes, and, finally, I have appreciated the magic of sound on CDs and iPods. I have waded in the Atlantic Ocean at Isle of Palms in South Carolina and in the Pacific Ocean at Latigo Beach in Southern California *on the same day.* I have seen and heard and done these and many other seemingly impossible things; so why should we Muggles assume there is a limitation and a finiteness to the possible? Once again, Arthur C. Clark has written, "The only way of discovering the limits of the possible is to venture a little way past them into the impossible." Magic, somehow, as Rowling seems to show us in subtle ways, helps us make that venture into the impossible.

Nobel-prize laureate Isaac Bashevis Singer, in his story "Gimpel the Fool," has his narrator say, "I wandered all over the land, and good people did not neglect me. After many years I became old and white; I heard a great deal, many lies and falsehoods, but the longer I lived the more I understood that there were really no lies. Whatever doesn't really happen is dreamed at night. It happens to one if it doesn't happen to another, tomorrow if not today, or a century hence if not next year. ... Often I heard tales of which I said, 'Now this is a thing that cannot happen.' But before a year had elapsed I heard that it actually had come to pass somewhere" (in *The American Tradition in Literature, Concise Twelfth Edition* 1922). Old Gimpel had lived long enough to become wise enough to see the impossible become possible time and time again. Lord Byron (as well as others) has reminded us that truth is stranger than fiction, and Thomas Hardy wrote long ago: "Though a good deal is too strange to be believed, nothing is too strange to have happened."

While almost all of what I have just been focusing on in the wizarding and Muggle worlds blurs the distinction between magic and science, our next lesson in Rowling's Muggle Studies 101 involves what I think is the closest parallel between the unplugged wizarding world and the very much plugged-in contemporary Muggle world. In short, think of electricity (not to be confused with "eckeltricity") as Muggle magic. If you accept this comparison, by the way, magic folk have, presumably, been magic for thousands of years while Muggles have been electrified for barely over two hundred years in the laboratory and just over one hundred years in everyday life. To say this another way, the wanded have forever been unplugged, but the wandless are ever so recently plugged in. In present times, if we were all to be unplugged, the magic folk would not know the difference, and yet we Muggles would be decimated.

In *Goblet of Fire* when Harry theorizes that Rita Skeeter may have used Muggle-like surveillance devices to get information at Hogwarts, the exasperated Hermione explains to Ron and Harry: "All those substitutes for magic Muggles use—electricity, computers, and radar, and all those things— they all go haywire around Hogwarts, there's too much magic in the air" (*GF* 548). Let us face facts: when Hermione mentions computers and radar "and all those things," we are talking about electricity as the ultimate and primary source of Muggles' "substitutes for magic"; almost everything comes down to Arthur's favorite collectible, the plug. So, just to put things into perspective, if we tacitly assume Muggle superiority with regard to science over magic, plugs over wands, consider this: how do the most advanced civilizations in the Muggle world do even temporarily without their power sources? We cannot get our twenties out of an ATM; we are unable to pump gas into our cars; we can only go online or text or tweet as long as our batteries hold out; we cannot microwave a frozen dinner; and, worst of all, we cannot turn on the television to see what other Muggles without the magic of electricity are unable to do. You may recall that Hermione's Muggle Studies professor assigns an essay on this topic: "Explain Why Muggles Need Electricity" (PA 250). As I mention in my book *Repotting Harry Potter*, I have an idea for writing this essay. This might fall a few feet short of the assigned length, but that essay could come down to "Muggles need electricity because they don't have magic."

Rowling's next lesson for those of us enrolled metaphorically in her Muggle Studies 101 course has to do with what I call "My Group Awareness." This is both an awareness that we are different and distinctive and are members of a group within the whole, like witches and wizards living among Muggles; but it is also, among the good magic folk, a sensitivity to the common humanity of us all. Rowling creates the all-important International Statute of Wizarding Secrecy, originating in the late seventeenth century; thus magic cannot be used against (or, we assume, even for) Muggles with their awareness of it. So in a sense, in the Potterverse, we wandless Muggles are even more wandless than goblins because we do not even know there *are* wands.

If we consider the shibboleths within the group, the understood code language, the commonalities of where the group members go to school, live, socially interact, marry, and are acutely aware of who is one of them and who is not, then we might see parallels between magic folk and the Amish, the LDS, evangelicals, Jehovah's Witnesses, the gay and lesbian community, neo-cons, Tea Party people, or any one of dozens of other groups I could name. I am not meaning in any way to suggest that these groups feel themselves to be different and *superior*—or different and *inferior* for that matter—but just different from the whole. They have a high level of self consciousness and self awareness that contrasts with their perceived view of others. Even though they may, to a greater or lesser degree, be assimilated into the whole, the individual in such a group thinks of my group.

Rowling takes these ideas of "differentness" and sameness to a new height and teaches us a powerful Muggle Studies 101 lesson in the radio broadcast in *Deathly Hallows* when the voice of "Royal," the voice of Kingsley Shacklebolt, the voice of the future Minister of Magic, speaks: "Muggles remain ignorant of the source of their suffering as they continue to sustain heavy casualties. . . . However, we continue to hear truly inspirational stories of wizards and witches risking their own safety to protect Muggle friends and neighbors, often without the Muggles' knowledge" (*DH* 440). When Lee Jordan asks, "And what would you say, Royal, to those listeners who reply that in these dangerous times, it should be 'Wizards first'?," Kinglsey answers, "I'd say that it's one short step from 'Wizards first' to 'Purebloods first,' and then to 'Death Eaters' . . . We're all human, aren't we? Every human life is worth the same, and worth saving." These are words written, understandably and powerfully, by a woman who once worked with Amnesty International.

The next lesson in our course in Muggle Studies 101 I entitle, for lack of a better phrase, "Magic As Opposed to What?" As we reread the Potter books, what are some of the words that come to mind as being the opposite of magic? What would Vernon Dursley's opposite word be but "normal"? The Dursleys are obsessed with being normal, as well with as being rich, but that is normal in their world—being rich, making a good impression, having a new car, going to Majorca, not seeming odd in any way to their neighbors—all this is Dursley normal. Some of us might conclude that Vernon has a *boring* job, working at Grunnings *drills*; drills *are* for boring. One of Rowling's first details about Vernon in Sorcerer's Stone, by the way, is that he is "picking out his most boring tie" to wear to work (*SS* 2). From the beginning Rowling emphasizes Dursleyism as the antithesis of anything magical. James and Lily are described as being "as unDursleyish as it was possible to be" (*SS* 2), and McGonagall essentially describes Vernon and Petunia as the most thoroughly Muggled Muggles in all of England, telling Dumbledore, "You couldn't find two people who are less like us" (*SS* 13).

The lesson to be learned, and I doubt that it is lost on even the youngest of readers, is that we should not aspire to the Dursleys' kind of normalcy. Rowling satirizes Dursleyism in the first sentence of the first book, telling us ironically that the Dursleys are "perfectly normal, thank you very much" (*SS* 1). The family at number four, Privet Drive exists as do those people Thoreau describes in *Walden* as leading lives of quiet desperation. Of course there is a self-selection process at work here too: are Potter readers, avid Potter re-readers, in any real danger of being normal? Is it normal among Muggles to feel about these books as we do? Are we not just a wee bit eccentric—like Luna? In fact, maybe Luna is to the wizarding world as we are to the Muggle world. So, based on the characters in the Potter books, who would want to be normal? Are not most or all of the cool people in the Potter books magic folk? Can you name a cool non-magical person? Are not most or all of the nice people magic folk? Can you name a nice non-magical person? (You may recall Holden Caulfield's delineation of *nice*; it is the opposite of phony in his world.)

Do you remember the old three-part joke "What do you call a person who speaks several languages? Multilingual. What do you call a person who speaks two languages? Bilingual. And what do you call a person who speaks one language? An American." In the spirit of that joke, I would like to propose this one: "What is bad about being a Muggle? You can't do magic. What is worse about being a Muggle? You can't see magic. And what is worst about being a Muggle? You can't imagine magic." A magic person who cannot do magic is a Squib; we have all known that since we first found out Filch's secret. Typically, it is an excellent Rowling word since *squib*, among other things, means an explosive or firework that fails to go off, a *dud* as we might say. The one word Squib says it all for the magic-born non-magicals. But we have no word for Muggles like us who cannot do magic, cannot see magic, but can at least *imagine* magic. We need a name. What are we? Nitwits? Blubbers? Oddments? Or Tweaks? I like to think of us as the latter—Tweaks. In our minds whenever we choose, we can tweak reality into magic—hopefully not in excessive and delusional ways. We do have to work at our Grunnings, but with the money we make selling drills, we can buy wands.

Here's the next lesson I see in Rowling's Muggle Studies 101: we Tweaks, those of us who can imagine magic, might well consider *imagination* as Muggle magic. Some readers of the Potter books seem to feel that Rowling elevates the mind over magic. Former Notre Dame philosophy professor Tom

Morris praises Rowling's treatment of logic and reasoning
in his book *If Harry Potter Ran General Electric*. Citing
Hermione's solving the riddle in Book 1 and Harry's dealing
with the Sphinx in Book 4, Morris writes, "The mind can do
things that no magic can match," adding that Rowling shows
us "the more-than-magical effectiveness of the human mind at
work . . ." (195-96). David Baggett and others have written on
parallels between magic and a special kind of imagination, faith
(Baggett's essay, "Magic, Muggles, and Moral Imagination," is
in the anthology *Harry Potter and Philosophy*). St. Paul saw
faith as the essence of things unseen, as in things imagined,
by which I do not equate *imagined* with *imaginary* or *unreal*.
Danish philosopher Søren Kierkegaard contended that absurd
was not that which is logically impossible, but that which
is humanly impossible. Kierkegaard saw faith as beginning
precisely where thinking leaves off, as the work of a lifetime,
and as a monstrous paradox, the opposite of logical and
rational thought, more perhaps like magic than logic. He wrote
extensively on Abraham and Isaac, in whose story we have a
logical absurdity (that Isaac will be killed, yet through Isaac
Abraham will be the father of multitudes). There will have to be
magic on Mount Moriah, and believers believe that there was.

So if we can at least imagine that which we cannot see,
how sad are those Muggles in the Potter books (and elsewhere)
who will not see what they *do* see? There are Muggles who
do not see the Knight Bus, though it be tearing through the
neighborhood; Muggles who deny their keys are shrinking
until they disappear; Muggles who insist that cats cannot
read maps and that motorcycles do not fly—just as there were
Muggles who insisted the earth was flat, that the sun revolves
around the earth, that there are four planets, and that if people
have certain diseases, they need to be bled back to health with
leeches. Once more, think of two antithetical kinds of people
in Rowling's books: magic folk and Dursley Muggle (in the
latter case, those who do not or will not see anything that is
not normal). In Rowling's magic category I would place the
poetic, the imaginative, the creative, the whimsical (and
we Tweaks would fit there); and in *this* Muggle category I

would place those with no imagination, no music, no poetry in their souls. They represent the worst of Muggledom; they are the prosaic, and Vernon is their patron saint.

Those Dursley Muggles among us want an *either/or* answer to what is, arguably, Harry's most famous question in all forty-one hundred pages of the Potter books: "Is this real? Or has this been happening inside my head?" (*DH* 723). Dursley types demand, "Which is it—real or imaginary, truth or fiction, non-magic or magic?" Dumbledore's unforgettable response to Harry reminds us one last time that real and imagined are not *either/or* but *both/and*. It is happening inside Harry's head *and* it is real. This is Mark Twain's twist on a well-known line: "Truth is stranger than fiction, but it is because Fiction is obliged to stick to possibilities; Truth isn't." Rowling's dialogue between Harry and Dumbledore at King's Cross addresses the false dichotomy of imagined as opposed to real and underscores what we re-readers of her books and countless others have long known—that great literature deconstructs the boundaries of reality and imagination, facts and truth, actuality and fiction. Part of the magic of the Potter books is that apparently for many millions of readers Rowling has created things that are happening inside our heads—fictive things, not factual—which, nevertheless, have truths within them and have their own reality.

Again, I will quote Hagrid's comment in *Sorcerer's Stone* as he and Harry try to negotiate London: "I don't know how the Muggles manage without magic" (*SS* 67)? To which I say, "Hagrid, the smart ones *don't* manage without magic; they don't even try." They get their magic wherever they can find it—and not necessarily from going to the Post Office, riding escalators, or plugging in some new electric device. Smart Muggles, cool, nice, and imaginative Muggles, aka Tweaks, find magic in music and painting and sculpture and books and calculus and compounds and conundrums and whatever else engages their hearts and minds. And they find their magic in and through love—just love—which is the same in both worlds, magic and Muggle alike. I would like to elaborate on two powerful matters which seem virtually the same in the wizarding world and in our own—music and love.

Headmaster Dumbledore, moved to tears by the students' singing at the Opening Feast Harry's first year at Hogwarts, proclaims, "Ah music . . . A magic beyond all we do here!" (*SS* 128). Who among us has not felt the power of music, felt what D. H. Lawrence called "the insidious mastery of song"? Maybe we would not be moved to tears by hearing all of Hogwarts sing the school song to hundreds of different tunes at the same time, but I like the symbolism of that. We all sing (and love hearing sung) music to our favorite tunes. In the final chapter of *Walden* Thoreau writes, "If a man loses pace with his companions, perhaps it is because he hears a different drummer. Let him step to the music which he hears, however measured or far away" (in *The American Tradition in Literature, Concise Twelfth Edition* 763). In one of Edgar Allan Poe's earliest reviews, having spent his wrath on reviewing bad poetry, poetry without music in the lines, Poe asks, "What was meant by the invective against him who had no music in his soul?" (*The Portable Edgar Allan Poe* 542). In other words, why rant against a poor poet who has no music in him? Such a one is doomed and suffers enough already, I suppose Poe must have felt.

In a much later work, a magnificent essay called "The Poetic Principle," Poe seems to be suggesting that there is magic in music even, in Dumbledore's terms, a magic beyond all we do here—not here at Hogwarts, but here on earth. Poe contends that when we encounter something ineffably beautiful in poetry or music, when we are moved to tears by the power of it, we weep "not . . . through excess of pleasure, but through a certain, petulant, impatient sorrow at our inability to grasp now, wholly, here on earth, at once and for ever, those divine and rapturous joys, of which through the poem, or through the music, we attain to but brief and indeterminate glimpses" (*The Portable Edgar Allan Poe* 561). Poe, who felt intensely that music is the ultimate source of beauty among mortals and whose aesthetic theory is essentially indistinguishable from his theology, affirms further: "We are often made to feel, with a shivering delight, that from an earthly harp are stricken notes which cannot have been unfamiliar to the angels." It would seem that the appreciation of the magic of music is not limited to witches and wizards, or Muggles, or even, according to Poe, mortals.

In a passage near the end of the Old Testament book of *Proverbs* (30: 18-19), the writer confesses to being amazed or, according to other translations, filled with wonder with regard to four things. He ponders how these things can be explained— who can understand them, he wonders: the way of an eagle in the air, the way of a serpent on a rock, the way of a ship in the midst of the sea, and the way of a man with a woman. Long ago we have come to understand the aerodynamics of a bird's flight, the mobility of reptiles, and the principles of buoyancy. Yet, why *this* man loves *this* woman, or why *this* woman is willing to die for *this* man, or why *this* man and woman both know they wish to be together until eternity, remain mysteries—mysteries of a deeper nature than Harry or Rowling or any one of us could ever solve.

How often in poetry and song written long after *Proverbs* has a writer resorted to *magic* to explain the mystery of love. Old Blue Eyes alone sang of "that old black magic called love" and proclaimed that "it's witchcraft" that has caused him to fall in love (Old Blue Eyes, for those who may not know, was the Chairman of the Board—Frank Sinatra). Remember in the film *Sleepless in Seattle* when the talk on the radio is of love, and Tom Hanks's character on the radio and Meg Ryan's character in her car say simultaneously that love is magic? (By the way, I think that at any given moment of every night or day, some cable channel somewhere is showing *Sleepless in Seattle*.)

Speaking of movies, Richard Quine's 1958 film *Bell, Book and Candle*, based on John Van Druten's hit Broadway play of the same name, provides some interesting contrasts for us Potterites. The witches and warlocks in the play, in addition to having magical powers, differ from non-magicals because they do not weep and they do not fall in love. Van Druten created tearless, loveless magical folk who are more zombie-like than they are Rowlingesque. The non-magical folk in *Bell, Book and Candle* are called "humans," which really makes us appreciate the word "Muggles"; and the plot revolves around a witch who uses magic to make a man fall in love with her. He finds out about her witchcraft and rejects said witch, who later *loses* her magical powers *because* she has fallen in love for *real*, just as humans do.

In stark contrast to Rowling's magical folks' views on and abilities to love just as Muggles love, then, Van Druten's work reserves love just for humans (or, in Rowling's terms, love is just for Muggles). How sad and limiting this is; and how much more do we appreciate love among Rowling's magicals and Muggles alike. Love—or as Dumby likes to say "just love"—is a magic we fools share in both worlds. In predictable romantic-comedy-happy-ending-style, the film adaptation of Van Druten's play concludes with the human man (played by Jimmy Stewart) embracing the now *former* witch (Kim Novak), who is now crying and loving and who is therefore now a human woman rather than a witch. The human man tells her that *this* time their love for each other is real, adding "Or has it been real all along? Who's to say what magic is?" That rather lame line makes me appreciate the depths of love among Rowling's magic and Muggle folks all the more.

In addition to my examination of how Rowling lets us see Muggles from a magical perspective in the Potter books, how she enrolls us in Muggle Studies 101 in a sense, I would like to examine a few Muggle-related matters from her ancillary books, *Fantastic Beasts and Where to Find Them, Quidditch Through the Ages*, and *The Tales of Beedle the Bard*. (I encourage readers who may not own these books to get copies and enjoy them; remember that sales benefit Comic Relief UK and the Children's High Level Group.) So, now as we focus on Muggle matters in these three brief books, it is almost like enrolling in Muggle Studies 102—team taught by Newt Scamander, Kennilworthy Whisp, and Beedle the Bard, though really by the master teacher herself.

Let us first focus on a few Muggle-related references and implications in *Fantastic Beasts*. In Newt's account of Muggle awareness of magical beasts, he mentions that medieval Muggle artists depicted "real" creatures like dragons, centaurs, unicorns, and griffins—beasts that contemporary Muggles are now convinced are "imaginary" (*FB* xiv). Newt goes into the history of magic folk taking great pains to conceal fantastic beasts from Muggles in modern times   He then points out that certain beasts, like the creature Muggles call "Nessie," are sighted far too often since the Loch Ness monster "appears to have developed a positive thirst for publicity" (xvii). Similarly, far too many yeti have let themselves be seen by Muggles, especially in Tibet. Such sightings are the rare exceptions, however, mainly because Muggles tend to be "satisfied with the flimsiest non-magical explanation" for something fantastic they have seen (xvii). Newt informs us that Professor Mordicus Egg has written a book on this subject; it is entitled *The Philosophy of the Mundane: Why the Muggles Prefer Not to Know* (published by Dust & Mildewe).

All this is consistent with Muggles in the Potter books preferring not to believe in cats reading maps and keys shrinking. When a Muggle does try to convince someone he has seen a magical creature, Newt explains, he is "generally believed to be drunk or a 'loony'" (xvii). With Luna Lovegood, often called "Loony," coming up in Rowling's next Potter book after *Fantastic Beasts*, I find Newt's phrase especially interesting. Luna is loony to many in the magical world because of her talk of nargles and Crumple-Horned Snorkacks, getting the same reaction in the wizarding world as Muggles do in theirs when they have seen something that others have not or cannot or will not. By the way, Rowling has said that Luna's husband is Rolf Scamander, Newt's grandson, a detail that seems quite fitting.

Four other beasts have links to the Muggle world as well. Newt tells us that the Mooncalf dances on its hind legs at night in wheat fields, leaving "geometric patterns behind . . . to the great puzzlement of Muggles" (30), who, in their puzzlement have concluded that aliens or hoaxers have made the patterns. The beast known as a Billywig, which Xenophilius has used to improve Rowena Ravenclaw's diadem, is an Australian insect with its wings on the top of its head. It is a stinging insect, and being stung by a Billywig, Newt writes, results in "giddiness followed by levitation" (4). He continues, "Generations of young Australian witches and wizards have attempted to catch Billywigs and provoke them into stinging in order to enjoy these side effects . . . ." No explicit Muggle parallels here are drawn by Newt and will not be drawn by me, but note the pleasant high following a spell of giddiness. I'll just say what Dumbledore says at one point in *The Tales of Beedle the Bard*: "Make of that what you will" (106).

A specific Muggle reference is a part of Newt's discussion of another beast, the Chizpurfle. These tiny pests infest and ruin cauldrons and wands and can also "attack electrical objects from within" (7). Newt concludes by saying: "Chizpurfle infestations explain the puzzling failure of many relatively new Muggle electrical artifacts." So now we Muggles know that when the GPS malfunctions or when we cannot get a DVR'd program to fast forward, it is not bugs, gremlins, or glitches causing the trouble; it is the work of a Chizpurfle.

One more beast reminds me of Muggle matters: the Nundu, the "most dangerous" beast of all, is, according to Newt, a giant leopard that "moves silently despite its size" and breathes a virulent breath that causes a disease so deadly that it "eliminate[s] entire villages" (31). This beast can only be subdued by more than a hundred skilled wizards "working together." Though almost all of the beasts in Newt's book have comic implications, I think the Nundu suggests quite serious parallels with Muggle woes and maladies. After all, there is many a Muggle disease that "moves silently despite its size," which is microscopic, that is virulent and is often fatal to whole villages, and that has "never yet been subdued" even by hundreds of scientists and researchers and Nobel laureates working over many decades to conquer incurable fatal diseases still moving silently among us.

Kennilworthy Whisp turns his attention to Muggle relations, devoting an entire chapter in *Quidditch Through the Ages* to the subject. This chapter, called "Anti-Muggle Precautions," is the shortest in the book, however (again, we are just not that interesting). It deals mainly with the history of efforts to conceal the wizarding game from Muggles. Early players of Quidditch were first required to play at least fifty miles from a Muggle town, later changed to a hundred-mile distance (17-18). One early writer advised magic folk to "play [Quidditch] at night" (15). That reminds me a bit of a certain night-time secret vampire baseball game, which may ring a *bell* with some of my fellow Potter readers.

In my book *Rowling Revisited: Afterthoughts on Harry, Fantastic Beasts, Quidditch, and Beedle the Bard* (Zossima

Press, 2011), in the chapter on Kennilworthy Whisp's history of Quidditch, I draw a number of parallels between this magic sport and various Muggles sports. (By the way, that was another kind of Muggle plug.) So, here are a few parallels between Quidditch and games we Muggles know quite well. Since only the Chaser carrying the Quaffle may enter the scoring area (25), we have a rule somewhat like offside in soccer (viewers of the 2010 World Cup matches surely know what being offside is in soccer—or do they?). Quidditch fouls (28-30) like Blagging violations (grabbing the tail of an opponent's broom to slow him down) seem like holding in American football; Cobbing (vigorously elbowing an opponent) would likely elicit a referee's whistle in basketball as well. And Quaffle-pocking (altering the Quaffle so it "falls more quickly or zigzags" (30) is reminiscent of baseball pitchers who do funny things to the ball so it will do funny things on the way to the plate. Kennilworthy also mentions that the Seeker usually receives the most severe injuries and that the opposition seeks to do him special harm. As Brutus Scrimgeour, author of *The Beaters' Bible* advises, "Take out the Seeker" is the first rule of Quidditch. Readers and movie-goers familiar with *The Blind Side* will see the parallel to Muggle quarterbacks and the linemen who try to keep them from being taken out.

Magical and Muggle worlds in many ways collide in *The Tales of Beedle the Bard*. We have magical Hermione as translator, magical Dumbledore as commentator, Muggle Rowling as the annotator and illustrator all contributing to a volume of stories dealing with both magical and Muggle characters. In her introduction, Rowling contrasts elements in magic and Muggle fairy tales, noting that witches in Beedle's tales often take matters into their own hands, as opposed to "taking a prolonged nap or waiting for someone to return a lost shoe" (ix)—offense intended for Aurora and Cinderella.

In "The Wizard and the Hopping Pot," a Muggle-friendly father has a Muggle-hating son, or at least a trouble-hating son, and trouble comes in the form of Muggles and their needs and problems, until the son repents and helps them, living in harmony with his Muggle neighbors. Dumbledore's commentary mentions how unusual it is that such an early pro-

Muggle tale survived. In "The Fountain of Fair Fortune," a non-magical Sir Luckless is the one who bathes in the Fountain on that June day. A major underdog named for having no luck is the winner, against all odds; anything can happen to a witch or a Muggle, especially if love is involved, and Sir Luckless has fallen in love with a witch named, appropriately, Amata. The magic is between Amata and Sir Luckless, not in the waters of the Fountain. In Dumbledore's commentary on this tale, by the way, he has to deal with the outrage of Lucius Malfoy, who feels the story promotes "*interbreeding*" of magic and Muggle (40).

Dumbledore calls the king in "Babbitty Rabbitty and Her Cackling Stump" a "foolish Muggle" king (82). That seems an accurate phrase since this Muggle planned to master and monopolize magic in his kingdom, and what are the chances of *that*? With the help of the witch Babbitty and according to the charlatan's plan, things are going pretty well for the king as he tries to convince his subjects he is magic: the Lady's hat disappears, the horse flies, but the dead dog stays that way. Sabre the dog cannot be brought back to life; for, as Beedle tells us, "no magic can raise the dead" (72). Somewhat melancholy in his commentary, Dumbledore mentions that it was this story of Beedle's that taught him that sad fact (78). He goes on to say that magical children at first believe that their parents "would be able to awaken our dead rats and cats with one wave of their wands." So, in addition to the beauty of music and the wonder of love, magic and Muggle folk have in common the finality of death.

Beedle's other two tales have much less to do with Muggles; in fact, "The Tale of the Three Brothers" is concerned exclusively with magical lore. Though "The Warlock's Hairy Heart" deals only with a warlock and the witch he intends to marry, the implications for Muggles are rich indeed. Wishing to avoid the effects of falling in love, the warlock locks his heart away. When he and the maiden look upon his protected, casketed heart (50), they see an ugly, hairy heart, one that had "never fallen prey to beauty, or to a musical voice, to the feel of silken skin." I might add too that the heart had never been broken or felt pain, or grown stronger because of these things. I am reminded of Nathaniel Hawthorne's story "Ethan Brand" about a character, isolated from humankind, whose heart turns to stone, or of this line from W. B. Yeats's "Easter 1916: "Too long a sacrifice can make a stone of the heart." In T. S. Eliot's "The Love Song of J. Alfred Prufrock," Prufrock decides not to ask the "overwhelming question," not to proclaim his love, not to sing his love song and give away his heart. Prufrock seems to resolve that he will lead a careful, controlled, and, obviously, lonely life.

The warlock, Ethan Brand, J. Alfred Prufrock, and many other literary characters stand in contrast to millions of us "fools who love," as Dumbledore calls us; and, saddest of all, those like Beedle's warlock are heartless yet still not invulnerable to pain. To love is to hurt, and, as Dumby tells us in his commentary, "To hurt is as human as to breathe" (56). Another gem of Dumbywisdom from this commentary follows: "in seeking to become superhuman this foolhardy young man renders himself inhuman" (59). This is an understandable comment from one who witnessed Tom Riddle becoming Lord Voldemort.

I'd like to quote once again Robert Burns's lines from "To a Louse," this time adding the last few lines of the poem, again in modern English: "O would some Power the gift give us/ To see ourselves as others see us./ It would from many a blunder free us/ And foolish notion/ What airs of dress and bearing/ And even pridefulness." Seeing ourselves as others see us, seeing Muggles as magic folk see us, results perhaps in our being a bit more free from "pridefulness." Pride has been viewed by countless millions over many centuries as the deadliest of the seven deadly sins. Aristotle identifies overweening pride in the *Poetics* as the tragic flaw that can bring the downfall of the great. Benjamin Franklin says in his autobiography that of the thirteen moral virtues he sought to acquire, humility was the most difficult. Franklin adds that if he ever achieved it, he would probably be proud of his humility.

We Muggles do have much to be proud of, but reading Rowling reminds me that as wonderful and unique as we are, we are not alone on the earth, we are not infallible, we are not invincible, we are not perfectible in this mortal form, and we are living paradoxes. It is to our deepest shame and to our utmost credit that we are capable both of killing and of dying for our own kind. And acts of both extremes permeate the pages of Rowling's books. Like Voltaire, Jonathan Swift, Mark Twain, and other great social satirists, Rowling knows us well, keeps our pride in check, and constantly reminds us of our burdens and our blessings—love being preeminent among those blessings. Rowling's works, Muggle Studies 101 and 102, teach me that life is rich, that much can be endured, and that even more can be enjoyed to the fullest because we have our real Muggle friends in our lives *and* our real magic friends inside our heads.

Bibliography

Baggett, David and Shawn E. Klein, eds. *Harry Potter and Philosophy: If Aristotle Ran Hogwarts.* Chicago: Open Court, 2004.

Kennedy, J. Gerald, ed. *The Portable Edgar Allan Poe.* New York: Penguin, 2006.

Morris, Tom. *If Harry Potter Ran General Electric: Leadership Wisdom From the World of the Wizards..* New York: Doubleday, 2006.

Perkins, George, *et al.*, eds. *The American Tradition in Literature, Concise Twelfth Edition.* Boston: McGraw Hill, 2009.

Technological Anarchism:
The Meaning of Magic in Harry Potter

Joel Hunter

H ISTORY TEXTBOOKS THAT ACKNOWLEDGE humans
used to believe in magic invariably do so in order to isolate
magical thinking and experience to prescientific ages. Magical
belief, so the conventional story goes, was common during
humanity's period of intellectual immaturity but now that we
have scientific explanations for scary and wonderful things
magical beliefs are no longer appropriate for serious, clear-
thinking people. Magic, if it is regarded seriously at all, is little
more than a quaint subject about which eccentric historians or
anthropologists muse over in their spare time, or the feignedly
rebellious ventilations of the privileged classes descanting on
their boutique spirituality. There is no doubt that the Scientific
Revolution established a categorically different way of understanding nature and our place in it. The "disenchantment of the
world" swiftly began to displace from the world its supernatural realties and spiritual forces with the fully explicable world of
immutable natural laws and causal mechanism.

The magic at work in the Harry Potter (HP) series has more in common with these principles of modern science than with the historical magic that anthropologists study.[1] The correspondence between HP magic and modern science can also be found when we examine the nature of science's twin: technology. Suppose we adopt the conventional meaning of technology—a tool or instrument, an object found or fabricated to make use of for some task. It is "good" technology if its design and construction are effective means to achieve the desired end. In 1973, Arthur C. Clarke rounded out his two "laws of prediction" with a well-known third: "Any sufficiently advanced technology is indistinguishable from magic." Demonstrate the use of a cigarette lighter to a primitive hunter-gatherer society, so the clichéd example goes, and the amazed simple-minded onlookers will regard the lighter as a talisman wielded by the stranger, who obviously is an extraordinary, powerful magician. The conceit of Clarke's law is that only one of the parties has the correct understanding of the process that accounts for the lighter's performance. Scientific and magical explanations can't both be true. One of the parties has a defective understanding of what is *really* going on, of the real causes for what occurs when the operator uses the tool. Advanced technology and magic are at most superficially similar; their actual principles of operation have nothing in common. Thus, Clarke's third law implies that there is a radical dissimilarity and separation between magical and technological thinking.

But if we want to understand real rather than illusory similarities between magic and technology, then Larry Niven's inversion of Clarke's third law is more informative: "Any sufficiently rigorously defined magic is indistinguishable from technology." Niven's maxim is superior because a *rigorously defined* magic requires that it be a *rational system of knowledge*. The magical rules and operations that J. K. Rowling has devised in the HP series are a rational, cause-and-effect system obeying mechanistic laws. Insofar as HP magic is described by Niven's law, it shares an elementary logic with modern science and technology. And because the magic in HP is functionally equivalent to technology, Rowling has placed in our hands a tool with which to critically examine technology in our world from a fresh perspective.

Why is it taken for granted that "the newest technology" is an improvement? Is "cutting-edge" technology ever objectionable? The technological mind reasons: technology is always improving, so the more society is saturated technologically, the more society is improving. What, if any, are the flaws in this logic of technological ideology?

What additional powers does technology bestow on us? If we attend to the message broadcast by marketers and merchants of the latest schemes, styles, and gadgets, what are the recurrent themes? It will satisfy my desires. It will enhance my experiences. It will improve my quality of life. It will relieve my boredom. It promises to transform society for the better. If we develop it, it could well advance the course of human history on the steep climb of progress. Technology can save us from harm, restlessness, sadness, wastefulness, ruin, and meaninglessness. How well has technology delivered on these promises? To answer these questions we need more than technical information. We need to examine technology as a social and historical phenomenon. Only with the critical distance that such a perspective provides can we hope to analyze technology's character, claims and consequences with any accuracy.

For the thesis I am advancing in this essay I will be calling upon the work of some of my favorite writers and a few key theorists in the fields of sociology, social and cultural theory, and philosophy. But if I frog-march you into a full frontal assault of this specialized material, I will only engage your intellect. Since my argument is informed by a work of imaginative literature, I don't want to risk disfiguring the HP stories by distilling bloodless abstractions from them. It is your imagination that I wish to spark, for it is there that the magic in the HP series gives us a foothold from which to clarify the relationship between technology, history, society and the character of our contemporary lives. If I am successful in my argument, then you will have been interacting with some sophisticated and complex critical theory by letting Harry

Potter's magic shape (and I hope disturb) your perception and appraisal of technology.

Technology: Its Character and Claims

The idea of comparing the magical world of the HP series to our technological world is not new.[2] Benjamin Lipscomb and W. Christopher Stewart (2004) adopt the familiar characterization of technology as "applied science," the conventional meaning of technology I discussed above. But I do not think that this description is sufficient to understand technology as a social, human and spiritual fact. The HP series allows us to perceive the ways in which technology can be— and often is—opposed to personal autonomy, justice, and conviviality. Ivan Illich (2001) uses the term *conviviality* to describe a harmonious commonweal. Conviviality is living together in peaceable and joyful concord. The term evokes a cluster of meanings also attached to the Hebrew *shalom*. This is one standard by which to determine what is responsibly limited technology. *Does the technology diminish or increase conviviality?* An absolutely convivial society would consist of only those technologies which do not distract from or destroy social concord, individual initiative, or the free use of one's natural abilities.

When we think of technology we usually think of devices—*gadgets* that help us communicate, navigate, entertain, and occasionally be more productive at work. Technology makes demands on our resources, energy, attention, intellect, and desires; it carves the grooves into our material and virtual worlds along which we move, live and have our being. Because technological devices don't exist without a network of social forces and institutions developing, building and propagating them, we need to clarify the concept of technology beyond the simplistic association with devices. I shall adopt the general descriptions of Jacques Ellul in *The Technological Society*.

Technique is a method of action to accomplish some end. The applicability of techniques is limited, narrow, and local. As a result, individuals retain their freedom to choose among alternative techniques or refuse them altogether without diminishing their range of control and initiative. *Technology* is the totality, the systematic unity of all rationalized techniques. A technology is a *rational* method of efficient and effective action. It is not just the pursuit of human power over nature; it is this pursuit that aims for greatest efficiency. Because effectiveness and efficiency are its distinctive qualities, if we seek to develop *good* technology we must follow the rules to bring about those qualities. Once it is granted that the efficient and effective means of action are always justifiable, technology obtains its autonomous character. Technology acquires its irresistible power to mold individuals and society because individuals and communities have ceded their personal autonomy to defer always to the one best means to control and coordinate their environment. The electronic book reader has more than a value-neutral instrumental existence; its effective material and functional qualities require specific skills, aims, effort, and response from us. We must adjust what we value to conform to what the electronic book reader renders valuable.

Since technique preceded science, it is incorrect to limit the meaning of technology to "applied science." Scientific research requires that technique precede it. The modern study of astronomy required the material and craftsmanship of glassmaking and lens grinding. There is no search for fundamental particles without the large, expensive, and sophisticated technical apparatus of the particle accelerator and the industrial complex that supports its construction and operation. Max Weber argued that there are techniques for every human activity and purpose: techniques for battle, for love-making, for prayer, for dance, for writing. The means to achieve the desired ends of these activities may be spontaneous, tentative, intuitive, or esoteric to whatever degree chosen by an individual, or in accord with cultural mores or the rules of a tradition. Techniques become technologies when the activities are subjected to rational operations like abstraction, conceptualization, generalization, formalization, and proliferation, which are by their nature indifferent to cultural and traditional boundaries. The results of these operations are then elaborated theoretically and implemented systematically.

The aim of technology is to seek and determine *the one best means* independent of private judgments and all contingent factors. New techniques and materials might allow us to improve the one best means in the future, so the rationalized techniques that constitute technology have a ceiling to their power and sophistication determined by the particular level of development in the society.

Primitive magical societies, too, often have elaborate worldviews and highly structured systems of action and interaction. "Rational" is the appropriate term for such a society because it is the product of ordered and conscious thought. But the narrower sense of rationality I am employing in my argument is the specific "one best means," the modern scientific sense associated with mechanics, mathematical formulae, and logical analysis.

The rational element is introduced to technique by requiring that the technique be the one best means to the desired end. Then the one best means can be sought and applied to every possible field of inquiry and activity: business, government, education, communication, entertainment, child rearing, dying, and so on. Technology is the science of techniques: the comprehensive and systematic elaboration of rational, efficient actions. Therefore, magic in the HP world is not only a set of favored or culturally defined techniques, but is technological in the strict sense I am employing. Wizards have systematized magic into a compendium of practical and theoretical knowledge. Thus, magic can be explained and taught to any student. Although magical technique is universal in scope and absolute in its applicability, the success of any particular wizard or witch in exercising it depends on his or her natural abilities and capacity to improve those abilities. This is why OWL examinations have both theory and practical components.

According to Ellul, the logic of technique is inexorable: when a technical possibility exists, it *must* be applied. The force of this practical logic is perhaps most evident in the development of military and medical technologies. The power of technique to extend promises of new abilities and achievements creates and imposes new needs and habits on people. Consider the way in which the mere possibility of making a Philosopher's Stone must have changed Nicholas Flamel's life. Relationships, financial resources, daily activities, safety, and attentiveness all had to be reoriented in order to complete the project. Once the knowledge, skill and material were attained, it *had* to be made— the possibilities it promised to yield were irresistible. And once made and used, the technology again reshaped and redirected Flamel's life (although we are not given any information about the side effects of these results, with the notable exception that he comes to see the virtue of dying a "natural" death). Voldemort's desire for the Stone is a threat to society precisely because he wishes to wield its power but without the moral constraints embraced by Flamel. The justification for developing, building, and proliferating a technology always comes *after* its effectiveness and efficiency is already proven. The desired end is extending one's life indefinitely; a technique is devised to accomplish the end. The technological solution is the most efficient means to realize the goal. Whether it is a magical technique to acquire immortality or a material technique to double our life expectancy, the logic of technique impels us to develop and use the technology and worry about long-term consequences or justifying our actions (if at all) after we have at our disposal the means to realize our goal.

Technology: Its Consequences

Magic and technology are both techniques for solving a problem. As Postman (1997) observed, when applied they frequently create new problems. Automobiles solved a mobility problem. As more and more people used them, however, new problems were created, especially aesthetic and environmental problems. With the automobile we see the further irony that the very problem solved becomes worse instead of better. The automobile provided greater mobility, which, when its use was multiplied, created the distinctive aggravation of traffic jams, a new form of *im*mobility.

The same principle applies in the HP world: magical techniques are devised which solve a problem but create new problems. The owl is an amusing example. Owl mail overcomes the problem of keeping and using detailed addresses for people when you want to send someone a letter or a package. What new problems does it create? Since they are animals, they require training and control—domestication, which has both practical and ethical consequences. As we learned in *Order of the Phoenix*, the Ministry of Magic "used to use owls, but the mess was unbelievable..." (110). Other techniques, some which bestow astonishing, sometimes catastrophic power are so obviously dangerous that the wizarding community prevents access to them (the Time Turner and the Resurrection Stone) or knowledge of their manufacture (Horcruxes).

It can be very difficult to foresee the problems that await us over the horizon—not all technologies impose their power in the way that a hydrogen bomb and the Elder Wand do. Indeed, one desirable characteristic of most technology is that it *not* be noticed. Neil Postman recounts the story of the 13th Century Benedictine monks who invented the mechanical clock.[3] They wanted to improve the accuracy of timekeeping so that they could pray the hours on a more precise schedule—pious and gentle aims to be sure. The abstract time established by their mechanical clocks was a more efficient and effective means to mark time than the unreliable and imprecise means provided by the Sun and the natural environment. However, if they had been given a vision of the future six hundred years hence, when their invention would be used to strictly regiment the working day of hourly wage earners and assembly line laborers, or to coordinate and regulate working shifts in twenty-four-hour continuously operating manufacturing plants, they may have had second thoughts and been content with their sundials and water-clocks. The long-term effects of a technology are not problems solved by greater technical proficiency. They require us to develop both a philosophy of technology (what principles govern technological change?) and a socio-historical awareness (what were the social effects of previous technologies?). Then we are better equipped to ask: Which institutions benefit and which are harmed by a technological solution? Who are the winners and losers in the struggle for power, security, wealth, and influence? Will this technology permit us to balance the benefits of an effective technique with the traditional values of conviviality and personal autonomy?

I expect that we find it difficult to answer such questions—or even imagine technology in the service of other qualities like joy, justice, and beauty—because technological "solutions" for every personal wish and social improvement have proliferated and spread globally. Why are wizards and witches, the dominant culture of magical peoples, mostly blind to the social destruction wrought by their exchange of conviviality for effectiveness? They have allowed magic to diminish freedom by specializing, institutionalizing and centralizing the control and use of magic. As the effects of these forces accumulate and harden into standardized practices, products, and institutions, people are "repurposed" as accessories to the system that administers, legislates, and enforces the development and use of magic. Once magic is systematized throughout every level of society, it acquires the force of impersonal machinery. Magic gradually consolidates the entire collection of these institutions into an autonomous and self-augmenting network. This process is compatible with the occasional free-range innovation by the odd wizard or witch. The system can tolerate a family or two like the Lovegoods. Some people will use their creativity, technical resources, and intuitive skill to solve whatever problem is at hand. If the solution is effective in more than a one-off situation, then it will be absorbed by the system for institutional custodianship. Impersonal Magic acquires a will of its own as its logic is embraced and its rationalized methods accumulate. Magic attains its autonomy because of its inner rational principle to unify all efficient and effective means to achieve the desired ends. People may specify those ends; however, their pursuit of them is not free or human so long as priority is given to working out the means according to the doctrines of technology.

What is lost as technology expands and fills the human world is the question of ends. "I want to do X" is often a sufficient goal to initiate the drive that will deliver a technical solution enabling me to do X. But *why* do I want to do X? Will it be good for me? Will it be good for my family, my neighbors, my community? Never mind: X can be done, and done efficiently and effectively. It is technology's bewitching success, its irresistible expediency, that impels me to the inevitable conclusion that because X *can* be done it *ought* to be done and it *will* be done. This is the logic of the technological imperative taken to its natural conclusion. To refuse technology's effectiveness and efficiency would be irrational. But perhaps Thoreau was right when he criticized the utopian enthusiasm for machine technology's eschatological promises, "all our inventions are but improved means to unimproved ends."[4] It is easy for us to be dazzled and enthused by what can be done and fail to ask what is worth doing. Whither shall we go for guidance to know what to wish? By what light can we choose or reject what is technically achievable? Without a genuine alternative, a different imperative and hope for a less deterministic destiny, how are we to imagine or conceive improved *ends* to accompany our ever more powerful means? Is pragmatism the only ideology with which to evaluate the goals set by engineers and industries? The good, the fulfilling, the communally beneficial, the convivial—do these all reduce to the feasible, the realistic, the marketable? Can we resist the technological imperative, or has the technological system so intoxicated us that we can no longer see beyond our nose? "To navigate by a landmark tied to your ship's head is ultimately impossible."[5] If the technological imperative is the rudder for individuals and our social institutions, then society will eventually shipwreck on the shoals of either despotism or triviality.

The Technological Imperius Curse

When you hear that the latest "cutting-edge" device is about to hit the market, what does the news of it and details of its capabilities evoke in you? Do you anticipate and evaluate its likely social effects, that is to say, the social effects its use will have on others? (I do not mean the assistance or improved means it will provide you in managing and coordinating your interaction with people.) The bewitching charm, the "gee-whiz" attraction of gadgetry functions like an Imperius curse. Who is employing this curse? Those who stand to gain power and money from you. Who is under the curse? Those of us who neglect to evaluate the personal and social effects of it.

The devious nature of the Imperius curse in the HP series is that its victim doesn't know her will is being bent to the purposes of another. What shapes her desire and what determines her actions? The will of her unseen controller intrudes into her perception and judgment. It violates her human agency and therefore her dignity and autonomy. Note well: the victim of the Imperius curse isn't a robot—the controller doesn't have to micromanage every single decision and action of the victim. The victim has a limited range of free action. The important parallel with technology is that the controller sets the task to be done and imbues it with the addictive force of necessity, all while the victim is convinced that she has chosen voluntarily what she is up to. The Imperius curse alters the victim's capacity to make her own considered judgments or pause to reflect on whether or not the goal she strives for is right and good. Once the victim is convinced that the goal must be reached, she is all but unable to refuse to pursue it as she occupies herself with the details of how to successfully carry it off, of the means to reach the desired end that burns ever more intensely the nearer she gets to it. Harry has the unusual ability to resist the Imperius curse; we can develop that power, too.

The powerful want the powerless to remain unaware that they are powerless. When losers believe they are winning, when those being harmed believe they are being helped, they are all the more ensnared to the will of another and alienated from their own soul. Suppose every new laptop manufactured has a built-in webcam. This accessory is very helpful for some things I might like to do. I find it convenient to be seamlessly integrated with the computer. I don't have to think about it and it functions unobtrusively. That this increases the monitoring and surveillance power of some institutions—education, business, law enforcement—well, if I don't pay any attention to it, if I just behave normally, then do I really lose anything? Authorities will ensure that no one exploits its possible harmful uses. And so I participate in building an upscale, 3D, high definition digital concentration camp. This is not a camp with a fenced enclosure or arbitrary violence, yet our range of free action has been limited. It is a panopticon where the inhabitants don't notice that their choices, desires, and behavior have been reshaped and redirected by the wardens. From the point of view of the authorities and citizens whose technological reflection goes no deeper than to ask if the object or technique works effectively, to challenge or resist such a society is irrational. After all, if we want to eradicate *all* crime we need to supervise everybody. If a policing technique can be applied everywhere and not just hit-and-miss to criminals, then our objective is within reach.

Should we be this concerned about technology's effects upon our ways of life, social institutions, and mental and emotional habits? To be categorically anti-technology is idiotic. In the wizarding world it would be equally stupid to be categorically anti-magic. We no more want to get rid of technology (or magic, if we are wizards) than we want to get rid of medicine. But even something necessary for survival and beneficial for society isn't an unqualified good. Ingesting too much medicine, ignoring side effects, and chasing after the high it might produce can poison or kill instead of cure. Medicine, magic, and technology can be life-enhancing, but they aren't always. The task is not to get rid of technology but of transcending it by determining its responsible use. As long as our wishes, desires, perception, and judgment are determined by the possibilities which technology alone extends to us, then we live in self-imposed servitude to it. We must first become conscious that our actions are not free and then understand the properties of technology that rob us of that freedom. We may need help to do this. Many believe such help comes in the form of education.

Technology and Education

Hogwarts School of Witchcraft and Wizardry, Durmstrang Institute, and Beauxbatons Academy represent the rationalized idea of schooling: one effective, efficient method applied to everyone. This approach to schooling, the rational monopoly, is then the singular path to knowledge, employment, and social advancement within the system. Even Voldemort graduated from Hogwarts. We see this idea of schooling reflected in the one glimpse we're given of the Muggle world as well: the Dursleys. Vernon and Petunia's pride in Dudley's introduction to the societies beyond Number Four Privet Drive is a function of his entering the system through a socially desirable institution like Smeltings. But schooling has failed to renovate Dudley's soul, a failure of which Vernon and Petunia are blithely unconcerned. The evidence in the HP series suggests that schooling in its present form is an area of social malignancy in both the magical and Muggle worlds. Rowling has signaled to us that the same spirit drives social institutions within both worlds. They are in need of reform, or better, of liberation from that which undermines their conviviality.

Popular views of technology consider it to be a value-neutral tool. A technology cannot be good or bad, so this way of thinking goes—only the use to which it is put can be good or bad. So any value that attaches to technology is credited exclusively to the good or bad intentions of the human user of the tool. My argument, however, is for the contrary claim that technology's inner principle—rational efficient and effective action—induces people to shape their aims, attitudes, and wishes to the recommendations of instrumental reason: what is practical, feasible, and "realistic." In previous generations, the value-neutral view focused on the machine as the neutral object and man as its master. The emblematic technologies today are the computer and the Internet. As technologies proliferate and are used for more and more purposes, we alter our actions, desires, values, and manners toward our technological environment and with our companions to accommodate the demands of the architecture and agenda of the technological medium. In the recent past the network of technologies meant the linking between factory, road, rail, and telephone. Today's technological network consists in the power generation plant and distribution grid, communication cabling, radio transmitters and receivers, and satellites. Even though technologies become obsolete, the principles that govern them do not. Their social force is constant. The computer network, even though it is designed and constructed by human ideas and effort, modifies society according to its own inherent principles.

If technology is the most significant social fact of our day, and if it is not value-neutral, then what are its effects upon traditional moral categories? We can predict what they *should* be given the defining property of technology already set forth. A technique is a method of action to accomplish some end. Technology is the rationalized technique of the "one best means," universally applicable—the method of efficient and effective action for a given stage of development. Accordingly, the greatest injuries to a technological society's operations are inefficiency, disarray, and impotence. Therefore, the moral categories of *bad* and *evil* will manifest themselves in terms like "problem," "disorder," "uselessness," "failure," and the like. Evil is an obstacle to fix or remove, not the traditional inclinations to corrupt, deceive, or deface. Likewise, the moral category of *good* will manifest itself as "solution," "practical," "success," and so on.

If we were to test our prediction in the educational system, what results would we get? Do we cast moral judgment of things, events, and people *primarily* in the terms of technological value? What makes one student better than another in the eyes of the public? Is the 'A' student better than the 'C' student? Does society, through its education system, reward or convict the student on this basis? *Excellence* means achieving maximum results in a standardized curriculum. The excellent student is commended not for her character, initiative or creativity, but her measurable effectiveness in accomplishing the work given to her. Just ask Hermione Granger. She will have free rein in the professional wizarding world—not on the basis of her sturdy Gryffindor moral fiber, but on her technical competence to understand and use magic.[6]

Technology demands that the educational system embrace a Slytherin House. Salazar Slytherin and Voldemort, as master practitioners of the Dark Arts, unfetter efforts to expand all knowledge for the sake of greater control over the natural and social environments. As Voldemort boasts to Dumbledore, "I have experimented; I have pushed the boundaries of magic further, perhaps, than they have ever been pushed." The Sorting Hat proclaims that those bound for Slytherin are "cunning folks [who] use any means, to achieve their ends." A clever, cunning, or shrewd wizard may use magic effectively, but doing so "using any means" implies that the pursuit occurs without moral restraint or boundaries. Amorality is institutionalized in a technological society. Rowling associates our rationalizations for a tool or technique (they're efficient, useful, effective, etc.) to the rationalizations offered by Voldemort. He has achieved "progress" precisely by refusing to be governed by any moral regulations which might constrain him. When we fail, either by omission or commission, to be morally responsible for a technique we acquire and use, our humanity sinks to Slytherin's dungeons.

Hogwarts exists to produce young energetic witches and wizards to service and maintain the institutions of the wizarding community. It restricts as well as disseminates knowledge. Illich has argued that we ought not equate education with schooling. Harry gets his *schooling* from Hogwarts; he gets his *education* from Dumbledore, his family (Sirius and the Weasleys), his friends (especially those in Dumbledore's Army), and the Order of the Phoenix. Hogwarts, Durmstrang and Beauxbatons are formal, ritualized, sacred cows in the wizarding world, as are schooling institutions in our world. These institutions do more than supply access to knowledge—they inculcate every student with the primary values of the governing technocratic socio-political-economic system: success or failure, effectiveness or uselessness.

Knocking down Hogwarts is not the solution to liberating education from the institution of universal mandatory schooling. An anarchic curriculum is an alternative, but not an anarchism that expunges the wisdom of the past. A constructive anarchic alternative to the standardized and ritualized education system would be to disestablish compulsory schooling so that young people from any community can access the store of knowledge locally through the preexisting bonds of human fellowship in families, friends, mentors, and community leaders. These often already function locally in the context of the student's existing and enlarging convivial society.

Voldemort: The Spirit of Technology

The character of Lord Voldemort confronts us with a human will disconnected from any moral sensibility. Everything is permissible—it is only a question of whether he has the means to accomplish what he wills to do. What does such a spirit, the technological spirit, will to do? What is the ultimate boundary for it to transgress?

> I miscalculated, my friends, I admit it. My curse was deflected by the woman's foolish sacrifice, and it rebounded upon myself. Aaah . . . pain beyond pain, my friends; nothing could have prepared me for it. I was ripped from my body, I was less than spirit, less than the meanest ghost... but still, I was alive. What I was, even I do not know... *I, who have gone further than anybody along the path that leads to immortality. You know my goal – to conquer death.* And now, I was tested, and it appeared that one or more of my experiments had worked ... for I had not been killed, though the curse should have done it.[7]

Why does Voldermort wish to conquer death? What does Voldemort have against Death? Why is Death Voldemort's enemy? Is it because of the physical and psychic pain that Death causes? Is he grief-stricken by the loss of friends, children, or mentors? Although his life began in a social setting where suffering and brokenness were common, he had no direct personal experience with suffering. No, Voldemort's desire to conquer Death is because Death is the universe's ultimate winner. Death wins—eventually—against everyone. Voldemort's outrage at Death's overwhelming power is not fueled by the cosmic injustice of lives wounded and torn asunder, but by the inescapable fact there exists a power greater than any Voldemort himself commands.

Voldemort's wounds are not caused by his compassion (if ever he had any). It is his pride that is offended and which urges him on. But to seek to master the eminent qualities of Death—power and invincibility—one must transform into something that Death cannot defeat. One must outdo Death at His own work. So in order to defeat Death Voldemort makes himself Death's pupil and servant. Voldemort is convinced by this inward-spiraling logic that he can turn the tables and become Death's master. But what can a human being—even the most powerful—do that Death cannot? There is one thing: Death cannot bring about Its own death. That power is something Voldemort *can* acquire. So his goal requires that he kill whatever is weak and vulnerable in himself. He must put to death his self. Note well the distinction in Voldemort between physical and psychic self-annihilation—the former is physical suicide, which is but a dull, awkward imitation of the inner suicide, the murder of one's own soul. All that remains is the sheer, naked will that chooses and acts toward the goal of invincibility. That Voldemort might defeat Death is his great act of self-justification and self-delusion. The goal is impossible—a parody of godhood—if one follows the logic of technology. There is no "one best means," no mechanism, that can vanquish Death. The only result from the effort is a progressively diminished soul and destruction of all that loves and is loved in the world. We arrive at a nihilistic terminus: where technology is pursued to solve every natural and human problem, when it is the final arbiter of what is to be done in every case, its imperative crumbles under self-negation.

What is the "solution" to the "problem" of the person with a will strong enough to subdue "any internal distress or doubt when one inflicts great suffering and hears the cry of it?"[8] Nietzsche seems to have foreseen Lord Voldemort. Ollivander agrees with Nietzsche that one like Voldemort is "great" (although Ollivander places some value in the social niceties that Nietzsche disdains, for he quickly adds "terrible, yes, but great"). Why would he regard Voldemort's deeds as belonging to greatness? Ollivander's craft is at the very heart of wizarding society. He is not only a wand-carrier, he is a wand-maker. He makes the instruments necessary for wizards to wield magic effectively. The value inherent to the magical-technological society, rational effective and efficient action, makes Ollivander a member of the most elite professional class. He esteems any wizard—no matter how "terrible"—who maximizes magical expertise and power. And what of the moral or spiritual cost of attaining that greatness? "Who can attain to anything great if he does not feel in himself the force and will to inflict great pain?"[9] Like Nietzsche, Ollivander understands that performing terrible deeds is the price that a truly great wizard likely must pay. The impasse in Ollivander's moral reasoning is his inability to comprehend why Voldemort's cruelty actually outweighs the value of his effectiveness.

Since Voldemort embodies the technological spirit in its purest and most explicit form it is easy for us to think the connection irrelevant in "the real world" because, after all, *we're not Voldemort*. But Voldemort is an exaggeration. What of the human condition does he magnify? Some, like Nietzsche's great man and Voldemort, scoff at ethical demands that, in their estimation, attempt to extort what they believe they've earned and deserve by "having pushed the boundaries further" than anyone else. Their goal is self-actualization, not compassion, magnanimity, or a peaceable, convivial society. "That which Voldemort does not value, he takes no trouble to comprehend." But in *Deathly Hallows* we're given a glimpse behind the terrifying appearances of Voldemort's greatness and power to see his true identity, his soul as it really is:

> Then a noise reached [Harry] through the unformed nothingness that surrounded him: the small soft thumpings of something that flapped, flailed, and struggled. It was a pitiful noise, yet also slightly indecent. (…) It had the form of a small, naked child, curled on the ground, its skin raw and rough, flayed-looking.[10]

In King's Cross station, Harry sees the real Voldemort, the small, disfigured, miserable creature unaware of his condition and surroundings. It is who Voldemort has chosen to be. A lifetime of self-glorifying choices, of pusillanimity and ignorance cloaked in a bully's boastings and banal cruelty— Voldemort, the consummate self-made man, in reality a wretched, quivering, self-mutilated soul.

Voldemort's path is a temptation for the best of us, the Albus Dumbledores among us:

> Oh, I had a few scruples. I assuaged my conscience with empty words. It would all be for the greater good, and any harm done would be repaid a hundredfold in benefits for wizards.

> And at the heart of our schemes, the Deathly Hallows! How they fascinated [Grindewald], how they fascinated both of us! The unbeatable wand, the weapon that would lead us to power! The Resurrection Stone—to him, though I pretended not to know it, it meant an army of Inferi! (…) our interest in the Cloak of Invisibility was mainly that it completed the trio, for the legend said that the man who united all three objects would then be truly master of death, which we took to mean "invincible."[11]

Dumbledore shocks Harry with his tearful confession that Harry's beloved mentor, the man he believed to be the most powerful and morally upright wizard in the world, was at one time no better than Voldemort. And why? "Master of Death, Harry, master of Death!" Dumbledore, like Voldemort and Grindewald, sought the power that would conquer Death. Not with the full, explicit commitment of the evil villains, but with the well-meaning pieties of a savior. What makes Dumbledore more threatening than the archvillain is the depth of his self-deception: the unapologetic power seekers in the world—the Voldemorts and Grindewalds—lack the duplicitous sincerity and false humility of the self-righteous improver of humanity. Dumbledore shows that even the best, most decent human being harbors the ambitions of godhood within the deepest folds of his heart. Dumbledore and Harry experience redemption in their respective ordeals because they choose to confront and, with help, overcome the Voldemort within them.

Voldemort had his predecessors—Grindewald, the Peverell brothers, Salazar Slytherin—and he will have his less obvious successors, too. The logic of the "one best means" is absolute and universal. If my application of Niven's maxim to magic in the HP series withstands critical scrutiny, then it should be revealing if we substitute technology for magic in this dialogue between Voldemort and Dumbledore that Harry witnesses in the Pensieve:

> Voldemort's expression remained impassive as he said, "Greatness inspires envy, envy engenders spite, spite spawns lies. You must know this, Dumbledore."
>
> "You call it 'greatness,' what you have been doing, do you?" asked Dumbledore delicately.
>
> "Certainly," said Voldemort, and his eyes seemed to burn red. "I have experimented; I have pushed the boundaries of magic further, perhaps, than they have ever been pushed—"
>
> "Of some kinds of magic," Dumbledore corrected him quietly. "Of some. Of others, you remain…forgive me… woefully ignorant."
>
> For the first time, Voldemort smiled. It was a taut leer, an evil thing, more threatening than a look of rage. "The old argument," he said softly. "But nothing I have seen in the world has supported your famous pronouncements that love is more powerful than my kind of magic, Dumbledore."
>
> "Perhaps you have been looking in the wrong places," suggested Dumbledore.[12]

The boundaries of technology are pushed out further every year. We who trust that it shall one day yield all the secrets of happiness, health, pleasure, wealth, and immortality—is there knowledge—lore—that we have chosen to neglect and of which we remain "woefully ignorant?" Do we suspect Dumbledore to be deluded in his "old argument"? Does he really know something or is he bluffing? Where is the evidence? I look around the world and I see plenty of counterevidence: it appears that it is the problem-solvers, goal-achievers, and other winners who get things done, who succeed, who are in command of their own destiny. In spite of this it still might be true that I am looking for evidence in the wrong places. Dumbledore's allusive and open-ended response invites us to find out for ourselves, to reflect on our choices, on the next decision we face, and if need be, turn from soul-corrupting means and ends.

Prophets of a glorious technological future have been with us since the Industrial Revolution. I'm with Dumbledore: the means to pursue such a society are "real, and dangerous, and a lure for fools." The Hallows are the material summit of magical power. If the possibility to make the technological equivalent of the Hallows is within our reach, then the logic of technology urges us to apply that knowledge. But who shall be the master of the impersonal dynamics of technology, or rather, who would try to master them? We will not have to contend with a Grindewald or a Voldemort. It isn't the evil power of an archvillain that will threaten us with the technological utopia. It is the tyranny of bright and optimistic people, those who mean us well with their dreams of improving humanity that will build Pandora's new box and unleash it on the rest of us for our own good.

Shall we advocate policies that seek to improve human beings by technologically transforming them? The proponents of transhumanism—eugenicists for our more enlightened age—aim to apply technology to enhance our natural abilities for more than ameliorative or healing benefits. The human body and brain are to be enhanced and augmented by more robust and powerful mechanisms. Biotechnologies promise to reduce and eventually eliminate disease, aging, and even death. Voldemort is their prophet: his unlimited drive to augment and extend his powers to the point of invincibility is the personification of the logic of technology at its extreme and bitter end, a logic which is submerged in our social institutions and systems. Technology mediates our interaction with our natural and social environments. Because we are immersed in the technological medium and thrive (in some ways) with its many concrete advantages, no standard—not the good, just, beautiful, or true—can challenge the technical standard— rational efficiency—without unforeseen intervention on its behalf. It will be difficult to resist our improvers.

Conclusion

Is there an alternative use of technology? Yes, but we must raise the kind of questions that admit other than conventional, preordained answers. We cannot cook the books to get answers that preserve in advance and at all costs technological proliferation. We cannot underestimate the difficulty of this task. Institutions and bureaucracies resist change. They define our social environment and technology's demands are expressed through them. They function as a collective superego to preserve the technological values of survival, consumption, and daily busyness. The alternative uses of technology in which social integration and conviviality are produced may not be difficult in principle, but they are difficult to imagine because of the restricted vision a technological society imposes. How do we develop and use technology responsibly and encourage outbreaks of conviviality in our homes, neighborhoods, cities, schools, businesses, and other social institutions?

In *Tools for Conviviality*, Ivan Illich suggests four questions to ask of any technology; I have responded with the social effects we observe in the wizard magic of the HP series:

Does the technology extinguish the free use of the natural abilities of the members of the society?

The range of activity, creativity and initiative available to "other" rational magical beings—house elves, goblins, centaurs—is restricted by the dominant class.

Does it isolate people from each other and lock them into a human-made shell?

Families are estranged (the Blacks, the Dumbledores); squibs have to get by in the margins of society;

discrimination against other magical beings increases social and cultural Balkanization.

Does it promote extreme social polarization and splintering specialization within the community?

Centralized schooling, house sorting, and ordering of students from Head Boy to inferior ranks below entrenches ethnic and class prejudices; vocational possibilities are restricted by OWL and NEWT examination scores.

Does the acceleration of techniques (their complexity, power, etc.) enforce social change at a rate that rules out legal, cultural, and political precedents as formal guidelines to present behavior?

The Ministry of Magic multiplies departments to manage every conceivable social contingency; policing, prison, and the justice system underscore the preeminent values of efficiency and order over human dignity and other traditional values; the rule of law is tenuous at best in the wizarding legal system.

We can ask these questions of our technological tools and environment as well. How can we tell when our tools overwhelm our natural abilities? I might become aware that I exist for the tool rather than the tool existing for me. I might be vaguely uneasy that my day-to-day life is isolated from whole groups of people. Does magic in HP, or at least certain magical practices, tend to do this? Let's take a closer look at a final example.

Harry and Griphook have a conversation in *Deathly Hallows* that might have been the first of its kind between a wizard and a goblin. What was operative in that moment between them, what common language or attitudes provided the means for them to, if not overcome, suspend the hostilities and suspicions between their opposed peoples? Harry had earned Griphook's hesitant appreciation ("You're a very unusual wizard Harry Potter") because Griphook had observed Harry's equal regard for non-wizard magical peoples—Dobby the house elf and Griphook himself. For his part, Harry simply treated Griphook as a person due the same respect and dignity as other persons. Their conversation hinted that some profound breakthrough in magical society was possible, perhaps just around the corner (Hermione senses this, too, and joins their discussion). Their rapprochement—even though tentative and tainted by ulterior motives—destabilized some of the permanent ways in which magical values and imperatives had been institutionalized. They found that past wrongs had poisoned the trust and cooperation that mark a true convivial society of equals. And what were those injustices rooted in and marked by? The wizarding community, "wand-carriers," had withheld wand-lore from all other magical beings. And wand-lore is the body of technical, specialized knowledge—technology.

No one is as utterly wicked as Voldemort. But if I've accurately described the parallels between the magical society of HP and our technological society, then Rowling is warning that we all have a piece of Voldemort within us that prefers technocracy over freedom. Perhaps we don't entertain grand utopian illusions. Perhaps we don't believe that technology will make us fully invincible or fix every human and social problem. But we need to examine ourselves and our society with a finer instrument than the blunt tool of a Voldemort. We prize some things as humanly desirable in general—has technology been instrumental in developing and establishing those values?

Do we nurse the delusion of control and exercise it over others in miniature tyrannies?

Do we resent our finitude and endeavor to transcend the plain fact that we have limits, perhaps by indulging in the folly of consuming and accumulating more?

Do we turn to technology to satisfy our immediate urges? To protect us? To give us something to do? To distract us from the activity and people around us?

Do we comply with what technology recommends as best and default to its mediation of our natural and social environment as preferable?

From answers to such questions we may begin to observe the consequences of our technologically determined attitudes, actions and habits, and anticipate what more of the same will produce. What kind of society are my technological commitments helping to build? Is it one of greater trust, cooperation and conviviality? Does my allegiance to technology encourage magnanimity, initiative, *shalom*, and creativity? We are not shown such a society in the HP series, not even after the defeat of Voldemort.

Many readers of the HP series are dissatisfied with the tame, conventional lives depicted in the epilogue. But the end of the series rings true to me. The great threat is over; the healing and rebuilding is underway. It is still an open question whether the wizarding community will radically reform the place and use of magic in their ways of life, institutions, and social practices. Great deeds need to be remembered and wrongs confessed. Injustice and distrust—the seeds of further enmity—remain amongst the magical races. The Malfoys and the rest of the vanquished Death Eaters await their penalties—what will the "good" side do with its enemies? The unconscious arrogance of sincere and well-intentioned people still injures those who are close to them. The series ends with the convivial magical society an as yet unknown land and unfulfilled possibility. There are signs of hope but much difficult work to be done. And so it is in the technological society.

French mathematician and philosopher Blaise Pascal called the predicament in which humans find themselves the "triple abyss:" (1) we are enslaved by our egotistical self to our instinctual desires; (2) we lust for power over others and over nature; (3) we crave intense sensation and manipulative knowledge, knowledge that is primarily used to increase our own power, profit and pleasure. The HP series is an examination of Pascal's triple abyss and the ease with which we slip further down into its depths—but also the help that has intervened and is near in friends and mentors. The characters of the HP series must face the ever-present temptation to declare their allegiance to the power offered by magical technique—as Percy Weasley discovered, signing up to be a Death Eater isn't the only way to assist Voldemort in his aims. The principle of technology urges us to embrace the bondage of its imperatives as well. But Rowling's mythology also displays a moral sensibility that we can appropriate and with which we can take stock of technology's character, claims, and consequences. We can envision other possibilities than those determined by the absolute logic of technology. From the deepest pits of the triple abyss the voices of self-destruction call us to develop and apply every technical possibility and worry about its cost to our humanity later. Compared to the impressive control and power with which technology equips us—the exciting promise it offers for permanent security, boundless comfort and amusement, and longevity—an alternative which questions, much less *resists* the obligation to apply the rational methods of efficiency and effectiveness at all levels of society seems romantic and irrational. But with collective and critical effort, we can refuse the technological imperative, disestablish the technological society, and return technology to its role as the servant to human flourishing as we seek peaceful companionship, enriching relationships at all levels in a community, and renewal for society's failures and losers. From the perspective of a world in which technology is sovereign, principles which demote technology's authority make as much sense as Arthur Weasley's fixation with Muggle techniques of illumination and transportation. Of what use are plugs and batteries at the Burrow? Why, none at all! But it is a small beachhead for freedom, an outpost for wonder and delight in useless things.

Acknowledgements

Many thanks to Travis Prinzi and John Granger for their conversation, encouragement and penetrating literary insights; to Kimberly Condoulis for her assistance in researching Harry Potter "technology" and tracking down references in the series; and to the students in the Harry Potter Society of Arizona State University who love to talk Potter with their peculiar faculty sponsor.

Notes

References

Berry, Wendell. The Way of Ignorance: And Other Essays. Berkeley, CA: Counterpoint, 2006.

_____. Art of the Commonplace: The Agrarian Essays of Wendell Berry. Ed. Norman Wirzba. Berkeley, CA: Counterpoint, 2003.

_____. Sex, Economy, Freedom & Community: Eight Essays. New York, NY: Pantheon, 1994.

Ellul, Jacques. The Technological Bluff. Grand Rapids, MI: Eerdmans, 1990.

_____. Propaganda: The Formation of Men's Attitudes. New York, NY: Vintage, 1973.

_____. The Technological Society. New York, NY: Vintage, 1967.

Illich, Ivan, et al. Disabling Professions. London: Marion Boyars Publishers, 2000 (1977).

Illich, Ivan. Tools for Conviviality. London: Marion Boyars Publishers, 2001 (1973).

_____. Deschooling Society. London: Marion Boyars

Publishers, 2000 (1971).

    Jacobs, Alan. "Harry Potter's Magic," First Things 99, 2000: 35-38.

    Lipscomb, Benjamin and Stewart, W. Christopher. "Magic, Science and the Ethics of Technology," in Harry Potter and Philosophy: If Aristotle Ran Hogwarts. Ed. D. Baggett, et al (Chicago: Open Court Publishing, 2004), 77-91.

    Ostling, Michael. "Harry Potter and the Disenchantment of the World," Journal of Contemporary Religions 18:1, 2003: 3-23.

    Postman, Neil. "Defending Ourselves Against Technology," Bulletin of Science, Technology & Society 17:5-6, 1997: 229-33.

    _____. Amusing Ourselves to Death: Public Discourse in the Age of Show Business. New York, NY: Penguin, 1986.

    Stivers, Richard. Technology as Magic: The Triumph of the Irrational. New York: Continuum, 2001.

Endnotes

1   I agree with Michael Ostling (2003) that magic in the Harry
    Potter series reflects Max Weber's "disenchanted" world of mo-
    dernity, and that, therefore, the Harry Potter series presents the
    wonderful and extraordinary as demystified and mundane. Thus,
    Ostling suggests, the series is popular precisely because its "mag-
    ic is disenchanted," "ordinary" and "unchallenging." However,
    I think Ostling's helpful analysis only takes into account the
    surface narrative and the rules J. K. Rowling established for the
    series' magical world. It may be overreaching to claim, as some
    commentators do, that "Harry fulfills our hunger for enchant-
    ment, our search for something numinous beyond the real," but
    I do think that, while not fulfilling such yearning, it arouses it.
    This is partially attributable to the "deeper magic" that Ostling
    acknowledges is present in the series and which is not intrinsi-
    cally explicable. It is also attributable, as I will argue in this es-
    say, to the subversion of the instrumental magic within the series.
    This is only possible if there is a didactic layer below the surface
    narrative and logic. If we treat magic in the Harry Potter series as
    a symbol, then we have a key with which to access its moral sub-
    surface and the embedded critique of our technological world.

2   Lipscomb and Stewart (2004).

3   "Defending Ourselves Against Technology," 231.

4   "Paradise to be Regained" (1843), by Henry David Thoreau, a re-
    view of J. A. Etzler's *The Paradise Within the Reach of All Men,
    Without Labour, by Powers of Nature and Machinery: An Address
    to All Intelligent Men* (1842). The transcendentalists understand-
    ably opposed the ideas of utopian socialism. For Thoreau and
    some contemporary proponents of localism, notably Wendell
    Berry, any system which demands that machinery replace man-
    ual labor wherever possible devalues physical work and thereby
    subverts conviviality.

5   *Man and His Future: A CIBA Foundation Volume.* Ed. Gordon
    Wolstenholme (Boston: Little, Brown, 1963) 268.

6   Note well how actions that are exceptions from this rule stand out.
    For example, in the conclusion to *Philosopher's Stone* Dumbledore
    awards house points to the Gryffindor students for the particu-

lar moral qualities they exhibited in thwarting Voldemort on the basis of traditional notions of good character traits. And again in *Goblet of Fire*, most of the judges agree to reward Harry's self-less act of rescuing Gabrielle Delacour on the basis of its showing his "moral fiber." These exceptions prove the rule that ambition, cleverness and willpower are the ordinary means to succeed in life—extraordinary means require intervention from outside the system.

7   *Harry Potter and the Goblet of Fire*, 269. My emphasis.

8   Friedrich Nietzsche, *The Gay Science* (1882), §325.

9   Ibid.

10 *Harry Potter and the Deathly Hallows*, 596.

11 Ibid, 604.

12   *Harry Potter and the Half-Blood Prince*, 267

"Merlin's Pants!"
The World of Wizarding Insult

Kathleen Langr

W HEN WE THINK OF what it takes for an author to build a world of fantasy, it is easy to consider only the completed imagery. Characters must have a background, a distinct physical description, a particular way of interacting with others, and so on; social hierarchies must exist; the settings of character interactions must be complete in every way imaginable. However, creating a brilliantly complete fantasy world is not just the simple task of putting an image into words to be later translated back into an image by a reader. There is a plethora of background details that must be carefully allocated by an author in even the most mundane situations. Among these necessary details lies the unbounded idea of language.

Rowling's works have been linguistically analyzed several times over, but most of what is dissected lies on the topic of her neologisms. Indeed, her method of creating spells, places, and even character names is effective and brilliant, but there are language systems lying deeper than nomenclature that play huge roles in creating new cultures. One such system, rarely considered on its own, is that of insult and expletive. Though insult does not necessarily belong to "lower" culture or wit, it tends to be looked down upon as a counter-culture practice, since the routes of peace or neutrality are the wiser. Nonetheless, fantasy worlds are required to be neither wise nor perfect, so an insult system is important.

The simplest way to use a system of insult and expletive in any sort of work would be to borrow entirely from one's mother language, in Rowling's case British English, but where would lie the fun in that? The system would be closed to outsiders of different languages and cultures. Therefore, the easiest solution is to draw from the culture created within the work, and build a whole new set of expletives and system of insults. Rowling does not necessarily create her own from scratch: since she is writing in British English she certainly has the right to build from what she knows. However, she carefully modifies the ordinary into something of a different world. The following sections will take a look at Rowling's artistry in this facet of linguistic adjustment; we will see what she starts with, how she creates new cultures, and how she manipulates the interactions of those cultures into new forms of insult.

Rowling creates more than one culture?

The Muggle readers of Rowling's series do not live in the same world as non-human creatures that are able to understand and speak human languages; to the knowledge of these readers, everyone of human intelligence is probably human. Therefore, within Muggle society, there exist rifts only between members of different religions, ethnic backgrounds, homelands, or other group divisions. On the contrary, Rowling's world not only contains as many ethnicities and religions as the readers' Muggle world, but it includes hundreds of other species otherwise unknown to members of the latter. Throughout the series readers learn of dozens of species, many of which are capable of human speech, and see their interactions with Wizards.

It is at this point of interaction that Rowling begins to

build her world of insult and expletive. Not only does she give each featured culture a colorful depiction (I say "featured" because there are many other species that are merely glanced upon but not dimensionally complete), but she allows us to observe their lifestyle decisions, how they are viewed by others, and how they react to certain situations.

So how do we know what insult is?

Before it is possible to even glance at the insult system surrounding the different social structures in the Wizarding world, one must have a firm grasp on what insult actually is. Unfortunately, there is no set-in-stone way to define it, as dictionaries can only provide so much. What I have provided, for the purpose of simplicity, is a short explanation of insult and offense. Here is a basic chart:

> Insult = from one to another (action)
> Offense = perception of insult (state)

In other words, per my definition, insult and offense are directly related to one another. Offense always lies in the eye of the beholder, since some may try to offend but fail and others may not try at all but still deliver a smashing blow. Insult is the action of delivering this offense; it does not have to be on purpose.

Before moving on into more complex matters of wizard insult, I will demonstrate the idea by applying the above chart to three quotations from the *Harry Potter* series.

Scenario one: Attempted insult, failed offense

In *Sorcerer's Stone*, Harry catches his first Snitch by way of his oral cavity while trying to stay on his out-of-control broomstick. Draco is less than pleased:

> Disgusted that the Slytherins had lost, he had

tried to get everyone laughing at how a wide-mouthed tree frog would be replacing Harry as seeker next. (*Sorcerer's Stone* 195)

Here, Draco has attempted to get other students to laugh at Harry in order to hurt Harry's feelings. But, as readers remember, everyone is too impressed with Harry staying on his bucking broomstick, and Harry experiences elation more than any other emotion.

Scenario two: Unattempted insult, confirmed offense (i.e. accidental insult)

In *Order of the Phoenix,* Harry discovers that Bellatrix Lestrange is related to his godfather, Sirius, and expresses his astonishment, which most likely occurs because Harry cannot imagine Sirius being related to such a horrible person. Even though Harry intends no harm, Sirius takes offense to Harry's surprise:

> "You never said she was your…"

> "Does it matter if she's my cousin?" (*Order of the Phoenix* 114)

Sirius immediately forgives Harry, but this issue touches a nerve in Sirius, based on a predominant "cultural" mentality of good morals versus poor idealism (to be discussed shortly).

Scenario three: Attempted insult, confirmed offense

A beautiful example of a successful insult shows up in Snape's encounter with the Marauder's Map. Four insults are lined up for him:

> "Mr. Moony presents his compliments to Professor Snape, and begs him to keep his abnormally large nose out of other people's business."

"Mr. Prongs agrees with Mr. Moony, and would like to add that Professor Snape is an ugly git."

"Mr. Padfoot would like to register his astonishment that an idiot like that ever became a professor."

"Mr. Wormtail bids Professor Snape a good day, and advises him to wash his hair, the slimeball." (*Prisoner of Azkaban* 287)

Even though Snape does not react to a particular insult or rise and jinx everything in sight, he expresses his upset through his attempts to punish Harry and based upon the claim that the map is clearly full of dark magic.

As can be seen from the above scenarios, Rowling demonstrates usage of all three possible insult-offense combinations, which is consistent with her tendency to complete character backgrounds rather than present two-dimensional cutouts. She therefore fulfills the first requirement for creating an effective insult culture: being able to provide a variety of insult-offense combinations.

How could a character possibly feel offense?

Requirement two in the world of insult is for the subject of the insult to be applicable to the intended (or unintended) recipient. If the recipient thinks the name "butthead" is more humorous than anything else, why would he feel insulted? Then again, what if "butthead" were traditionally used in a more damaging sense, rather than to just tease?

Sociolinguist Geoffrey Hughes demonstrates this concept with the following example:

Imagine the following exchange:
X: Rapist!
Y: Bastard!
X: Child molester!
Y: Son of a bitch!

X: Plagiarist!
Y: Cretin!
X: Embezzler!
Y: Coward!

Clearly, X's epithets are, technically, more damaging since they stigmatize his enemy in powerfully anti-social terms, but Y's have greater impact, not because they are more critical, but because they have acquired a weight of tradition in the speech community. (Hughes 22)

The "weight of tradition" is the key feature when attempting an assault of personality. Not only must an insult be applicable, but it must also carry a greater stigmatization than merely being socially unacceptable. So how does this relate to Rowling's world? To put this theory into play, I'll use another Snape example:

> "Kill me then," panted Harry, who felt no fear at all, but only rage and contempt. "Kill me like you killed him, you coward – "
>
> "DON'T – " screamed Snape, and his face was suddenly demented, inhuman, as though he was in as much pain as the yelping, howling dog stuck in the burning house behind them – "CALL ME COWARD!" (*Half-Blood Prince* 604).

Snape is a complex character, to say the least. He despises Harry and his Gryffindor companions, is wholly trusted by Dumbledore, and his history grows increasingly sinister as the series unfolds. Even though he is an enigma for the majority of the books, at the end of *Half-Blood Prince* the reader sees a part of him that rarely appears in other characters: that which upsets him more than anything else in the world.[1]

---

1. I could imagine that Rowling's relationship with Snape and her hatred of cowardice would put her in a position to agree with Hughes: even though being a child molester implies that one has done terrible things, being called a coward puts question to one's character and how he has built his life.

Even though we rarely see reactions full of such emotion as Snape's reaction to "coward" as a result of most insults in the books, the majority of the human characters (Muggle or not) have something that sets them off in a state of high dudgeon. Building these individualized reactions is no simple task, but Rowling takes them even further. The characters of other species throughout the series also react animatedly to different prompts. Elves, werewolves, goblins, and more react differently to their respective perceptions of insult; I will return to this concept shortly.

How is Wizard language different from Muggle language?

After gaining a basic idea of what builds a general insult, it is important to take a closer look at what sets apart the insults of Rowling's world from those of Muggle communities. The characters all speak British English as Rowling does, but the reader still gets the sense that he is in an entirely different world. I will explain this phenomenon by demonstrating the presence of "Wizard-isms."

In every language there are slang phrases, idioms, and wizened quips that are supplied by mothers and elder family members and passed generation-to-generation. From an outside perspective, these may make no sense at all. The meaning of the idiom "a bird in the hand is worth two in the bush" has always escaped me, and I expect that many visitors from outside cultures find it just as silly as I. But nonetheless, English speakers hear phrases like this all the time. They relate to past cultural practices and societal beliefs. Therefore, if a culture were to lack such idioms, would it not seem a bit strange? Rowling recognizes this necessity and supplies the reader with the following beauties:

> Harry smiled feebly. Deliberately causing mayhem in Snape's Potions class was about as safe as poking a sleeping dragon in the eye (*Chamber of Secrets* 186).

This simile appears at about the time Harry begins

demonstrating a higher level of comfort in wizard society.

> "Poisonous toadstools don't change their spots," said Ron sagely (*Order of the Phoenix* 235).

This idiom is actually my favorite Wizard-ism – it is a reference to Snape and the likelihood of him not being surly and greasy.

> "And don't tell anyone what you're doing. Just stick to Malfoy like a couple of wart plasters." (*Half-Blood Prince* 422).

This phrase is Harry communicating precisely how much he would like Dobby and Kreacher to tail Malfoy in his suspicious activities. A simile such as this can be easily related to phrases many English speakers use in normal conversation. Generally, one would stick to something like glue, but "wart plasters" is a stronger term, since warts tend to permanently hold.

The above selections are but a few of the Wizard-isms that Rowling supplies, but all of them demonstrate differences between Muggle language and wizard language.

How does Rowling create her base for insult?

So far I have touched lightly on how Rowling sets up individual characters to be insulted, but have yet to cover the overall map of insult exchange. Just as the book is set up into different "Us versus Them" mentalities, so are the main insult groupings. There are quite a few, but three main selections stick out: Muggles versus Wizards, Death Eaters versus Anti-Voldemort Personnel, and The Ministry of Magic versus the Order of the Phoenix. Not only do the individual characters of each of these groups have different tics that relate to their respective selves, but they may also be provoked by the enemies of their chosen group.

Muggles versus Wizards

In the very first book, *Sorcerer's Stone*, readers learn that the Dursleys have a heavy prejudice against wizard-kind. Petunia calls her own sister a freak, and Vernon, who only understands as much of the Wizarding world as Petunia has chosen to disclose, speaks of wizards in the most degrading terms: "Oh, these people's minds work in strange ways, Petunia, they're not like you and me" (*Sorcerer's Stone* 40). The reader is immediately willing to sympathize with wizards, for Vernon freely accepts his wife's prejudice as his own, and it is a rare occasion that another Muggle aware of the presence of wizards shows up throughout the remainder of the series. In addition, phrases like "these people" and "your lot" are striking because they show complete unwillingness to even attempt to understand. Overall, the Muggles in the first book do not establish the best reputation for themselves.

It is easy to side with the magical world; fantasy worlds often seem like utopias to readers because characters encounter problems outside of mundane reality. However, like any good fantasy author, Rowling uses the front of her magical world to confront the same issues that her readers face daily. None of the characters in *Harry Potter* are perfect – all wizards and magical creatures included. This very situation is addressed by the fact that all wizards carry prejudices against Muggles, no matter their societal archetype.

To begin, the reader meets the stereotypical "bad guys": the Malfoy family. In Harry's first encounter with Draco, he learns of his prejudice against Muggle-borns: "But they were our kind, weren't they?...I really don't think they should let the other sort in, do you?" (*Sorcerer's Stone* 78). Not only is this an immediate exclusion of a certain group that completely ignores the character of an individual, it implies a prejudice against Muggles as well. If the magical offspring of Muggles are filthy, what does that make Muggles? In addition, there is a heavy resemblance between Draco's statement and Vernon's "these people."

Unfortunately, the Malfoy family believes in the idea of "greater" and "lesser" wizards and Wizarding families.

Within one chapter of meeting Harry at Madam Malkin's robe shop in *Sorcerer's Stone*, Draco expresses a prejudice against wizards of low monetary status: "Think my name's funny, do you? No need to ask who you are. My father told me all the Weasleys have red hair, freckles, and more children than they can afford." (*Sorcerer's Stone* 108). Here, Draco is expressing an opinion that many pure-blood, high-status wizards share (as the reader discovers further into the series): even in a world of magic, having a large family that does not promote the welfare and exclusivity of a certain society invites resentment. This opinion of members of society in lower status is reflective of Muggle society. Even Muggles who do not exhibit such evil or self-promoting activities as the Malfoys express some disdain for members of the lower class who "take" and give little in return.

Furthermore, the Weasley family is doubly bad-for-society because of how much they adore and accept Muggles. Even though both the Weasleys and the Malfoys are "pure-blood" families, the Weasleys do not exhibit much care for the tradition of the status. For this, other pure-blood families that believe in the power of being pure-blood, such as the Malfoys, have little respect for those who "dirty" their pureness by admiring Muggles (or merely respecting them as equal human beings). The first blatant expression of this disdain comes in the *Chamber of Secrets* from dear Draco: "Arthur Weasley loves Muggles so much he should just snap his wand in half and go join them" (222). This small statement carries a lot of weight – a wizard's wand symbolizes his power, and by suggesting that Arthur abandon his power and revert to a more archaic state, Draco implies that Arthur is unworthy of the honor of being a wizard.

It is unsurprising that Draco continues to make similar comments about the Weasley family and Muggles throughout the series; however, the reader does not receive another jolt of Wizarding disrespect until *Deathly Hallows*, when Harry, Ron and Hermione learn the true meaning of the phrase "Magic is Might":

Harry looked more closely and realized that what he had thought were decoratively carved thrones were actually mounds of carved humans: hundreds and hundreds of naked bodies, men, women, and children, all with rather stupid, ugly faces, twisted and pressed together to support the weight of the handsomely robed wizards.

"Muggles," whispered Hermione. "In their rightful place." (242)

The imagery in this one paragraph is enough to make even the most wizard-struck of readers understand wizards' capabilities for terror. First, the Muggles are naked: a barbaric state that implies vulnerability. This nudity is not the artistic beauty that one would generally find in Greek art, but rather a cold representation of how Muggles should be. Second, the Muggles are ugly: even though every reader knows that wizards and Muggles are physically the same, the Ministry's lack of respect for Muggles translates evenly into grotesque facial expressions. Third, the Muggles are forced together to support wizards: there is a considerable amount of symbolism in this feature of the statue, but it is most important to recognize how much higher in esteem wizards hold themselves to their non-magical counterparts.

Not all insult of non-magical humans is necessarily grotesque, nor must it follow the "attempted insult, succeeded offense" pattern. Of all wizards expected to insult Muggles, the members of the Weasley family do not seem to be the type. But alas, Arthur Weasley's adoration of Muggles and Muggle things could be taken quite negatively by a Muggle bystander: "'Muggle magic tricks!' said Fred happily, pointing them out. 'For freaks like Dad, you know, who love Muggle stuff'" (*Half-Blood Prince* 118). In short, Muggles are almost considered the cute pets of wizards, existing to be studied. The Weasleys, of course, mean no offense at all, but the patronizing nature in which we see Muggles addressed throughout the series is a hint at wizards' inherent opinion of them.

Death Eaters versus Anti-Voldemort Personnel

The most obvious insult-provoking rift that appears in the *Harry Potter* series is that of "the good guys" versus "the bad guys" (think back to the good-and-bad separation that Sirius considers when reminded that Bellatrix is his cousin). The disdain of one side for the other is so obvious throughout the series that the insults do not come as deeply layered as those of Muggles versus Wizards. The main distinction between the two themes (Death Eaters versus Not and Wizards versus Not) is that the latter is a subtle prejudice, while the former requires the overt selection of a "side."

Once again, the Malfoy family poses as a good example of a bad thing. Even at the young age of fourteen, Draco has already taken on a thorough mimicry of his parents' beliefs, and he seems wholly pleased at the return of the Dark Lord: "'You picked the losing side, Potter!...Too late now, Potter! They'll be the first to go, now the Dark Lord's back! Mudbloods and Muggle-lovers first!'"[2] (*Goblet of Fire* 729). A reader of the full series understands that Malfoy has not really thought over his position at this point in time (hence the "bad faith" implication of his name), and he will eventually realize the stupidity of blindly following a superpower. However, insult does not necessarily have to function at any point in history; at the presented point in time, Malfoy fully supports his interpretation of what would happen under the Dark Lord's rule.

The Anti-Voldemort side expresses similar hatred to that of the Pro-Dark Side. Voldemort-bashing is a frequent occurrence. One example of such bashing utilizes a manner of insult I have not yet covered: tone of voice. Generally, it is difficult to express "tone" through text without the use of descriptor words ("scathingly," "disdainfully," "exuberantly" and so on), but Rowling does not yield to such limitations. Powerful manipulation of language and the use of insult expressed primarily through tonal inflection appear in a phrase uttered by Professor McGonagall: "You Death Eaters

---

2   I will return to the "M" word shortly – a slur this powerful deserves its own evaluation.

have your own private means of communication, I forgot" (*Deathly Hallows* 597). A few key words help her out. First, the word "you" preempting "Death Eaters" has an implied separation. McGonagall is not distinguishing the Death Eaters merely as separate beings, but pushing the entire group away from what she defines as civilized. The repetition of this same idea occurs in "your own private," three words that even alone imply separation. Finally, "I forgot" reeks of sarcasm; it is almost possible to imagine the eye roll that might accompany such an utterance.

The Ministry of Magic versus the Order of the Phoenix

Like any government organization, the Ministry of Magic is complex and nonsensical even at the best of times. Readers of the *Harry Potter* series get to experience all of the wavering levels of Ministry control, from bumbling to Stalin-esque, all in the short period of a few books. And, since the Order of the Phoenix is (originally) led by Dumbledore, there is a natural aperture between this rogue organization and the government. The relationship changes over time, as do the insults thrown by each side. The two books in which the opposition between Ministry and Order is at the forefront, *Order of the Phoenix* and *Deathly Hallows*, hold in common the price on Harry's head.

In *Order of the Phoenix*, it is important that the Wizarding world know that Harry is an attention-seeking, crazy liar. The Ministry does a superb job of spreading this opinion, and, more importantly, Harry takes offense to what is being said about him:

"They keep slipping in snide comments about you. If some far-fetched story appears they say something like 'a tale worthy of Harry Potter' and if anyone has a funny accident or anything it's 'let's hope he hasn't got a scar on his forehead or we'll be asked to worship him next." (*Order of the Phoenix* 74)

Harry makes it abundantly clear that he does not want to be worshipped and his friends believe him, but Dolores Umbridge, the woman readers love to hate, pushes Harry along the edge of "crazy":

> "Oh no....Oh no, no, no. This is your punishment for spreading evil, nasty, attention-seeking stories, Mr. Potter, and punishments certainly cannot be adjusted to suit the guilty one's convenience." (*Order of the Phoenix* 265-266)

Overall, the Ministry does quite a job on the Order throughout *Order of the Phoenix*, as both its symbol (Harry) and its leader (Dumbledore) are made out to be absolute nutcases.

There is some return of insult from the side of the Order; most of these come from the younger "members." These teenage insults function in a more lighthearted manner. One of the better scenes of this is when Harry's picture on the front of *The Quibbler* is blown up and made to spit out phrases like "Eat dung, Umbridge," and "The Ministry are morons" (*Order of the Phoenix* 584).

Much of the government-related insult in *Deathly Hallows* is related to Muggles and Muggle-borns; the anti-Muggle propaganda was discussed in the section on Muggles versus Wizards. However, in *Deathly Hallows*, Harry runs into the small problem of being branded "Undesirable Number One." Even though Harry is used to being stigmatized by certain groups of people and was expecting as much from the Voldemort regime, the reason the Ministry gives for his wanted status is what triggers a state of offense in Harry. It is implied that Harry was associated with the death of Albus Dumbledore in a malicious way (rather than merely being present at the scene of the crime). To Harry, the assault on his relationship with Dumbledore is more insulting than being made into a ward of state.

What about prejudices and slurs?

As previously mentioned, the different species of Rowling's series all have individualized reactions to different situations, and they take offense to implications that a normal human might not otherwise find offensive. The reader will find that this is one of the more impressive aspects of Rowling's sociolinguistic culture; the insults are multidimensional and the reader sees the insult *and* the reaction of the insulted. It is not merely a hierarchy of "here are these inferior creatures, here is what we have to say about them," but rather a glimpse into the biased viewpoints of Wizarding society. Since basic wizard and Muggle insult was covered in previous sections, I will only delve into some of the more highlighted part-human and non-human creatures.

Dangerous half-breeds

A few of the so-called races that Rowling builds can be categorized as what Umbridge would call "filthy half-breeds;" the idea is that their blood has been tainted. Despite this basic commonality, each species experiences a different prejudice.

Werewolves are stigmatized by society because of how dangerous they become at full moon, and are viewed by Wizarding society as nothing but what they become for that short time period. Lupin, who is a wholly good man, cannot help what he becomes once a month, yet even Ron judges him when he finds out what he is: "*Get away from me, werewolf!*" (*Prisoner of Azkaban* 345). Werewolves accept their stigmatization in an interesting way: they become what wizards imagine them to be. Since they are so shunned, many begin to live the life that wizards already believe they have, turning more animal simply because they are assumed to be as such.

The general opinion of **centaurs** is that they are odd; they are intelligent, but keep to themselves and make strange comments on the surrounding world. There are, of course, some who view them as less than even this, simply because they are half-beast. Umbridge is a shining example: "Law Fifteen B states clearly that 'Any attack by a magical creature who is deemed to have near-human intelligence, and therefore considered responsible for its actions - '" *OOP* 754. Centaurs take great offense to being deemed less intelligent than wizards. However, true to the multidimensionality of Rowling's characters, they return the favor to wizards by not directly answering questions and consistently commenting on humans' inability to see the broad perspective.

Outcasts

Some creatures of the Wizarding world share less of a personal affiliation with the human species (in other words, they are not part human), but still retain human association in some sense.

Goblins are an interesting race in the series. The way they are viewed by some of the more prejudiced wizards bears an uncanny likeness to some medieval views of Jewish people. Goblins work with money, which is something that few wizards (and, in the past, few Christians) deal with, as it is considered a "dirty" thing. Travers explicitly gives this description in Deathly Hallows: "'Gold, filthy gold! We cannot live without it, yet I confess I deplore the necessity of consorting with our long-fingered friends'" (*Deathly Hallows* 528). Not only does Travers allude to the dirtiness of the Goblins' work, but he also draws attention to a characteristic of the race that sets them apart from wizards. In return for such offenses, goblins keep many secrets from wizards, and strive to perpetuate animosity. Both parties are to blame in this situation.

Giants, outcasts that consort little with wizards, are still influenced by the prejudices of Wizarding culture. Although they prefer their space and privacy, wizards have forced them to live near one another, resulting in the slow extinction of the race. Their banishment says much to the opinion of those who recognize the existence of giants, and even if the species is not intelligent enough to grasp the insult, a reader of the series can understand the presence of said insult.

House Elves

     Elves are a special group that we as readers get to see a good deal of due to Harry's relationship with Dobby. Rowling does a particularly fine job of developing their culture and the linguistic features of elf culture, both in the way elves speak and in the way they perceive the world around them. They are extremely loyal to the Wizarding community, despite the fact that they are treated as inferior by almost all within it. Therefore, it is no surprise that elf offense is different from that of all other groups that appear within the series.

     The majority of elves consider it the highest dishonor to be free. Even though the human-based societies in the series consider clothes to be a symbol of status and honor, elves prefer to remain in their unclothed, inferior state. Dobby is the only exception to this rule (there is always the odd one out). However, even Dobby is uncomfortable with being treated as equal to a wizard; despite his desire to be free and wear whatever he pleases, he does not enjoy the idea of receiving considerable pay for a work he enjoys. In elf culture, receiving payment for doing a task that comes naturally or that the doer enjoys is simply insulting.

     Despite the fact that many elves are treated poorly within their families, elf loyalty consistently shines through. Elves cannot speak ill of their masters, both due to binding contract and to self-censorship. They understand the idea that they are frequently the most trusted members of a family, and are not likely to leave the family out to dry. Again, Dobby is an exception; he is not always blinded by his loyalty to the Malfoys, and over time he openly speaks of how terrible they are.

     As with all races and groups in the series, elves display a certain set of reactions to comments and implications that insult them. Winky, who is at one point Barty Crouch's house elf, gives a prime example of "taking offense":

"And how much is Professor Dumbledore paying *you*, Winky?" Hermione asked kindly.

If she had thought this would cheer up Winky, she was wildly mistaken. Winky did stop crying, but when she sat up she was glaring at Hermione through her massive brown eyes, her whole face sopping wet and suddenly furious.

"Winky is a disgraced elf, but Winky is not yet getting paid!" she squeaked. "Winky is not sunk so low as that! Winky is properly ashamed of being freed!" (*Goblet of Fire* 379).

Even though the elf perception of freedom is precisely opposite of what most humans have come to accept as ideal, it is easy for the reader to understand Winky's perception of what Hermione has said as insulting. In a few short books, Rowling was able to create a convincingly real species whose societal norms are completely different from that of humans.

Squibs

The word "Squib" is odd. It sounds like an insult, it *is* an insult, and yet Squibs and Wizards alike use it to refer to non-magical wizard-borns. First we hear it from Filch: "'He did it, he did it!' Filch spat, his pouchy face purpling. 'You saw what he wrote on the wall! He found - in my office - he knows I'm a - I'm a - ' Filch's face worked horribly. 'He knows I'm a Squib!' he finished." (*Chamber of Secrets* 142). At this point in time, the reader only recognizes that a Squib is a bad thing to be. But four books later, it shows up as a slur being spat from Marvolo Gaunt's mouth: "'Lucky the nice man from the Ministry's here, isn't it? Perhaps he'll take you off my hands, perhaps he doesn't mind dirty Squibs...'" (*Half-Blood Prince* 206).

The perception of "Squib" is best left to the reader, mostly because of the odd reaction that Squibs give. They seem to accept their position as inferior (similar to the way elves accept their enslavement), yet ministry members such as Bob Ogden, who is present during Marvolo Gaunt's utterance, do not react kindly to the use of the term. In the end, the term is probably not "politically correct" but it still remains the most salient way of naming such an individual.

M*dbl**ds

The foulest word to appear in the series and the greatest example of a slur adopted by a group that considers itself superior is that which refers to Muggle-born wizards. The reader first learns it from Draco when Harry is only 12 years old: "No one asked your opinion you filthy little Mudblood." (*Chamber of Secrets* 112). Shortly after, Harry learns that it means bad blood, dirty blood, and that it is "about the most insulting thing [one] could think of." (115). The term is not so much a swearword as a way of telling someone who is equal in every way possible except for their birth that they are considered inferior. "Mudblood" is terribly reminiscent of the infamous "N" word in modern American English.

Though Hermione most often falls victim to the word throughout the series due to her prevalence as a character, the changes in government at the commencement of Voldemort's rule begin pushing the term into more common use. Propaganda such as the Ministry of Magic pamphlet "Mudbloods and the Dangers They Pose to a Peaceful Pure-Blood Society" (*Deathly Hallows* 249) pop up to kindle fear in society. It becomes a more common-use word, yet the effects are no less-damaging: "'Spare us,' spat Yaxley. 'The brats of Mudbloods do not stir our sympathies.'" (259).

Blood-traitor is similar to Mudblood in that it contains a heavily unappealing term – however, the Weasleys, the "biggest blood-traitors of all," embrace their enjoyment of Muggle concepts and company. All the same, we still hear characters such as Bellatrix Lestrange express heavy disdain for them: "'If she dies under questioning, I'll take you next… Blood traitor is next to Mudblood in my book.'" (*Deathy Hallows* 463).

What about Wizarding expletives?

There is always a time and a place to throw in a few good swears, especially if one is a young wizard living out a hefty number of adventures. Although Rowling's books are, in most senses, suitable for young ones, she still manages to squeeze in some swears that a young speaker of British English might hear on occasion:

"**Blimey**, a baby!" (*Deathy Hallows* 514)

"Oh **damn**, that'll be the books." (*Deathy Hallows* 162)

"NOT MY DAUGHTER, YOU **BITCH**!" (*Deathy Hallows* 736)

Not only does the reader experience explicit swears, such as the ones above, but Ron is the lead purveyor of swearing inexplicitly, censored as such:

…there was a particularly tense moment when Ron stubbed his toe only yards from the spot where Snape stood standing guard. Thankfully, Snape sneezed at almost exactly the moment Ron **swore**. (*Chamber of Secrets* 259)

Wizard swears follow the same patterns as British English swears, but, like insult, they are more relevant to Wizarding lifestyle. Here are a few of the more creative ones:

"Why weren't you at the match? Your elf was saving you a seat too – **gulping gargoyles**!" (*Goblet of Fire* 133)

"Down in the old – but they told me – **Merlin's beard** - " (*Order of the Phoenix* 134)

"But you don't **give a rat's fart**, do you…" (*Deathly Hallows* 308)

Overall, wizard swears give a heftier number of references to animals and creatures. And of course, we see "Merlin," whose name stands in for "God" in quite a few situations:

> "And are they getting married in my bedroom?...No! So why in the name of **Merlin's saggy left** - " (*Deathly Hallows* 92)

> "Snape in Dumbledore's study – **Merlin's pants!**" (*Deathly Hallows* 226)

> "And what in the name of **Merlin's most baggy Y Fronts** was that about?" (*Deathly Hallows* 227)

What better way to avoid religious confrontation than to use Merlin, the most historically famous wizard, as the deity of reference?

Unfortunately, not all sociolinguistic features can be as lighthearted as the Wizarding expletives that appear in the *Harry Potter* series. An insult system is important to creating any convincing society, and it must touch on dark, sensitive subjects. In the case of a fantasy world, every prevalent species that appears must also hold its own prejudices and defenses. By confronting such issues, Rowling goes beyond creating just a "fairy tale" to bringing to life an entire fantasy world.

Works Cited

Hughes, Geoffrey. *Swearing: A Social History of Foul Language, Oaths and Profanity in English.* London: Penguin Books, 1998.

Rowling, J.K. *Harry Potter and the Chamber of Secrets.* New York: Arthur A. Levine Books, 1999.

---. *Harry Potter and the Deathly Hallows.* New York: Arthur A. Levine Books, 2007.

---. *Harry Potter and the Goblet of Fire.* New York: Arthur A. Levine Books, 2000.

The Wizarding World of Harry Potter:
From Book to
Embodied Myth

Priscilla Hobbs

AUTHOR'S NOTE: THIS ESSAY is adapted from a presentation I gave at Infinitus 2010, a Harry Potter conference. On the date of my talk, July 17, the Wizarding World of Harry Potter had just turned one month old – it opened June 18, 2010 – and Disneyland in Anaheim, California, was celebrating its 55th birthday. While I realize that it seems a little weird to talk about Disney in a Potter essay, especially since the Wizarding World is a part of Universal Studios, as the two corporations have a long history of rivalry, it is nonetheless essential for the groundwork of the essay. Without Disneyland there would be no Wizarding World of Harry Potter.

Theme Parks & Embodiment

Disneyland was the first American theme park. Drawing from the history of amusement parks and World's

Fairs, the vision for the park was of a place where adults and children could equally have fun together while simultaneously addressing some of the more common Disney fan questions, notably "where does Mickey Mouse live?"An amusement park differs from a theme park in that an amusement park concentrates on fun and recreation, not on the stories that a theme park conveys. The World's Fairs were seen as a showcase for new technologies and products, relying on a "wow" factor to amaze and amuse patrons.[1] Many of the attractions of a traditional amusement park or World's Fair were either specifically for adults or specifically for children, with the occasional walk-through attraction for all ages. Walt Disney, who, I believe, would have been sorted into Slytherin house had he gone to Hogwarts for his overwhelming ambition and drive for success (but he would have been one of those nicer ones that wouldn't have become a Death Eater), originally conceived of his park as a walk-through showcase of miniatures (one of his favorite hobbies) with a train circling around it (another one of his hobbies) adjacent to the Disney Studios, but his vision quickly grew too elaborate for such a small scale.[2] As the idea for the park grew, he wanted it to deviate from the standard thrill ride plus Midway games (those carnie games you play to try to win a stuffed animal or a similar prize) formula, both of which dominate Universal Studios Orlando. He wanted instead for the rides in his park to both retell the Disney stories and to make the guest a character in the story. For example, guests could ride through Snow White's story as if they were in her slippers or fly to Neverland as the Darling Children to join Peter Pan in his heroic rescue of Princess Tiger Lily from Captain Hook. They could journey to the moon or take a cruise through the jungle. They could even take a tour of the Western Frontier on the backs of mules. Much has changed from Walt

---

1   See Neil Harris, "Expository Exposition: Preparing for the Theme Parks" in *Designing Disney's Theme Park: The Architecture of Reassurance* edited by Karal Ann Marling, Paris: Flammarion, 1997.

2   Marling, Karal Ann. "Imagineering the Disney Theme Park." *Designing Disney's Theme Park: The Architecture of Reassurance.* Ed. Karal Ann Marling. Paris: Flammarion, 1997. 50.

Disney's original vision of Disneyland. The mules and moon are gone, but he once declared that Disneyland would never be completed as long as there is imagination in the world, a statement also important for the Potterverse as the stories will never end as long as there is imagination left in the Fandom.

Disneyland offers an opportunity to *embody* what have become some of the key images of American myth.[3] In the traditional sense, embodiment is defined as "a new personification of a familiar idea," such as the new heroes of Young Adult literature representing the hero archetype (such as Harry Potter, Percy Jackson, Katniss Everdeen or Buffy Summers), or "a concrete representation of an abstract concept," such as how evil is characterized by Lord Voldemort. Similarly, embodiment is the process actors use to "become one" with their character, such as Alan Rickman's embodiment of Snape. In order to fully become Snape, he sat with J.K. Rowling to find out his character's motivations and fate long before the final book of the series was written. He was the only actor to know, and this was essential for his portrayal. However, the type of embodiment I am describing is one where the myths become embodied such that we can physically interact with the story – embodied in a space, not so much within ourselves. When we read a book, the most physical contact we have is turning the page. When we watch a movie, that contact is made through the environment of the theater, but we can't jump in the screen and play along. The rest of the experience is left to our imagination, which isn't a bad thing, but every now and then, it's nice to put the book down or pause the DVD and get out for awhile. It's not easy to take an 800 page hardcover everywhere, and watching a portable movie in public can be considered rude in many situations.

Historically, mythologies had a fair amount of physicality. For example, when one would listen to a story by a fire, the darkness of the cave or campsite enclosed the storyteller and listeners in a private space, one where the magic could happen. Similarly, if one was performing in a ritual, it would

---

3   By myth, I am referring to the potent stories and experience of humanity, not to the idea of lies or pagan religions.

take place somewhere different than everyday transactions. This pattern of separation-magic-return is prevalent in many of the myths and rituals of the world, such as the often-discussed Hero's Journey. A theme park fulfills this pattern in the modern world: One is separated from the outside world by the design of the park. It has clear boundaries and the creators go to great lengths to keep the outside world from leaking in.

The theme park *experience* induces a sense of magic and wonderment, akin to Harry's first tour of Diagon Alley. Like Harry's wizarding world, theme parks don't follow the rules of conventional Muggle wisdom. They challenge us to rethink what we consider real, and pull us into a world we once thought was fictional. After riding a theme park ride, one cannot help but feel at least a little connected to the story, or, if the ride successfully generated a lot of excitement, maybe very connected. I know many of my friends, or PotterPeeps as I call them, didn't want to leave Hogwarts.

As Harry Potter fans, we are well aware of the need for physical contact with the Potter myth. Throughout the history of the Fandom, fans have been trying to find ways to interact with the stories and separate them from the pages of the books: some people write filks or wizard rock, some write fan fiction, some do crafts, some hold Potter Parties, some use the ideology of Potter for social activism such as the Harry Potter Alliance, some dress in full or partial costume at "odd" times and places, some hang out in online forums forming deeply rooted friendships, some make or listen to podcasts, and some attend conferences. There are some who devote their academic careers to Potter, and still others who do all of the above. And none of us are afraid to admit it.

This need is fueled by the power of Harry Potter as a myth: The story excites the imagination to a point beyond "regular" fanaticism. We feel something different within ourselves at the end of the book, and now that the series is over, we naturally create rituals to keep the mythic fire of Hogwarts burning. It's not that the books are simply "popular," but that they speak to a deeper need for a guiding mythology that, even though bleak at times, still gives us a better understanding of our world and hope for the future. One does not have to be an English boarding school student to understand this experience.

The corporate media outlets have tried to accommodate this need: Warner Brothers gave us movies, movie tie-in toys and games. Hot Topic sells clothes for when our robes are inappropriate. EA Games made us video games complete with Wii wand action. Lego made us toy sets. TT Games made us a Lego video game, which is very fun once you acquire your wand. But in all of these examples, we are still separated from the environment of Hogwarts castle and Hogsmeade. We cannot be enclosed in the castle walls, take a stroll through the hustle and bustle of Hogsmeade, and we can only speculate what Butterbeer tastes like. At least until now.

The Main Attraction

The Wizarding World of Harry Potter is a land within the Islands of Adventure area at Universal Studios Orlando. There are six shops, one restaurant, and three rides. The shops and restaurant are deliberately themed after Hogsmeade rather than Diagon Alley. While Diagon Alley is more familiar to passive Potter participants who have only seen one movie or two, Hogsmeade is the village nearest to Hogwarts, which is the central attraction of the park. Additionally, Hogsmeade is the one aspect of the wizarding world that Harry almost did not get to experience because he didn't have a permission slip. As such, he sneaks there to be with his friends. While Diagon Alley is one of Harry's entrance points into the wizarding world, Hogsmeade, the only true wizarding village in the UK, is a place where his mischief blossoms. This is a place where he has to sneak around (at least before he gets his permission slip) and later becomes the place where he defies authority, realizes that Cho really isn't the woman of his dreams, and then becomes the access point for the Rebel Alliance to sneak back into Hogwarts for the final battle. It's a logical theming choice because Harry grows up in Hogsmeade, whereas Diagon Alley is more like the reminder that school is about to start. Luckily, our tickets into the park function as permission slips, so we don't have to wear that invisibility cloak in the hot Orlando summer sun.

Let me take you on a tour, beginning with the shops:

Dervish and Banges is inspired by the shop in Hogsmeade that sells and repairs magical objects. At Wizarding World, it also carries Quidditch supplies, clothing and stationary items.

Filch's Emporium of Confiscated Goods, a very clever name, looks like Filch decided to make a few extra galleons by selling stuff taken from students, in addition to various souvenirs of their Wizarding World visit. It is located at the exit of the *Harry Potter and the Forbidden Journey* ride.

Honeydukes, the famous sweet shoppe in Hogsmeade, is enough to make Hermione's parents fret. This is our chance to try some of the goodies we read so much about: chocolate wands, Chocolate Frogs, and Bertie Bott's in bulk, among many other sweet delights.

Ollivander's allows us to get the wand we are really meant to have in an interactive selection process. It is also the place for wand collectors to find movie replicas. I never stood in line for this, but according to someone who did, the interactive presentation is only for one person in a group of 15, usually a small kid, and the wait time was 2 hours.

Zonko's has all of your fun magical gags and jokes, including Pygmy Puffs, Extendable Ears, and Shrunken Heads.

Finally, the Owl Post is the place to send all of your stuff home with an authentic Hogsmeade postmark. This would be a good spot to ship items home so we can save headaches with TSA, but I didn't see a reliable shipping zone.

My major criticism of Hogsmeade, one shared by others I have spoken to, is that the area is too small for what Universal aims to accomplish. This is especially evident in the lack of crowd control. In many of the shops, there can be up to a two hour wait during peak times to enter. Capacity inside the shops is maybe half of what they allow in, so shoppers are literally bumping shoulders with other shoppers and disabled people are severely limited. In Honeydukes and Zonko's (connected stores) the merchandise is limited to many of the same things – as though, by the time of my visit in mid-July, one month after the park opened, they had already sold out of certain items and were compensating by filling the shelving holes with overstock of other products.[4]

The limited dining is the Three Broomsticks, Hogsmeade's most preferred haunt, at least, by Hogwarts students. There is a nod to the Hog's Head in the back of the restaurant with an array of "adult beverages." Universal was more successful in the delivering of ambiance in these two connected places than in the shops. Walking into the Three Broomsticks and Hog's Head, one is cut off from the hustle and bustle of an overcrowded Hogsmeade - which, despite the snow-topped buildings, is still hot and muggy during Orlando's summer - into the kind of eating atmosphere that promotes leisurely dining, not the eat-and-go of quick service locations. The noises outside are drowned out by the noises of diners and the clank of silverware. It gives the impression of a pub-like atmosphere. The food invites savoring, with a menu inspired by English tradition, including Shepherd's Pie, Cornish Pasties and roast chicken. I had the Cornish Pasties, which are little dumpling-shaped finger pies filled with beef and gravy, and was happy to find that the overall quality is much better than typical family theme park fare for the price. Here is the place for Butterbeer with or without alcohol. Without alcohol, the butterbeer is the best cream soda ever.

Let's continue our tour of the park by looking at the rides:

The two outdoor attractions, *Flight of the Hippogriff* and the *Dragon Challenge*, already occupied the area before Wizarding World was envisioned, but their queue space was redone to fit into the Potter theme. The space around Hippogriff is meant to look like Hagrid's front yard, including a non-walk-through replica of his hut and Beaky's nest. As one walks through the queue, we are taken on a labyrinthine journey reminiscent of Hagrid's garden. The ride itself is a training flight on a Hippogriff inspired by Harry's flight in the movie adaptation of *Prisoner of Azkaban*. This is a family coaster, so

4   Much of the merchandise in Borgin and Burkes and the Owl Post (again connected stores) is targeted towards the immensely popular Gryffindor and Slytherin.

it's not very intense. And it's very short, clocking in at less than minute. In *Dragon Challenge*, the queue is designed to resemble a portion of the castle, though removed from it, leading to a dragon pitch. It encloses us fully, such that we cannot hear the screams from the ride, but we do hear a music loop and the echoes from other potential passengers. As a warning, those who are claustrophobic will find the queue difficult to tolerate if the ride goes down. The closer one gets to the front of the line, the more narrow the space becomes, only slightly wider than one-and-a-half people. Since the ride went down to allow Orlando's daily shower to pass while I was at this point in the line, claustrophobia is the main reason why I chickened out from riding it. The ride is inspired by the first task of the Tri-Wizard Cup. Choose your dragon and hold on tight. It consists of two roller coasters running simultaneously, and each dragon offers a different experience, namely in regards to intensity and acrobatics.

These rides were redesigned from existing rides rather than reconstructed, impairing the overall quality of the ride experience, because the story is forced to fit the architecture rather than the other way around. The story experience is organic, and is enhanced by freshness in the telling, even if it's a familiar story. But when the story is being told using old tools, it's like wearing Dudley's hand-me-downs or Ron's second-hand dress robes. This does not make for an excellent experience, but it does save money for the attraction that is the center of the Wizarding World, which is where Universal really got it right: Hogwarts Castle and the ride inside, *Harry Potter and the Forbidden Journey*. Regardless of Universal's master plan for the park, their attention to the castle betrays their main intent for the area. The ride is housed inside Hogwarts, which one enters in the dungeons near Snape's classroom, and the queue takes us on a tour of the castle, leading to the Room of Requirement, or the boarding area. We visit the Herbology greenhouse (the only part of the queue outside), walk past the griffin hiding the staircase to Dumbledore's office, pass by some talking portraits. While not all portraits move, the ones that do are well done, making excellent use of digital technology to bring the paintings to life in a believable way. We work our way through Dumbledore's office and then one of the classrooms, featuring a projected Dumbledore and Trio, respectively, giving us the impression that they are really in the room with us. Through the Gryffindor Common Room, past a Sorting Hat that tells us the safety information for the ride – in rhyme of course – to the front of the attraction queue. If one is stuck in the line, there is plenty detail to observe to keep from being overwhelmingly bored.

      This ride is the one that Universal has been the most quiet about. Spoilers about this ride follow. If you want to remain surprised, please skip to the next paragraph. The most crucial element to a successful theme park attraction is the story, and the story of the *Forbidden Journey* is that a dragon has gotten loose from Hagrid's keep and is running loose in the grounds around Hogwarts. The Trio decides to help Hagrid catch it before anyone gets hurt, but they need our help. So we get into a vehicle that will simulate flying without the discomfort of riding on a broomstick and with all the necessary safety restraints. Hermione casts a spell to ensure our vehicle will take off, and we are launched on the journey. The attraction combines IMAX-type 3D technology with vehicular movement, so we feel as though we are flying. For the sake of keeping the ride moving, we are whisked to different screens. To maintain continuity of story, as we pass to a new screen, we pass through a scene of audio-animatronics. This helps break the tension of intensity without breaking the story. Audio-animatronics were designed by Disney Imagineers to simulate 3D animation using realistic technology. The three-dimensionality of audio-animatronics brings a cartoon or animated character to life or replicates animals without compromising on real life imperfections, so as to ensure a consistent performance all the time. We see many of the popular images and figures from the movies: Quidditch, Malfoy's taunting, Hogwarts castle, Aragog, the Whomping Willow (complete with smashed ride car at the base of its trunk), a dragon, Dementors. It is truly an immersive experience into the books. For those familiar with Disney attractions, it's like *Soarin'* meets *Indiana Jones*.

In a promotional video shown at the Infinitus 2010 "Night of a Thousand Wizards" event, Universal boasted that Hogwarts is the new Magic Kingdom, or, more accurately, the new Cinderella's Castle. I would hardly give it that kind of kudos, but I do think the attraction is one of the best I have encountered. Comparing the castles, it is important to consider that historically, a functional castle was constructed horizontally to the earth to be a fortress. The fairy tale castle is vertical, as though it is meant to be a bridge between earth and sky.[5] Disneyland's Sleeping Beauty's castle was modeled on the ultimate real life fairy tale castle: Neuschwanstein Castle in Bavaria, Germany, the model for all fairy tale castles since. When approaching either of these Disney castles, one walks through an opening ground level with the castle. Hogwarts, however, sits on top of a crag that overlooks the park and expects us to go through the basement.

As we know from the books, Hogwarts is a fortress, not just a school, and one of the safest places in all of Europe, breaking the fairy tale castle model. Symbolically, however, Cinderella's and Sleeping Beauty's castles, being ground level and vertical, invite us in, whereas Hogwarts is imposing and foreboding. This creates two perspectives: (1) the approach from Hogsmeade invokes the image that students see when approaching from the train, as though what lies inside will educate and transform us as Hogwarts does the students, but (2) that the castle is dominant, both within Rowling's wizarding world and within Universal Studios. Consider the Medieval European convention that the tallest building in town – usually the church – is the most important place in town; thus, Hogwarts is the most important building at Universal. Also, I question if the crag was meant to add height to the castle in the hopes of making it taller than or at least comparable to Cinderella's castle, but it fell short almost 40 feet.[6]

---

5   The Imagineers. *Walt Disney Imagineering: A Behind the Dreams Look at Making the Magic Real.* New York: Disney Editions, 1996. 79.
6   Hogwarts measures 150 feet, and Cinderella Castle is 189 feet tall.

Corporate Sell-Out?

When Universal announced its theme park plans for Harry Potter, I confess myself disappointed. Warner Brothers had been hoping for a theme park since they started planning the first movie.[7] This plan was WB's more so than J.K. Rowling's because they own the rights, but she did give it her blessing as long as Stuart Craig, production designer on the films, was involved. In the famous *PotterCast* interview, Rowling praised Craig's work because it mirrors "what's been in [her] imagination." She added that the theme park is as close to walking on a film set as most of us get. "Better, of course, because it's 3D and you can walk around the corner and look at the back and, you know – it's gonna be quite incredible. … Personally, I think it will be the best thing in the world of its type…."[8]

But wait a second, hadn't JKR said there would never be a park?[9] Isn't that the ultimate degree of selling out? Perhaps, but successful theme parks allow us to physically enter into a mythic space and, at least for awhile, satisfy our human need for contact with the physical myth. Could this little section of a Universal park accomplish what the Magic Kingdom does so well?

During my visit to the Wizarding World, I found myself feeling nostalgic for pre-movie Potter: the original hand drawn logos and cartoonish portrayals of the characters. Seeing and experiencing Wizarding World makes it very clear the extent to which Potter culture is now dominated by Warner Brothers' imagery. This does raise the concern for the corporate involvement over Potter as a myth. While I fully support J.K. Rowling's rights as an author, it is as though she allowed her

7   McGinty, Stephen. "Pottermania-Focus-Profile-J.K. Rowling," *The Sunday Times* (UK), Oct. 17, 1999. Retrieved from Accio Quote.

8   Anelli, Melissa, John Noe and Sue Upton. "PotterCast Interviews J.K. Rowling, Part Two." *PotterCast* #131, Dec. 24, 2007. Retrieved from Accio Quote.

9   For awhile, during the early negotiations, there was a lot of confusion about who would build the park, if anyone. Rumors suggested Disney, which were later denied, then nothing public until Universal announced its intention to build the Wizarding World.

stories to become corporatized to the point where the line between Rowling and Warner Brothers is blurred. For example, when *Sorcerer's Stone* was in its infancy as a film adaptation, it was important to her to have complete veto power over production decisions, yet by the third film that control was relaxed, noticeable in the fact that younger wizards wear muggle clothes and not the robes described in the books. Similarly, she allowed the fandom to grow and develop without restraint, except for the occasional interference by Warner Brothers. So, it is disconcerting that she once declared that there would be no Harry Potter theme park, yet here we are with a segment of a Universal park which she supports. If we consider Potter as a myth, as much Potter scholarship does, then the question of ownership should never arise. As described above, the Potter myth has been nurtured and loved by the community, and this passion – for the true Potter fan – is fueled by the corporate imagery but not owned by it.

A major criticism of theme parks lies in the expense of the experience and the costs of tickets, souvenirs, and refreshments, which often leads to the argument that the motivation of Universal or Disney seems to be driven by the capitalization of entertainment and the bottom-line. This does create a different experience, with a difference between "a really good time" and an immersion into myth. From my experience in the park, the Wizarding World succeeds wonderfully as an immersion into myth in some places, but not as well into others. The two outdoor rides, *Hippogriff* and *Dragon Challenge* are designed for a "really good time" - one can feel the wind in one's hair going up and down the hills, screaming with the other passengers in your car who are most likely also having a really good time (unless they're sick or scared), and that feeling of being on top of the world at the highest peak and seeing off towards the horizon. The overall ambiance of Hogsmeade is hindered by the lack of room, which prevents a more immersive experience. One has to concentrate on dodging the crowds and has to wait – sometimes for hours – to enter into the shops. People with disabilities cannot maneuver. During peak hours, it is claustrophobic and overwhelming. The lack of adequate space makes it difficult to enjoy the area. The outdoor area is not successful, when compared to *Forbidden Journey*, which is truly transformational: we enter Hogwarts from the bottom and work our way to the top (an apt metaphor for the journey of a student) and get sucked into a mission that makes us Hogwarts students. After all, Harry wouldn't have picked just anyone to help him out – he picked you, an unknown student! Leaving the ride and entering Filch's Emporium tells us that we are "in" and now it is time to buy supplies for the coming school year. There is even a photo to prove it!

In a promotional video on the Universal website, Rowling describes seeing the park during the Grand Opening festivities: "I'm used to walking onto film sets where at a certain point everything dissolves into scaffolding and lighting. So, I suppose that the completeness of the vision is what is very breathtaking."[10] This completeness of vision is what allows us to engage in the mythology of Harry Potter in a way that we hadn't been able to do before. For all of its downfalls and shortages, the Wizarding World of Harry Potter does succeed in bringing Harry Potter fans closer to the stories and films. It does this by bringing to life a fictional place that only exists either as we imagine it or as how it is imagined for us by the movies: a place that any Potter fan would like to be a part of but one that has no known muggle geographical place.

When any new theme park attraction opens, especially when there is as much investment, publicity and fan expectation as the Wizarding World of Harry Potter, the first year is the year during which kinks are worked out and corrections or expansion plans are made. The park attraction or area is expected to survive a couple of years before its fate is determined. Indeed, one can glimpse through Disneyland history, and the average shelf life for failed attractions is two to five years.[11] I will be very

10   "The Wizarding World of Harry Potter Grand Opening" from the Universal Studios Orlando, Wizarding World of Harry Potter news website.

11   See Chris Strodder's *The Disneyland Encyclopedia: The Unofficial, Unauthorized, and Unprecidented History of Every Land, Attraction, restaurant, Shop, and Event in the Original Magic Kingdom*. Santa Monica: Santa Monica Press, 2008.

interested to see if Wizarding World survives, how well it fares after the opening season of 2010, and what changes Universal will make to keep the attraction vital.

It is the hope of all theme park designers that everyone has the same magical experience they intended; however, in reality, magic happens for different people at different times and places. The theme park is a place where the context and ritual are designed to be magical. I am appreciative of Universal for the attempt they have made to try to embody Potter for us fans, and I do acknowledge that there is a margin of error for any infant project. I do hope they will consider revising the outdoor coasters and spacing out Hogsmeade so the entire Wizarding World can be as transformational as *Forbidden Journey*. I also hope that we, as Potter fans, can appreciate the attempt Universal has made to give us a pilgrimage site devoted to all things Potter, one that places us in the world as participants.[12] This is a place that the entire family can enjoy. And if they don't, Walt Disney World is right down the street.

---

12   In contrast to the travelling exhibit, which still keeps us at a distance from the experience. Potter is embodied in movie props and costumes, but we can only participate by seeing not by doing.

Cracking the Planetary Code:
Harry Potter, Alchemy, and the Seven Book Series as a Whole

Erin N. Sweeney (Caltheous)

A T FOURTEEN, I WAS taught the definition of alchemy in my high school chemistry class:

> A medieval forerunner to chemistry, based on the *supposed* transformation of matter. It was concerned primarily with the attempt to convert lead to gold.[1]

I immediately smirked at that "supposed" idea. Obviously the ancients understood little about the nature of matter if they thought they could magically convert one element to another.

Other definitions for alchemy did nothing to open my mind to understanding the underlying meaning of the art.

---

1   "Alchemy." *Oxford American Dictionary*. Online Apple Widget.

Another definition goes:

> *figurative* – a process by which paradoxical results are achieved or incompatible elements combined with no obvious rational explanation.[2]

Reading this one today makes me smile. That is exactly the way the word alchemy is used; the implication that it is irrational comes from our own figurative use of the term in the English language.

Since falling in love with the *Harry Potter* books in 1998, I have become a gradual student of the concept of alchemy. It was the much quoted comment of J.K. Rowling in a 1998 newspaper interview revealed in 2007 that led many of us to research the topic. She said:

> I've never wanted to be a witch, but an alchemist, now that's a different matter. To invent this wizard world, I've learned a ridiculous amount about alchemy. Perhaps much of it I'll never use in the books, but I have to know in detail what magic can and cannot do in order to set the parameters and establish the stories' internal logic. [3]

Apparently J.K. Rowling, my hero, wanted to be an alchemist? And I thought it was nonsense! I had to learn more.

After years of study, I now believe that I understand the inner truth or science behind alchemy. It appears so irrational to chemists today because it is not the science of chemistry, but the science of the soul. It is linked to chemistry in a deep, symbolic way that resonated with our human consciousness before we had an understanding of chemistry. Hundreds of years ago, people were able to equate the journey of our mortal lives to a chemical reaction that involves a catalyst, heating and cooling, desiccation and dissolution, the binding of components, and the transformation of the states of matter. When you think of alchemy that way, it is a miracle of the human mind. Further, if

---

2 *Ibid.*

3 Simpson, Anne. "Face to Face with J K Rowling: Casting a spell over young minds," *The Herald*, 7 December 1998

you are a person of faith, it is a message from God that teaches us, as it is said in *The Emerald Tablet,* wisdom and freedom from obscurity.

A year previously, on John Granger's recommendation, I had gotten many answers from *The Chemical Wedding of Christian Rosenkruetz.* So, again on his recommendation, I purchased a book by Titus Burckhardt called *Alchemy: The Science of the Cosmos, the Science of the Soul.* This book presents, towards the end, information that links the order of the *Harry Potter* books and the seven alchemical planets of Mercury, Saturn, Jupiter, the Moon, Venus, Mars, and the Sun. It also describes the meaning behind that order, allowing the underlying alchemical pattern in the seven Potter books to be clearly visualized. It is important to understand alchemy in order to make sense of this underlying meaning. The pattern does not follow the order of the stages that an alchemist would follow when performing the practical work, but instead represents a link of a person's soul with the Divine Spirit of God in the form of an alchemical wedding. In this analysis, I will use the meaning of soul and spirit following closely to Christian mysticism because that is how J.K. Rowling framed her imagery and themes.[4] This link between soul and spirit involves two parts: first the soul is purified and indicates it is willing to receive the spirit, then the spirit provides the willing soul with revelation.

---

4   There are differences between the mysticism in various faiths. In Christianity, the Spirit is Divine and written with a capital 'S'. The soul (which is linked to matter) is not. This was defined in the council of Nicaea in 787 A.D. I will use the terms in the Christian sense in this essay because I follow Burkhardt's explanation; however, I chose not to capitalize spirit. In other mysticism, spirit and soul are of equal value, true partners. The terms I use (such as "greater" and "lesser" work) are what appear to elevate spirit above soul, not Rowling's actual presentation. Please note this distinction between the use of the terms in my Christian analysis and Rowling's actual presentation, which does not demote soul beneath Spirit but celebrates both as equal partners in the alchemical wedding.

What is Literary Alchemy?

Alchemy has been around for thousands of years. It was known in ancient Egypt, ancient Greece and ancient India. Some say that it can be traced back to an Egyptian origin and a founder called Hermes Trismegistus. [5] A work known as *The Emerald Tablet,* attributed to Hermes (another name for the god Mercury), is worth reading; it is a short list of spiritual truths which outline the basic premise of alchemy.

Because the practice of alchemy was usually transmitted orally, it is difficult to know the history of alchemy precisely. The alchemical texts we do have often bear the names of authors who lived years previously so that determining a chronology or exact author is difficult. [6]

In "recent" times alchemy was adopted by the monotheistic religions of Islam, Judaism, and Christianity. Titus Burkhardt wrote:

> From the Christian point of view, alchemy was like a natural mirror for the revealed truths: the philosopher's stone, which turned base metals into silver and gold, is a symbol of Christ, and its production from the 'non-burning fire' of sulphur and the 'steadfast water' of quicksilver resembles the birth of Christ-Emmanuel. [7]

I do not know if the pious soul of a wise alchemist can literally transform matter into silver and gold, as Nicoles Flamel says he did in 1382 with his beloved wife Perrenelle. After years of "ceaselessly praying to God," "meditating on the words of the philosophers," and "accomplishing the various operations I divined from their words,"[8] Flamel wrote that he accomplished his goal. With his wife Perrenelle at his side, whom he was very clear to say, "understood it just as well as I did myself,"[9] he carried out the process of producing silver and gold with the use

5   Burckhardt, Titus. *Alchemy.* 16.
6   Burckhardt, Titus. *Alchemy.* 21.
7   Ibid. 18.
8   Ibid. 180.
9   Ibid. 181.

of the philosopher's stone. While claims like this make the modern mind turn away from the ancient practice of alchemy, look to the soul-work to correspond to the metallurgical work.

This soul-work represents a personal transformation that is the purpose of alchemy and the inner truth behind what Nicolas Flamel claims to have done. It is said that he could live forever and make gold. Flamel describes the secret book he used to achieve these feats in some detail. He says that the fourth page of the book depicts the god Saturn, holding an hour glass on his head and brandishing the sickle of death, chasing the winged Mercury around while attempting to cut off his feet.[10] Perhaps it depicts how people flee from both death and time. Our immortal life is born from an understanding of the eternal now, which forms a soul that shines like gold.

This image of Saturn and Mercury that Flamel described is just one example of how the alchemical texts tend to be cryptic and mysterious. When he shared the text with his wife, he wrote,

> "I could hide nothing from her, and told her everything, showing her the beautiful book, with which she fell in love just as much as I had done. Her greatest pleasure was to gaze on its beautiful covers, engravings, pictures, and representations, of which, however, she understood as little as did I."[11]

There are elaborate symbols, tiered stages, and color coding in works of alchemy. *Harry Potter* is no different in this regard. Some scholars say that the symbols and details of the steps are intentionally cryptic so that the alchemist must struggle in order to achieve success. Flamel even remarks that portions of the ancient alchemical text that he used as the foundation of his own efforts cannot be repeated because "God would punish me for this."[12] Trying to make sense of it all is overwhelming. It can bring on the sort of reaction a person has to trying to understand the size of the universe or the way time theory works; the brain just gives up and decides to watch *American Idol*. But alchemical works like *Harry Potter* get past this challenge by presenting the information as a story that we can live and breathe.

10   Ibid. 173.

11   Ibid. 176.

12   Burckhardt, Titus. *Alchemy*. 176.

Alchemy Primer

There are three basics steps of alchemy:

1. The Nigredo. An initial period of difficulty marked by depression or suffering. The color black, death, going underground.

2. The Albedo. A coming together of the skills or players needed to break through the difficulty. The color white, water, snow, ice.

3. The Rubedo. The battle that breaks you through the difficulty. The color red, fire, blood.

These are the three stages of overcoming an obstacle of some kind. We can probably all relate to these steps from personal experience.

The three original stages of nigredo, albedo, and rubedo are further broken into seven parts, just as the *Harry Potter* books number seven. The nigredo, or initial period of suffering, can be viewed as a passive stage of self-evaluation. This is seen as the "lesser work" and contains three stages: lead, tin, and silver. The rubedo, or battle that breaks you through difficulty, can be viewed as an active step that is seen as the "greater work". This step also has three stages: copper, iron, and gold. The albedo, or gathering of the skills or players needed for the battle, can be seen as an overlying aspect of the entire process – present at all steps – and is seen more as a catalyst than a stage: mercury. The presence of sulphur is a counterpart to mercury and also serves as an important catalyst. From this, the three larger steps above become seven: lead, tin, silver, copper, iron, gold, and mercury.

The ancients were able to see seven heavenly bodies from Earth with the naked eye. They were the Sun, the Moon, Mercury, Venus, Mars, Jupiter, and Saturn. Many cultures looked at this aspect of the heavens and gave these celestial bodies godly personifications and spiritual aspects. In alchemy, these heavenly bodies are related to the metals in each stage.

The process of transformation begins with lead (Saturn); it is converted to tin (Jupiter), then silver (the Moon), then copper (Venus), then iron (Mars), and finally to gold (the Sun). Mercury or quicksilver is the catalyst of all the stages, rather than a stage itself.

Mercury	Saturn	Jupiter	Moon	Venus	Mars	Sun
Mercury	Lead	Tin	Silver	Copper	Iron	Gold
☿	♄	♃	)	♀	♂	☉

Figure 1. The alchemical planets, metals, and symbols shown in order with mercury, the catalyst, depicted first.[13]

All of the symbols of alchemy are present in our culture today, so the symbols and stages feel familiar to us. Alchemy has a long tradition in British literature with use by authors like C.S. Lewis, J.R.R. Tolkien, and William Shakespeare. Continuing this tradition, Rowling drew not just from the ancient Greco-Roman concepts of the planets, but she also used Christian symbols to infuse her work because that is part of her culture.

In the symbols for each metal/planet shown in Figure 1 there is also meaning. The moon is a sickle shape, the cross represents the four elements of matter (earth, air, fire, water), and the circle represents the sun. Mercury, the catalyst, is symbolized by the union of the sun and the moon on top of the cross of matter. The first three stages: lead, tin, and silver are considered lunar metals; again, this is the "lesser work." Notice how their symbols represent an ascending action of the sickle shape of the moon up the cross of matter. Saturn shows the sickle under the cross but Jupiter shows the sickle on the left arm of the cross with the final stage just the sickle of the moon. The last three stages: copper, iron, and gold are considered solar

---

13   Burckhardt, Titus. *Alchemy*. 184.

metals, and again, they are called the "greater work." Notice how their symbols represent a descending action of the sun into the cross of matter. Venus shows the sun above the cross, Mars shows the sun below the cross, and in the end we are left with the circle of the sun.

Figure 1 depicts the symbols in chronological order as an alchemist would follow the steps. First the moon, which represents the soul, must pass from deep within to the surface, or consciousness of man, and make itself receptive to receiving the revelation of the spirit. Then the sun, which symbolizes the spirit, must pass from above to within in order to unite with our receptive soul; this union is called the alchemical wedding.

The Alchemical Wedding

In spiritual thought, there is a polarity to the universe – the concept of duality. In alchemy the polarity of masculine and feminine is united to make a whole through a process called the alchemical wedding. The masculine is symbolized by the sun, gold, and sulphur. Masculine is active, hot, muscular, conscious, dry, hard, rigid, expansive, is referred to as yang, and equates to the immortal form of a human known as spirit. The feminine is symbolized by the moon, silver, and mercury (also called quicksilver). Feminine is cool, wet, formable, creative, connective tissue, unconscious, contractive, is referred to as yin, and equates to the subtle power that unites the soul with the body. The details are summarized in Figure 2.

Masculine	Feminine
Spirit	Soul
The eternal part of you that moves you to action	The immaterial aspect that binds you to your material body
Sun	Moon
Gold	Silver
Sulphur	Mercury
Active	Passive
Hot	Cool

Conscious	Subconscious
Dry	Wet
Hard, rigid	Formable
Expansive	Contractive
Muscular	Connective Tissue
Yang	Yin

Figure 2. The division of masculine and feminine in alchemy

Titus Burckhardt writes that some authors use the terms soul and spirit in the opposite sense, which is why I am so specific about their meaning. He uses them in the sense that the spirit is an eternal part of every person, and the soul is the spiritual stuff that sticks you to your body. The process of alchemy is in unearthing the divine spark, spirit, within. In the sense used by Burkhardt, you use your soul to produce creative works because those are material. The soul deals with matter, but it is the spirit that actively guides you in so doing. In this sense, the passive soul is what actively creates and the active spirit is what passively inspires. Notice that this melting together of active and passive roles is an important aspect of alchemy and is symbolized well by the image of yin and yang shown in Figure 3.

Figure 3. Yin and yang.

I find this a beautiful and sensual notion. Based on the number of alchemical works of star-crossed lovers, I am not the only person to find the sensuality in the union of soul and spirit (for example: *Romeo and Juliet*, the *Twilight* series, and *The Story of Layla and Majnun*). We can think of creation as feminine in this context. Material objects, mother earth, and cycles of life can be seen as eternal but ever-changing, just as the female body has ever-changing cycles. The immaterial and spiritual can be seen as the masculine father: changing very little and very slowly and being linked invisibly to all matter, yet having its origin in a greater consciousness that we call God.

Think of feminine and masculine as two parts of any human being. All of us contain some of both male and female polarity. In an alchemical story, a feminine or yin symbol could easily be a male character. The important message is that a major part of the work of alchemy is the union of yin and yang. There is usually an external example of the union, such as a marriage (Bill and Fleur and then later Harry and Ginny and Ron and Hermione), and an internal part of the struggle in which the hero embraces parts of himself that have been dormant or unbalanced. In Harry's case, one example of this is at Dobby's burial when he makes the decision to trust Dumbledore and go after the Horcruxes, not the Hallows. In making that choice, Harry ended up accepting the more passive choice of death (a feminine symbol) over the more active goal of possessing the elder wand (a masculine, phallic symbol). Harry reflects on his choice with the thought:

The enormity of his decision not to race Voldemort to the wand still scared Harry. He could not remember ever before choosing *not* to act.[14]

The intention of alchemy is for each person to unite himself or herself. Man or woman, we all contain the essence of the universe within us; we are best when we are able to access both yin and yang.

The importance of the "lesser work" and the "greater work" to the *Harry Potter* series is that the first three books of the series represent the "lesser work" and the last three represent the "greater work." Those six books can be aligned in the alchemical wedding in a way that relates to the concept of the soul and the spirit. While each is an independent story, when

14   Rowling, J.K. *Harry Potter and the Deathly Hallows*. 406.

viewed as a union of lesser and greater they contain additional examples of literary alchemy.

The Planets and the Books

Because there are seven alchemical planets and seven *Harry Potter* books it is an interesting exercise to relate each book to a planet. The most natural way would be to assume that they follow the stages of the work as presented above. Attempting to align them that way proves frustrating, however, because the books do not follow that order, the order which an alchemist would be expected to follow when changing lead into gold. Let's take a look at how the books actually line up with the planets. Then we can examine why the books seem to be out of order by returning to Burckhardt, who gives us the reason the reason J. K. Rowling lined up the books in the seemingly disorganized way she has.

Mercury	Saturn	Jupiter	Moon	Venus	Mars	Sun
Mercury	Lead	Tin	Silver	Copper	Iron	Gold
☿	♄	♃	☽	♀	♂	☉
GoF	PS	CoS	PoA	HBP	DH	OotP

Figure 4. This figure depicts the books aligned with the planets/ metals. Goblet of Fire (GoF), Philosopher's Stone (PS), Chamber of Secrets (CoS), Prisoner of Azkaban (PoA), Half-Blood Prince (HBP), Deathly Hallows (DH), and Order of the Phoenix (OotP).

In Figure 4, I have shown the pairings of books with planets and symbols as my analysis fits best. Below is a description of how these pairings unite.

Mercury

The mercurial book is *Goblet of Fire* for several reasons. Mercury represents the keystone between the two sides of the alchemical process: the masculine side and the feminine side. Mercury is a joining of male and female and is considered an androgyne for this reason. In *Goblet of Fire*, Harry already contains a piece of Lord Voldemort inside him, though we do not learn this until the seventh book. When Lord Voldemort uses Harry's blood to take physical form, that piece of Harry within him seals the bond between them in a way similar to yin and yang. This matches the concept of mercury as an androgyne, containing both sun and moon and being joined to the cross of matter. Lord Voldemort finally attains a second physical body, matter, and this certainly represents a "key" to the whole series.

Additionally, the god Mercury, also known as Hermes, was "the messenger of the gods who accompanied the soul after its death – bodily or mystical – through all the realms of the world of shadows, to its final place of rest." [15] In *Goblet of Fire*, Cedric's "echo" [16] asks "'Harry … take my body back, will you? Take my body back to my parents …'" [17] Harry returns Cedric's body to his family, just as Hermes would have accompanied mortals after their deaths. Even the Defense against the Dark Arts teacher, Barty Crouch, Jr., is reminiscent of Mercury-Hermes in this book. He is a messenger for the Dark Lord and a man with two faces and two roles. As Mad Eye Moody, he plays the part of helping Harry succeed in the Triwizard Tournament; as Barty Crouch, Jr., he is the messenger who delivers Harry's body to Lord Voldemort.

Saturn (Lead)

Saturn (lead), the god of time and death, is the first step in the alchemical process. It is the step in which ash is formed. Burckhardt wrote:

> At the beginning of the work the most precious material which the alchemist produces is the ash, which remains over after the calcining [reduce, oxidize or desiccate by roasting or strong heat] of the base metal. By means of this ash, which has been divested of all passive

15 Burckhardt, Titus. *Alchemy*. 185.
16 Rowling, J.K. *Goblet of Fire*. 605.
17 Ibid. 579.

'humidity,' he will be able to capture the volatile 'spirit'.

The first stage of the work corresponds to the mythological meaning of Saturn in that Saturn-Chronos, who devours his own children, is the divinity who, through time and death, causes 'that which becomes' to return to its formless origin.[18]

In *Philosopher's Stone*, Harry holds the philosopher's stone in his pocket when he comes into physical contact with Quirrell, who is housing Lord Voldemort in his own body. This action burns Quirrell's flesh. After touching Harry, Quirrell's hands "looked burnt, raw, red and shiny."[19] Also, after Harry touches Quirrell's bare face, it is "blistering too."[20] When Harry's skin touches Quirrell's, it is as though he is turning Quirrell, who dies as a result, into ash. Burkhardt writes: "At the beginning of every spiritual realization stands death, in the form of 'dying to the world.'"[21] At the beginning of the *Harry Potter* series "stands" the death of Professor Quirrell. Harry's first Defense Against the Dark Arts teacher represents the darker side of Saturn-Chronos, by attempting to thwart death in his assistance of Lord Voldemort, he destroys himself.

Also, the *Harry Potter* characters of Nicolas and Perenelle Flamel choose death in the end of *Philosopher's Stone*. Of this choice, Dumbledore says:

> To one as young as you, I'm sure it seems incredible, but to Nicolas and Perenelle,[22] it really is like going to bed after a very, very long day. After all, to the well-organised mind, death is but the next great adventure. You know, the Stone was really not such a wonderful thing. As much money and life as you could want! The two things most human beings would choose above all – the trouble is, humans do have a knack of choosing

18   Burckhardt, Titus. *Alchemy*. 186.
19   Rowling, J.K. *Philosopher's Stone*. 213.
20   Ibid. 214.
21   Burckhardt, Titus. *Alchemy*. 186.
22   Perenelle is spelled with one 'r' in *Philosopher's Stone* and two 'r's in Burckhardt's text *Alchemy*.

precisely those things which are worst for them. [23]

In this one brief paragraph, Dumbledore really says quite a bit. He is defining the acceptance of death as the point of the opus, Harry's adventure, right up front; in the first stage of the alchemical process, Saturn (lead), two people who made the philosopher's stone accept death.

Jupiter (Tin)

Next, Jupiter, the son of Saturn, is born. This second stage of the 'lesser work', also called tin, is about bleaching the soul and removing dark liquid. Burckhardt quoted the alchemist Morienus as writing:

> "Whoever knows how to purify and bleach the soul, and allow her to rise upwards, guards the body well and has freed it from all darkness, blackness, and evil odour…" [24]

Burckhardt wrote that Jupiter is about "water and air" and corresponds to "sublimation."[25] The climax of *Chamber of Secrets* involves Harry guarding Ginny's body, her soul taken over by Tom Riddle. Harry frees her by stabbing Tom Riddle's diary with a basilisk tooth. Rowling writes, "Ink spurted out of the diary in torrents, streaming over Harry's hands, flooding the floor." [26]   Once the ink, the literal dark liquid, is purged, Ginny's soul is free to return to her body, purified of Tom Riddle's possession.

Also of note, the basilisk, according to Lyndy Abraham, is an alchemical symbol of the "elixir which could transmute base metals into gold." [27] The transformation that occurs in the climax of this story takes place in the presence of a symbol of the alchemical philosopher's stone.

23   Rowling, J.K. *Philosopher's Stone*. 215.
24   Burckhardt, Titus. *Alchemy*. 187.
25   Ibid.
26   Rowling, J.K. *Chamber of Secrets*. 237.
27   Abraham, Lyndy. *A Dictionary of Alchemical Imagery*. 16.

Ginny's romantic angst, her unrequited love for Harry, "how she didn't think famous, good, great Harry Potter would ever like her..." [28] is another important aspect of this story. This and the smarmy ladies' man Professor Lockhart infuse *Chamber of Secrets* with romantic overtones. Lockhart is similar to Jupiter-Zeus, who had a reputation as an incorrigible ladies' man. The romantic aspects of the story are important to understanding the feminine nature of the soul and Ginny's symbolic role in the story as Harry's future partner and, in pairing with him, his own symbolic soul.

The Moon (Silver)

The moon stage corresponds to the third *Harry Potter* book, *Prisoner of Azkaban*. In alchemy, the moon and silver symbolize the pure soul. The moon comes into play in the book with the introduction of Remus Lupin, a werewolf whose greatest fear is the full moon. Lupin's namesake, Remus, one of the founders of Rome, was considered the son of Mars and the grandson of Jupiter. It is interesting how Rowling chose to link the symbols of the metals in her stories to the gods in the form of family, just as the gods/planets of antiquity were considered family. She also links the Defense Against the Dark Arts teachers to the darker side of each of their associated planets. So in the case of Remus (grandson of Zeus) Lupin, she chooses a teacher whose soul is impure and that impurity, his condition as a werewolf, is exposed under the full moon. In addition, Artemis, the goddess of the moon and the hunt, is associated with a werewolf because it is a predator, an animal that hunts. The wolf itself is a symbol in alchemy of "the mercurial waters of life and death, the universal solvent which dissolves metals, then cleanses, purifies and regenerates them." [29] The term purified is the exact purpose of the moon stage of alchemy, to purify the soul. Another connection that exists between the moon and *Prisoner of Azkaban* is in the legends associated with the goddess Artemis – she turned the hunter Actaeon into a stag

---

28   Rowling, J.K. *Chamber of Secrets*. 228.
29   Abraham, Lyndy. *A Dictionary of Alchemical Imagery*. 218-9.

for watching her bathe naked.[30] Harry's stag Patronus connects with the pure soul in more ways than the legends of Artemis, the moon goddess, however.

The climax of the book occurs under the full moon in which Harry fights to save his soul using his stag Patronus:

> And out of the end of his wand burst, not a shapeless cloud of mist, but a blinding, dazzling, silver animal. He screwed up his eyes, trying to see what it was. It looked like a horse. It was galloping silently away from him, across the black surface of the lake. He saw it lower its head and charge at the swarming Dementors … now it was galloping around and around the black shapes on the ground, and the Dementors were falling back, scattering, retreating into the darkness … they were gone.
>
> The Patronus turned. It was cantering back towards Harry across the still surface of the water. It wasn't a horse. It wasn't a unicorn, either. It was a stag. It was shining as brightly as the moon above … it was coming back to him … [31]

The fleeing hart is a symbol in alchemy of quicksilver in the state known as *cervus fugitivus* that produces silver, again the symbol for the purified soul. Abraham writes, "The fleeing hart, one of the best known epithets of the alchemical Mercurius, also known as the deer, fawn and stag."[32] He adds, "In his role as the fleeing hart Mercurius serves as the messenger or soul which mediates between the spirit and the body, uniting them in the chemical wedding. The deer/soul equivalent is common in seventeenth-century poetry and emblem collections." [33] As I mentioned above, the moon symbolizes the purified and receptive soul, the fleeing hart also symbolizes the purified soul, thus the climax of *Prisoner of Azkaban* takes place in the

30   Zimmerman, J.E. *Dictionary of Classical Mythology*. 32 – 3.
31   Rowling, J.K. *Prisoner of Azkaban*. 300.
32   Abraham, Lyndy. *A Dictionary of Alchemical Imagery*. 32.
33   Ibid.

presence of the moon, with Harry fighting to protect his soul, using a symbol of a pure soul, the fleeing hart.

Venus (Copper)

Next in the stages of alchemy is Venus, copper, the goddess of love. Of Venus, Abraham writes:

> Although green is not one of the three major colours of the opus (black, white, and red) it is nevertheless a significant colour, representing new life, growth and fertility without which the philosopher's stone cannot grow. The green colour appears in the alembic after the black of the deathly nigredo and before the multi-coloured stage known as the peacock's tail. Green is also the colour of verdigris, which is often found on copper.[34]

Therefore, green is an important color in the copper stage, and is linked to love, not just because of what Abraham wrote above but it is also the color of the heart chakra in Hindu mysticism and the color we associate with envy and jealousy.

The book that best fits this stage is *Half-Blood Prince*. It is that story in which we experience Hermione, Ron, and Harry as they grow and mature physically and live through teenage romantic angst that eventually ends in committed relationships between Ron and Hermione and Ginny and Harry. Also, Snape, the Half-Blood Prince himself, is a pivotal part of this book. His reasons for helping Harry don't become known until *Deathly Hallows*, but he helps Harry out of love for Lily Evans Potter.[35] Hermione's jealousy of Ron and Lavender Brown and Snape's jealousy of James Potter connect with the concept of jealousy being green.

Rowling also uses green to end the life of Albus Dumbledore. When Harry and Dumbledore are Horcrux hunting together in the cave at the end of *Half-Blood Prince*, "Dumbledore approached the basin and Harry followed. Side by side they looked down into it. The basin was full of an emerald

34   Abraham, Lyndy. *A Dictionary of Alchemical Imagery*. 209.
35   Rowling, J.K. *Deathly Hallows*. 544.

liquid emitting that phosphorescent glow." [36] Then Dumbledore and Harry's "eyes met over the basin; each pale face lit with that strange, green light." [37] And then a little later, "Harry hesitated, looking into the blue eyes that had turned green in the reflected light of the basin." [38] Even the final curse that does Dumbledore in, Avada Kedavra, is "a jet of green light shot from the end of Snape's wand." [39]

Mars (Iron)

Mars, the god of war, is the fifth stage of the work, the stage of iron. In *Deathly Hallows*, the final battle for control of the wizarding world is fought and won. Burckhardt writes:

> The highest meaning contained in the sign of Mars –
> one which extends far beyond alchemy itself – is the
> 'incarnation of the Divine Word'. In a certain sense
> this implies a certain humiliation of the Divine, in
> that, as Light, it appears in the darkness of the world.
> Alchemical realization, however, can only be a distant
> reflection of this incarnation. [40]

Incarnation means "a person who embodies in the flesh a deity, spirit or abstract concept." [41] In the use as Burckhardt introduces it, he does not mean Christ specifically, although that is certainly an example of the incarnation of the Divine Word; instead he means any time the Divine comes to the world. In the case of the *Harry Potter* series, the main theme of acceptance of death is demonstrated in Harry's journey. Harry's journey then becomes the incarnation of the Divine Word. He makes the connection himself in Deathly Hallows, after seeing Snape's memories, Harry thinks:

36   Ibid., *Half-Blood Prince*. 530.
37   Ibid., 532.
38   Ibid.
39   Ibid., 556.
40   Burckhardt, Titus. *Alchemy*. 190-1.
41   "Incarnation." *Oxford American Dictionary*. Online Apple Widget Version.

Finally, the truth. Lying with his face pressed into the dusty carpet of the office where he had once thought he was learning the secrets of victory, Harry understood at last that he was not supposed to survive. His job was to walk calmly into Death's welcoming arms.[42]

This choice to sacrifice himself to save his friends by facing Lord Voldemort with the plan to die is that incarnation of Divine Word that Burckhardt writes about above.

The link between the Dark Arts teacher and the planets continues in this novel. The character of Amycus Carrows is named after Amycus of mythology, a son of Poseidon and a brutal boxer who challenged all travelers to fight him. [43] As the son of Poseidon, he was the nephew of Zeus and the grandson of Chronos. Again, the family of the planets/gods. His brutality as the Dark Arts teacher is described by Neville, "We're supposed to practice the Cruciatus Curse on people who've earned detentions – " [44] Once again, this brutality is the dark side of Mars, the dark side of the god of war.

The Sun (Gold)

This leaves us with the sun or gold. Rather than being the final book in the *Harry Potter* series, the book that fits best is *Order of the Phoenix*. Of the symbol of the phoenix, Abraham writes:

> A symbol of renewal and resurrection signifying the philosopher's stone, especially the red stone attained at the rubedo, capable of transmuting base metal into pure gold. [45]

Of sol, or the sun, Abraham writes, "sol symbolizes the red king, the hot, dry, active seed of metals, the male principle of the opus, which must be united with his sister luna."[46] He

---

42   Rowling, J.K. *Deathly Hallows.* 554.

43   Zimmerman, J.E. *Dictionary of Classical Mythology.* 20.

44   Rowling, J.K. *Deathly Hallows.* 462.

45   Abraham, Lyndy. *A Dictionary of Alchemical Imagery.* 152.

46   Ibid., 185.

also says that sol symbolizes the "red elixir, the red stone, the culmination of the opus."[47]

Symbols of the sun are most present in the Order of the Phoenix, the fifth book. The song "Weasley is our king," 48 about redheaded Ron Weasley, calls to mind the "red king" mentioned above by Abraham. Also, during the final battle between Dumbledore and Lord Voldemort, "Fawkes swooped down in front of Dumbledore, opened his beak wide and swallowed the jet of green light whole: he burst into flame and fell to the floor, small, wrinkled and flightless." [49] Another symbol of a star or sun is the orb of the prophecy itself. Rowling describes it as "one of the small glass spheres that glowed with a dull inner light" [50] and then later, when Harry holds it, it "felt as though it had been lying in the sun for hours as though the glow of light within was warming it." [51]

Dolores Umbridge, the Defense Against the Dark Arts teacher in *Order of the Phoenix*, relates to the concept of the dark side of the sun-Apollo. This is the side of the sun that would eclipse all other things, taking over completely. In the *Order of the Phoenix*, she becomes the Hogwarts High Inquisitor and works to take Hogwarts completely over from Dumbledore.

Another sun symbol comes in the form of Harry's godfather, Sirius Black, who is named after the dog star Sirius. Of this concept of a black sun, Abraham writes about an alchemical substance called *sol niger*:

> Sol niger (the black sun) symbol of the death and putrefaction of the metal [...] the metal or matter for the stone is 'killed' and dissolved into its prima materia so that it may be resurrected in a new form. At the death of the matter, darkness reigns. The light of the sun (gold) is said to be put out, totally eclipsed.[52]

47   Ibid.

48   Rowling, J.K. *Order of the Phoenix*. 618.

49   Ibid., 719.

50   Ibid., 687.

51   Ibid., 688.

52   Abraham, Lyndy. *A Dictionary of Alchemical Imagery*.186.

Sirius Black can be seen as equating to the black sun, *sol niger*. An essential part of the conclusion of this book is therefore the extinction of three symbols of the sun: Fawkes the phoenix is killed and reborn, the prophecy is smashed, and Sirius Black is murdered.

Dumbledore and Harry discuss the death of Sirius "the black sun" Black in detail at the end of *Order of the Phoenix*. In this conversation, four times the light of the sun is mentioned and three times it falls upon something silver. First:

> The sun was rising properly now, there was a rim of dazzling orange visible over the mountains and the sky above it was colourless and bright. The light fell upon Dumbledore, upon the silver of his eyebrows and beard...[53]

Then, "Harry watched the sunlight, which was sliding slowly across the polished surface of Dumbledore's desk, illuminate a silver ink pot and a handsome scarlet quill."[54] And again, "Dumbledore stared for a moment at the sunlit grounds outside the window."[55] And finally:

> The sun had risen fully now: Dumbledore's office was bathed in it. The glass case in which the sword of Godric Gryffindor resided gleamed white and opaque, the fragments of the instruments Harry had thrown to the floor glistened like raindrops, and behind him, the baby Fawkes made soft chirruping noises in his nest of ashes. [56]

Harry receives the truth from Dumbledore as, symbolically, gold is cast upon silver; the light of the spirit is illuminating the soul all around him.

---

53   Rowling, J.K. *Order of the Phoenix*. 728.
54   Ibid., 730.
55   Ibid., 736.
56   Ibid., 740.

The sun is a symbol of the Divine Spirit. It is Harry's spirit he fights for in the conclusion of Order of the Phoenix. When Lord Voldemort attempts to possess him and fails, Dumbledore speaks to Harry about the power of love:

> That power also saved you from possession by Voldemort, because he could not bear to reside in a body so full of the force he detests. In the end, it mattered not that you could not close your mind. It was your heart that saved you.[57]

In that moment, Harry passively defends himself from Lord Voldemort with the power of his love. *Order of the Phoenix* is indeed a sun book, but it also contains symbols, not of the completed work, but of the extinction of the sun (symbolized by Fawkes, the prophecy, and Sirius) as it descends into the body of matter so that the alchemist can bring it back again in a new purified form.

Completing the Marriage

Figure 5 makes sense of this apparently disorganized order of the planets and metals. This alternative method of depicting the alchemical symbols is shown in Alchemy by Titus Burckhardt. [58] Perhaps J.K. Rowling actually read this book and intentionally used this order for her work. The order is as follows:

---

57   Ibid., 743.
58   Burckhardt, Titus. *Alchemy*. 193.

Ascending	↑		↓	Descending
Soul		GoF		Spririt
Passive		☿		Active
PoA	☽		☉	OotP
CoS	♃		♀	HBP
PS	♄		♂	DH

Figure 5. The left side depicts the ascending soul and the right side the descending spirit. The books are shown lined up with the symbols for the planets / metals in the alchemical work. Mercury and Goblet of Fire (GoF) are shown at the top of the chart. The "lesser work" on the left is Philosopher's Stone (PS), Chamber of Secrets (CoS), and Prisoner of Azkaban (PoA). On the right is the "greater work" with Order of the Phoenix (OotP), Half-Blood Prince (HBP), and Deathly Hallows (DH). [See Titus Burckhardt's Alchemy, *chapter 15, 'The Stages of the Work,' for the origin and explanation of this chart.]*

The left column represents passive purification of the soul – the "lesser work." Recall that the soul and the moon are considered alchemically female. The first three books each end in an important soul cleansing act. In *Philosopher's Stone*, Harry shows he does not want the stone for eternal life or for the production of gold; at the same time, he releases Voldemort's spirit from the body it is possessing by producing ash. In *Chamber of Secrets*, Harry frees Ginny from the possession of

Lord Voldemort, purifying her soul, and at the same time Harry becomes aware of her passive interest in him. In the final book of the "lesser work," *Prisoner of Azkaban*, Harry must defend his own soul with the production of a Patronus that symbolizes the pure soul in the form of the fleeing hart or stag.

The right hand column in the chart represents the masculine or active progress of Harry's spirit. This "greater work" represents the sun, spirit, descending in order to join with the receptive moon, soul. First, in *Order of the Phoenix*, the black sun (Sirius Black) dies and the phoenix is born anew. Harry also defends himself, his spirit, from possession with the power of his love for the black sun and then he receives revelations from Dumbledore about his purpose. In *Half-Blood Prince*, Harry actively joins with the feminine side of his symbolic soul by beginning his romantic relationship with Ginny. In *Deathly Hallows*, he actively defeats Lord Voldemort after choosing the path of death.

If you look at the books as pairs, you can see that *Philosopher's Stone* and *Deathly Hallows* both show Harry facing Lord Voldemort in battle. In the first, Harry is protected by his mother's love and he only needs to passively demonstrate that he does not intend to use the stone in order to get it. Later, in *Deathly Hallows*, Harry must actively stand and fight and repeat his mother's sacrifice in order to protect his friends.

In the next pair, Ginny's soul is cleansed in *Chamber of Secrets* of Tom Riddle's possession and she makes it known that she is passively interested in Harry – as his symbolic soul, she has shown she is receptive to him. In *Half-Blood Prince*, Harry is finally able to act on his feelings for her when he becomes her boyfriend.

Then, in the final pair of moon and sun, the defense of soul and spirit is completed. In *Prisoner of Azkaban* Harry must defend his soul from the Dementors by actively fighting with the Patronus charm. In *Order of the Phoenix* Harry must prevent his spirit from being possessed by Lord Voldemort, which he does using his love for his godfather, the symbolic black sun. Interestingly, as happens very often in alchemy, the lunar book is in the passive column but Harry must be active to defeat the Dementors. By contrast, in the active column, Harry need only feel love for Sirius to prevent the active possession of his spirit.

You can see how *Goblet of Fire* presides over the top as mercury, the key to the entire work. Then the order of the others makes sense, not chronologically, but as an alchemical wedding in which each has a corresponding active and passive component that unites the ascension of the soul with the descending spirit. In the end, the result is gold.

Conclusion

Joseph Campbell defined myth as a metaphor that is "transparent to transcendence." [59] This means that in a modern myth such as *Harry Potter*, you get out of your head and into your heart, so you experience a transformation of the soul that is invisible, or transparent, to you. A reader who is uncomfortable with the term soul or the notion of personal transformation, can be unaware of such loaded terms and simply enjoy the experience itself. Thus, resistance to terms or concepts falls away; instead revelation occurs right alongside the hero. That is what literary alchemy does for the reader and it is one of the many reasons J.K. Rowling's work is such a successful example of literary alchemy.

As an essay editor for the online essay project Scribbulus,[60] I read many amazing examples of this soul transformation in essay after essay. I do not mean Harry's soul, but the soul of the reader who was moved to write about his or her experience with Harry's adventure. It does not matter if we are conscious of what is happening as we internalize the story about accepting death, dispelling evil with love, bravery, or the power of a whole soul – it still transforms us. When I attend Harry Potter conventions, it is present in every aspect of the amazing community that has formed around the books. We are a community of loving friends who celebrate together by dressing up, laughing, writing songs, singing and dancing

---

59   Campbell, Joseph. *The Hero's Journey*. 40.
60   www . scruibbulus .com

together, and raising money for international charities.[61] That is the eternal life and richness that results from well-presented literary alchemy.

References

Abraham, Lyndy. *A Dictionary of Alchemical Imagery.* New York: Cambridge University Press, 1998.

Burckhardt, Titus. *Alchemy, The Science of the Cosmos, the Science of the Soul.* Louisville, Kentucky: Fons Vitae, 1997.

Campbell, Joseph. *The Hero's Journey.* Navato: New World Library, 2003.

Meyer, Stephenie. *Twilight.* New York: Little, Brown and Company, 2005.

Nizami. *The Story of Layla and Majnun.* New Lebanon: Omega Publications, 1997.

Rosenkreutz, Christian. *The Chemical Wedding of Christian Rosenkreutz.* Boston: Phanes Press, 1991.

Rowling, J.K. *Harry Potter and the Chamber of Secrets.* London: Bloomsbury, 1998.

———. *Harry Potter and the Deathly Hallows.* London: Bloomsbury, 2007.

———. *Harry Potter and the Goblet of Fire.* London: Bloomsbury, 2000.

———. *Harry Potter and the Half-Blood Prince.* London: Bloomsbury, 2005.

---

61   Potter-grounded organizations like The Nerd Fighters, Harry Potter Alliance, and The Leaky Cauldron raise money for charities as part of their regular business.

———. *Harry Potter and the Order of the Phoenix*. London: Bloomsbury, 2003.

———. *Harry Potter and the Philosopher's Stone*. London: Bloomsbury, 1997.

———. *Harry Potter and the Prisoner of Azkaban*. London: Bloomsbury, 1999.

Shakespeare, Wiliam. *Romeo and Juliet*. New York: Washington Square Press, 1992.

Simpson, Anne. "Face to Face with J. K. Rowling: Casting a spell over young minds," *The Herald*, 7 December 1998.

Trismegistus, Hermes. *The Emerald Tablet of Hermes*. IAP, 2009.

Zimmerman, J.E. *Dictionary of Classical Mythology*. New York: Bantam, 1971.

Mars Is Bright Tonight:
A Deeper Look at J. K. Rowling's Use of Dante's First Canto

Lancelot Schaubert

I T SURPRISES SOME, BUT many embrace the literary significance of the Harry Potter series by now, thanks to the
great canon of literature Ms. Rowling draws from. Others disagree with the hype, namely Alan Jacobs, a Professor of English
at Wheaton who wrote at least one book about the life of C.S.
Lewis.1 Men like Stephen McGinty disagree with Jacobs, saying in the Scotsman Newspaper, "Anyone not interested in ex-
ploring why these books are as popular as they are, frankly, is
not a thinking person."2

---

1. Jacobs, Alan *First Things* "The Code Breakers" Aug/Sept 2006

2. http://news.scotsman.com/topics.cfm?tid=3&id=1201052007 -- McGinty
goes on to say, "My approach has been to 'take Harry seriously' as literature
rather than as a cultural artifact; my answer to the question of 'whence Potter-
mania?' is (a) the artistry of her work, (b) the postmodern themes that resonate
with the beliefs and concerns of our age, and (c) the transcendent meaning
she reaches at and hits in her use of traditional symbols and story points." I

Assuming that everyone still reading is both (a) on board with a deeper talk about Harry and (b) acquainted with *all seven Harry Potter books,* we now come to the matter at hand. John Granger, the Hogwarts Literary Headmaster, notes several ties from Dante to Harry including the use of the name "Firenze", hippogriffs, hermetic arts, memory[3], house rivals, and astrology, to name a few.[4] Though his explanation of Rowling's love-trumps-death motif bears no rival, he and others have missed a gaping hole, to no fault of their own.

In book one, *Philosopher's Stone/Sorcerer's Stone,* we are three-fourths into the action where Harry meets Voldemort for the first time in the Forbidden Forest. In the midst of insanity, we come across two separate centaurs, Ronan and Bane, who say thrice in one page "Mars is bright tonight," and once Ronan adds, "Unusually bright."[5] Some dismiss this much like Hagrid does, chalking the Mars comment up to Rowling's rejection of New Ageism and the Occult. "'Never,' said Hagrid irritably, 'try and get a straight answer out of a centaur. Ruddy stargazers.

---

am well aware that great, intelligent women have involved themselves, and contributed to, the canon of Harry Potter interpretation. I use the masculine singular such as "men like Stephen McGinty" throughout this article to cut down on wordiness.

3. Yates, Frances, *The Art of Memory* (University of Chicago, 1966)

4. Granger, John, *The Deathly Hallows Lectures* (Allentown: Zossima, 2008) 133-135. "Firenze" is the name of the "good centaur", and his name is Italian for Florence, as any dictionary search will show. Hippogriffs showed up in *Orlando Furiosio* and *Orlando Innamorato,* 16th and 15th century paintings. Hermeticism is the broader word for the specific use of literary alchemy, which Rowling claims, "[set] the parameters and [established] the stories' internal logic." Four rivals come from "the four Principal cities of the Peninsula: Florence, Naples, Venice, and Milan." Astrology points to Milan, 15th century.

5. Rowling, J.K., *Harry Potter and the Sorcerer's Stone* (New York: Arthur A. Levine, 1997) 253-254. I say "one page" not because it appears on one physical page, but because if Ms. Rowling deleted Hagrid and Hermione's line at the top of pg. 253, the line "Mars is bright tonight" at the top of 254 would fit right at the bottom of the previous page based on the current typeset. .

Not interested in anythin' closer'n the moon.'"[6] Review of the use of triple-epizeuxis within ancient literature leaves that trail of interpretation cold.

A triple-epizeuxis is a triple repetition for emphasis.[7] This word will not appear in Webster's New World College Dictionary for how little it crops up. It's an older style of prose, but still makes appearances in modern poetry. One of the familiar uses appears in that old, famous opera we've heard time and again, "Figaro! Figaro! Figaro!" More important, the Scriptures use it *only three times* in the sixty-six books of the canon, four if you count the repeat, and comes at a time when triple-epizeuxis was most common via Hebrew and Aramaic poetic forms. Mind you, no book has been translated and published more than Scripture. Regardless of our philosophical backgrounds, it would do us well, as mavens of literature, to probe this body of ancient literature, especially for something obscure like a triple-epizeuxis. The first usage comes in Isaiah 6:3 when the angels around the throne say, "Holy, holy, holy is the Lord Almighty; the whole earth is full of his glory."[8] The second occurs in Jeremiah 22:29, when the Lord rebukes Jehoiakim, king of Judah: "O land, land, land, hear the word of the Lord!" Jesus himself says the third, "Go tell that fox, 'I will drive out demons and heal people today and tomorrow, and on the third day I will reach my goal.' In any case, I must keep going today and tomorrow and the next day—for surely no prophet can die outside **Jerusalem!** O **Jerusalem, Jerusalem,** you who kill the prophets . . ."[9]

---

6. *Stone,* 254. The "anything closer than the moon" line comes from the Ptolemaic system. "The earth was the center of creation and was surrounded by nine heavenly spheres (nine heavens) concentrically placed around it. The moon was the first of these and therefore the smallest," see Alghieri, Dante, *The Inferno* – translated by Ciardi, John (New York: Signet Classics, 1954) 40. More on this later.

7. Moore, Mark, *The Chronological Life of Christ,* V.2 (Joplin: College Press, 1997) 56

8. This happens again in Revelation 4. All scripture quotations come from the New International Version.

9. Luke 13:32-34, emphasis mine.

Prophets use this repetition to gather the attention of either the reader or the hearer, sometimes from both. These examples show how it appears in an opera, or in prophetic poetry and oral tradition, but what would it look like if it were used in a twenty-first century children's novel published by American Scholastic and British Bloomsbury? One might spread it out a bit, and share the load between speakers, but keep it close enough together that it's all in sight. This is what we see, even though the last use of "Mars is bright" ends up as the first line on the next page in Chapter 15 of *Stone*. Surely Jo was tickled to death when she saw that, seeing how coy she remained about the meaning and plot of her books over the years. Placing that testimony in the mouths of two witnesses would hold up even in a Jewish court, let alone an English-speaking one.[10]

So "Mars is bright tonight" is important, but in what way?[11] As the subtitle tells, I believe a staggering connection links Dante and this seemingly thrown-away line in *Philosopher's Stone*, and we need not search far to notice it. In canto I, lines

---

10. 1 Timothy 5:19

11. Lyndy Abraham notes, "The reign of Mars is associated with the stage when the rainbow colours of the peacock's tail (*the cauda pavonis*) appear in the vessel, heralding the advent of the white stage or albedo." It is true that the appearance of Mars in this scene sets up the peacock test, but I believe this to be a secondary point. My primary rational is that the triple-epizeuxis is a much more obvious reason for Mars' cameo and the colors of the rainbow, in order, are less obvious. However, it should be noted that the rainbow appears inside this scene right after the triple mention of Mars' Brightness, and they appear in order: red as in "Red sparks" (*Stone*, 254), orange and brownish yellow as in the "rustling of leaves" (*Stone*, 254), green as in the "heart of the forest" (*Stone*, 255), "blue eyes" (*Stone*, 256), indigo "like pale sapphires" (*Stone*, 256), violet as in the combination of blue and red "[blue] eyes lingering on [the red] scar that stood out, livid, on Harry's forehead" (*Stone*, 256), and then the white of the unicorn to mark the completion of the spectrum, and beginning of the albedo (*Stone*, 256). Again, this is not the easiest comparison, so the more sensible understanding is that Mars has more to do with Dante, and less to do with Alchemy, however much I personally love the peacock test. Abraham, Lyndy *A Dictionary of Alchemical Imagery* (New York: Cambridge, 1998) 122.

37-39 of Dante's *Inferno*, we read:

> This fell at the first widening of the dawn
> As the sun was climbing Aries with those stars
> That rode with him to light the new creation[12]

Aries is the Greek god which the Romans adapted into their god Mars. Aries was the God of war.[13] This might seem weird to say, "Mars is bright tonight" in the Saturn novel[14], the age of innocence, the first book about our twelve-year-old orphan. However, John Ciardi reveals the key in his translation of *Inferno*. "The medieval tradition had it that the sun was in Aries at the time of the creation."[15] A bright Mars is synonymous with Saturn, *a bright Mars is a marker of life – full life.*

To understand this, we must think less chronologically and more symbolically. Of course, chronologically, war came after the fall of man in the narrative of the Scriptures. Symbolically, however, war represents chaos, and in Genesis chapter one, we have the description of the earth pre-creation: "Now the earth was formless and empty, darkness was over the surface of the deep, and the Spirit of God was hovering over the waters."[16] In other words, it was chaos – or war – God spoke into. "And God said, 'Let there be light,' and there was light. God saw that the light was good, and he separated the light from the darkness. God called the light 'day,' and the darkness he called 'night.' And there was evening and there was morning, the first day."[17] Out of chaos light is born. This is where the medievalists grabbed onto the idea that the Sun, a planet in itself, was inside Aries climbing up "to light the new creation." The Alchemical symbol for the first stage of the Great Work, the first book if

12. Alghieri, Dante, *The Inferno* – translated by Ciardi, John (New York: Signet Classics, 1954) 29.
13. Bulfinch, Thomas, *Bulfinch's Mythology* (New York: Dell, 1959) 17.
14. More explanation will follow concerning the use of planetary names for the seven books of the series. For the logic concerning this usage, see Ms. Erin Sweeney's article: *Cracking the Planetary Code*
15. *Inferno*, 32.
16. Genesis 1:2
17. Genesis 1:3-5

you're talking about a series, is Mars (chaos and matter) on top of the sun sign (God). One symbol, Saturn, comes from the Ptolemaic astrology overlaying on the alchemical framework as lead.[18] The other symbol, a bright Mars, comes from the golden chain of Homer, a series of symbols representing the stages of alchemy. A bright Mars, therefore, represents Saturn or *lead*. It's a circle with a dot in the center, topped with a smaller circle, and a cross on top. Mars is *carrying* the sun.[19]

This is important for two reasons. The first, which we will deal with presently, is the marking of Dante's work within the Genesis of the *Harry Potter* series, the Saturn novel. The second, which we shall deal with later, is the wedding of Erin Sweeney's alchemical/astrological framework (which holds up the logic of the Harry Potter series) and the Genesis one poem concerning the seven days of creation (which holds up the logic of scripture in general). Concerning the first, and moving toward the second, I give you my point: *when J.K. Rowling mentions the Forbidden Forrest, she is referring to Dante, and in so doing, generates her own perfect Easter.*

Dante and the Forbidden Forrest

John Granger, in his *Deathly Hallows Lectures*, argues that the Chapter 34 title in *Hallows* – "The Forest Again" – is referring to Dante:

Chapter 33, "The Prince's Tale," you'll recall, linked Dante and Severus, because each book or cantica of the *Commedia* is 33 cantos. Chapter 34, the story of Harry's walk into the woods to sacrifice himself to defeat the Horcrux within him and the enemy outside him, is his fantasy-story "Holy Friday" walk to Calvary. Dante's journey through *Inferno*, *Purgatorio*, and *Paradiso* begins with his walking in the woods on Holy Friday in the year 1300:

18. "*Saturn* (lead) *Jupiter* (tin) *Moon* (silver) *Venus* (copper) *Mars* (iron) *Sun* (gold)" Burckhardt, 184.

19. Liungman, Carl G. *Dictionary of Symbols* (Malmo: Merkur International 1991) 57-58This is the beginning of the *Catena aurea Homeri* – the golden chain of Homer, a chain of ten symbols representing the ten stages of esoteric Alchemy.

Midway in the journey of our life
I came to myself in a dark wood,
for the straight way was lost

Ah, how hard it is to tell
the nature of that wood, savage, dense and harsh –
the very thought of it renews my fear!

It is so bitter death is hardly more so.
But to set forth the good I found
I will recount the other things I saw.[20]

Before that quotation and argumentation, Granger writes, "There hasn't been a forest entry in a chapter title in any of the books, or mention of 'The Forbidden Forest' in a title since Chapter 15 of *Philosopher's Stone*. That *might* be the meaning of 'Again' in the Chapter 34 title in *Hallows*."[21] He goes on to quote the above, but why not both options? Why not mean both "Dante" and "see also chapter 15 of *Stone*"? Has Rowling not laden enough of her names, titles, and content with multiple meanings[22] to make us even a little suspicious of the word "again" appearing in the title of the single most important chapter she wrote? I beg a second glance.

Three signposts shout at the reader to pay attention to Chapter 15 of *Philosopher's Stone*. The first I've mentioned: that three times in one page Rowling, via centaurs – symbols of Christ[23], says, "Mars is Bright Tonight" and once adds "unusually

---

20. Granger *Lectures*, 148.

21. Granger *Lectures*, 147, emphasis mine.

22. Granger, John. *Looking for God in Harry Potter* (SaltRiver/Tyndale, 2004) 101-116. Granger makes a great argument that "the character names are delightful puzzles with hidden Christian meanings." Moreover, he has the best argument of the etymology of Harry's name. Harry Potter < (Cockney accent, like Hagrid or French accent like Fluer) 'Airy Pot'er < Heir y Pater < Heir of the Father. I will assume this later in the chart on the logic of the series.

23. Granger, *Looking*, 118. "As we saw earlier, the centaur is a symbol of a perfect man and an imaginative icon of Christ riding into Jerusalem."

bright." Take any random page from the forty-one-hundred involved in the entire series. You will not find any other four-word phrase repeated this frequently in this small of a space. This triple-epizeuxis is literary way of saying:

PAY CLOSE ATTENTION!

Secondly, we've heard of this dark wizard, but this is the very first time we've *seen* him. If Harry is to become a symbol of Christ[24], and if Voldemort is the Devil[25], then this is the first meeting of a symbol of Jesus and the symbol of Satan in the *Harry Potter* series. The first meeting of Jesus and Satan in the Scriptures is the desert temptations. Though Harry is not tempted in this scene, he is *tried* by coming face to face with the raspy breath of Lord Thingy. This scene sets the stage for future romps through the forest. In those future romps, Harry will be tried by symbols representing the three desert temptations: lust of the flesh, lust of the eyes, and the boastful pride of life.[26] The medieval words for these three groups of sin are incontinence, violence/ambition, and malice/fraud.[27]

Last, the title of the chapter gives away the Dante referent. "The Forbidden Forest" comes straight out of the first

---

24. Granger *Lectures*, 19. "In *Deathly Hallows*, Harry doesn't rise from the dead *in the presence of* a symbol of Christ. He rises *as* a symbol of Christ. I think it's safe to say here that all the previous deaths and resurrections were just pointers and prefigurings of Harry's ultimate victory, his "mastery of death." Ms. Rowling has said that the last third of *Deathly Hallows* was the fixed part of the storyline that drove every other element of the previous books. **All the stories do point to Harry's trip into 'The Forest Again.'"** Latter **emphasis** mine.

25. Granger *Looking*, 17. "Well, how about those Slytherin nasties then? Their connection with the devil is remarkable. Their mascot is a serpent, their founder's name – Salazar Slytherin – is full of hissing serpentine sounds and suggests the motion a snake makes on the ground (slitherin'; see Genesis 3:14), and their leader is the Dark Lord. I don't think this is coincidental. That Voldemort's intimates are called 'Death Eaters' is just icing on the cake. (The opposite of Death Eaters is 'Life Eaters' – and those who eat the body and blood of God, who is the way, the truth, and the *life*, are Christians)."

26. 1 John 2:16; Matthew 4:1-11

27. *Inferno*, 27.

canto. Here is the intro again, from an earlier translation:

> Midway in our life's journey, I went astray
> From the straight road and woke to find myself
> Alone in a dark wood. How shall I say?
>
> What wood that was! I never saw so drear,
> So rank, so arduous a wilderness!
> Its very memory gives a shape to fear.
>
> Death could scarce be bitterer than that place!
> But since it came to good, I will recount
> All that I found revealed there by God's grace . . .
>
> But at the far end of that valley of evil
> Whose maze had sapped my very heart with fear!
> I found myself before a little hill . . .[28]

If Dante lived today, had read the *Harry Potter* series all the way through, and had been asked to describe the Forbidden Forest in his own words, he'd quote himself. The Forbidden Forest is where people either fall astray, or go as punishment for having fallen astray. Dumbledore says early on, "'First years should note that the forest on the grounds is forbidden to all pupils. And a few of our older students would do well to remember that as well.' Dumbledore's twinkling eyes flashed in the direction of the Weasley twins."[29] Harry, Hermione, and Malfoy are in the forest in Chapter 15 *as a detention*. When Harry recounts the night to Ron, the "very memory" of the forest "gives shape to fear." "Harry went on feverishly, 'then Voldemort will be able to come and finish me off. . . . Well, I suppose Bane'll be happy.' Hermione looked very frightened. . ."[30] As for the last two stanzas, they are reminiscent of The Calvary/The Forest Again chapter in the last book. More on that later.

---

28. *Inferno*, 28.
29. *Stone*, 127.
30. *Stone*, 260.

With these three combined – the brightness of Aries/
Mars, Harry's beginning of his "desert trials", and the *forbidden*
nature of the forest – *J.K. Rowling is referring to Dante when she
mentions the Forbidden Forrest.*

The Forest Temptations

Within the series, Harry reforms his character. This
occurs in every book through the *nigredo* stage of the alchemical
framework, and in the *nigredo* of the series as a whole.[31] More
importantly, he is being filled with information in his passive
soul (from *Philosopher's Stone* to *Goblet of Fire*) so that his
active spirit can do what is right, rather than what is easy (from
Goblet of Fire to Deathly Hallows).[32] For this to happen, Harry
must rid himself of qualities that would hinder him as our hero,
or "repent of sins." What sins?
We get a glimpse of them right after the Mars line.
They are the Leopard of Incontinence, the Lion of Violence

31. Alchemy is a science of the soul whereby the corrupted state, "spiritual
lead," is turned into a perfected state, "spiritual gold." This process uses
three main movements: *nigreddo, albedo, rubido* or black, white, red. In the
black stage, the soul is purged of impurities. In the white stage, the soul is
filled with new information for purity. In the red stage, the soul becomes
active in the sanctification process and works out the purification until gold.
See Granger, John *Unlocking Harry Potter: Five Keys for the Serious Reader*
(Zossima, 2007) 49-76 for Alchemy 101.

32. "From this it is clearly to be seen that for every active aspect there is
a corresponding passive aspect. Saturn represents a passive 'abasement',
Mars an active 'descent'. The first sign expresses the extinction of the
ego-bound soul, the second the victory of the Spirit. On the next level,
Jupiter corresponds to a development of the soul's receptivity, while Venus
corresponds to the rising of the inwards sun. The moon and the sun
themselves embody the two poles in their pure state, and Mercury bears both
essences within itself." Burckhardt, Titus *Alchemy: Science of the Cosmos,
Science of the Soul* (Louisville: Fons Vitae, 2006) 193-195. Rowling's pairing
of these astrological signs with the corresponding Harry Potter books
(*Saturn-Jupiter-Diana-Mercury-Apollo-Venus-Mars*) was first recognized by
Erin Sweeney, editor of *Scribbilus*. This is important because it explains the
chiastic structure of the series.

and Ambition, and the She-Wolf of Malice and Fraud (canto I: 40ff). Incontinence could be called "lust of the flesh," Violence and Ambition could be the "lust of the eyes," and Malice and Fraud could be the "boastful pride of life" which put Lucifer himself at the lowest level of hell in the Comedy. These three are the three levels of hell Virgil leads Dante through in order to be purged of his corresponding sins.[33]

Three monsters give us a scare in the "Forbidden Forest" chapter and foreshadow repentance for Harry as a parallel of Dante. The first is the mention of werewolves by Malfoy, "We can't go in there at night – there's all sorts of things in there – werewolves, I heard." To which Filch responds, "That's your problem, isn't it? Should've thought of them werewolves before you got into trouble, shouldn't you?"[34] At first blush, we might pin this as the she-wolf of fraud, but that is only because of the word "wolf." What is important is the meaning behind the symbol, what the werewolf represents. The werewolf, or potential werewolf, represents utter terror for the children when they come face-to-face with this ominous forest. They are in trouble for staying out past curfew, a common peccadillo leading to other grievous sins for those who struggle with incontinence. Those who work at night tend to lust in their flesh, the struggle of the werewolf who pursues temperance above all else.[35] The potential werewolf might as well have been

---

33. *Inferno,* 27, 29-30. "These three beasts undoubtedly are taken from Jeremiah 5:6. Many additional and incidental interpretations have been advanced for them, but the central interpretation must remain as noted. They foreshadow the three divisions of Hell (incontinence, violence, and fraud) which Virgil explains at length in Canto 11:16-111. I am not at all sure but what the She-Wolf is better interpreted as Fraud and the Leopard as Incontinence. Good arguments can be offered either way." I believe it easier to accept that Dante made three beasts for each corresponding level of hell *in the order they would come. Inferno,* 32.

34. *Stone,* 249

35. Think of Remus Lupin, "This time tomorrow, the owls will start arriving from parents. . . . They will not want a werewolf teaching their children, Harry And after last night, I see their point. I could have bitten any of you. . . . That must never happen again" *Prizoner,* 423. Lupin says his intemperance

the potential Leopard.

The Lion is Draco himself. Not only does he embody covetousness as the Malfoy (bad faith) child, but he also terrifies Neville and sends up a false alarm.[36] This may seem trivial, but Harry and Hermione "stood looking at each other, very scared, until they couldn't hear anything but the rustling of leaves around them."[37] Their terror is the result of Malfoy's eye-pleasure, his delight in seeing Neville scared.

The third, of course, is Voldemort himself, and his malice and fraud is explained in Firenze's Eucharistic admonition, "Only one who has nothing to lose, and everything to gain, would commit such a crime. The blood of a unicorn will keep you alive, even if you are an inch from death, but at a terrible price. . . . You will have but a half-life, a cursed life, from the moment the blood touches your lips."[38] The frauds and malicious should not touch the blood.[39]

From the Forest, we now own a lens for interpreting other forest events. How many events are there in the saga? Five, actually three if you don't count the "entrance" into the forest (*Philosopher's Stone*) and the "exit" from the forest (*Deathly Hallows*).[40] Three sins for three forest encounters – now that's starting to sound like Rowling. Of course, we can't talk of three temptations without at least mentioning Jesus.

Literarily, there are three things we should note about

---

from the previous night got him expelled. He could have said, "they will not want a drunk teaching their children" or "they will not want a pervert" or "they will not want an abusive man" or "they will not want a compulsive gambler." Mind you, I did not say *card player*, but *gambler* in that last one. . .

36. *Stone*, 254-255.
37. *Stone*, 254.
38. Granger *Looking*, 118.
39. 1 Corinthians 11:23-29. Granger, *Looking*, 119.
40. Technically, Barty Crouch gets an honorable forest mention in book four, which we will deal with later. For the sake of argument, I do not include that simply because (a) we only find out about it during the denouement and (b) because it's not from Harry's perspective. The forest, in this scene, is actually intended to represent a different sort of purification. It still reforms Harry, not within the Dante-framework, but rather alongside it.

Jesus and the temptations. First, as I mentioned earlier, they come in waves of three – three major temptations for the three main categories of sin.[41] Second, this is Jesus' first face-to-face with Satan. Third, they occur in a desert fast, after which Jesus is ready to begin his ministry. If we see a desert time, followed by tempting, followed by a profound ministry and the hero's character – or a profound apathy and a hero's incompetence – then the author is saying something about preparation – or as the alchemists would say – *preperatorio.*[42]

This is in fact what we see. We see a desert time (Harry in trouble during no-soul's hour), a tempting time (three monsters are alluded to, but not yet revealed), and a profound ministry . . . of magic (i.e. the other six books, and the worldwide phenomenon known as "Pottermania"). But what about these three monsters? She alludes to them, three trials at the beginning. Does she allude to them so near the end of the trial or the climax of the series?

She does, even calling them "trials" in the *Goblet of Fire* and "hallows" in *Deathly Hallows*[43] – three of them. Think of the three trials. Dragons in a Chinese context can represent good will and fortune, but in an English context, they represent hoarding, greed, and lust. "The dragon of our Western tales

41. Again, these are (1) lust of the flesh (2) lust of the eyes (3) boastful pride of life. They parallel (1) incontinence (2) ambition/violence (3) fraud and malice – the three monsters in Dante, and the three levels of hell.

42. The greatest literary examples of the temptations, or trials, are Johann Wolfgang von Goethe's *Faust* and Christopher Marlowe's *Doctor Faustus.* The Faustian bargain spreads across the whole of the literary cannon to say something about the main character. Depending on whether or not they "sell their soul" – an appropriate topic for a series dealing with horcruxes – the main character gains, or loses, a boatload of virtue that is necessary for the journey. Elliot, Charles W. *The Harvard Classics V.19: Faust & Doctor Faustus* (New York :Collier & Son, 1909). See also the framework of the hero's journey, specifically the period of testing in Campbell, Joseph *The Hero With a Thousand Faces* (Novato: New World Library, 2008) 81-91.

43. The Hallows represent the three temptations the invisibility cloak cheats death (lust of the flesh), the stone projects shadows of the dead (lust of the eyes), and the Deathstick makes you unbeatable (boastful pride of life).

tries to collect and keep everything to himself. In his secret cave he guards things: heaps of gold and perhaps a captured virgin."[44] Mermaids, for Rowling, represent coveting, lusting of the eyes. Chapter 25 of *Goblet* is called, "The Egg and The Eye." As a conjunction liking to two, you could make a little equation out of the word 'and': "The Egg : The Eye" or even "The Egg = The Eye." The point of the trial is in the looking: "An hour long *you'll have to look and recover* what we took, past the hour prospect's black. Too late, it's gone. . ."[45] When we meet the mermaids, we find "their eyes [are] yellow."[46] Krum becomes like them, turning into a grotesque shark. Cedric and Fleur distance themselves from the mermaids with a wall of air. Harry, in typical Christ-like fashion, eats of their food, and becomes like them in form and appearance, but doesn't take on the form of coveting. He saves. As for the labyrinth, we could go into a lot of Grecian myth, but to spare you the time, I'll point out the symbol of the maze's point: The Sphinx. The Sphinx, historically, would love to kill you if you get the riddle wrong. She *hides* the truth (fraud) hoping you fail and become her supper (malice). She represents the maze, hoping to hide the cup (fraud) in order to make you lose (malice).[47] If Forest = Dante, then we might look at the other occurrences in the forest to get a good picture of what's going on. The occurrences happen in books two, three, and four consecutively. In those three we meet the monsters foreshadowed in the original forest encounter: the werewolf/Leopard of incontinence, the Malfoy ("bad faith")/Lion of violence and ambition, and Voldemort/ the She-wolf of fraud and malice.

In *Chamber*, *Aragog represents incontinence.* We had a

44. Campbell, Joseph *The Power of Myth* (New York: MJF, 1988) 184. "In his secret cave he guards things: heaps of gold and perhaps a captured virgin. He doesn't know what to do with either, so he just guards and keeps. There are people like that and we call them creeps. There's no life from them, no giving. They just glue themselves to you and hang around and try to suck out of you their life."

45. Rowling, *Goblet*, 463.
46. Rowling, *Goblet*, 497.
47. *Goblet*, 629.

hint of this in two realms. The first, as I said, came from the punishment for being out late. They were indulgent in the night, and must be punished with the night. Lust of the flesh always repays like with like. It punishes by over-consumption.[48] The second comes out in Hagrid's bold response to Malfoy:

> "I'm not going in that forest," [Malfoy] said, and Harry was pleased to hear the note of panic in his voice.
>
> "Yeh are if yeh want ter stay at Hogwarts," said Hagrid fiercely. "Yeh've done wrong an' now yeh've got ter pay fer it."[49]

He goes on to threaten expulsion. Kicked out of school for breaking curfew? In the next chapter they dive headfirst into the trapdoor, and they don't even get a smack on the hand for that? Why so harsh a rebuke? Because Hagrid *did* get kicked out of school, for the monster represented by the "werewolves" Malfoy's scared of. People thought Aragog was the Basilisk.[50] "I never saw any part of the castle but the cupboard in which I grew up. Our kind like the dark and the quiet."[51] Harry grew up in a cupboard, and he might have grown to love the dark and quiet, or secret, arts.[52] He might have been enticed by the pleasures of the night, but having passed this test, he leaves the forest once again, more temperate than before.

---

48. Think of the dragon, or of anyone with a compulsive addiction.

49. *Stone*, 249-250.

50. Rowling, J.K. *Harry Potter and the Chamber of Secrets* (New York: Scholastic, 1998) 277.

51. *Chamber*, 278.

52. 1 Thessalonians 5:5-10 "You are all sons of the light and sons of the day. We do not belong to the night or to the darkness. So then, let us not be like others, who are asleep, but let us be alert and self-controlled. For those who sleep, sleep at night, and those who get drunk, get drunk at night. But since we belong to the day, let us be self-controlled, putting on faith and love as a breastplate, and the hope of salvation as a helmet. For God did not appoint us to suffer wrath but to receive salvation through our Lord Jesus Christ. He died for us so that, whether we are awake or asleep, we may live together with him." Those who get drunk, *get drunk at night*. The night symbolizes lust of the flesh/incontinence.

In Prisoner, *dementors represent ambition and violence.* Malfoy's scaring Neville hints at the terror that sprouts up by the presence of dementors. We learn in *Prince* that it takes murder to posture the soul, to fracture it for the creation of a Horcrux. The number one "soul sucker" in the series is the raspy dementor's kiss. By association, this links violence to the dementors:

> A pair of strong, clammy hands suddenly attached themselves around Harry's neck. They were forcing his face upward. . . . He could feel its breath. . . . It was going to get rid of him first. . . . He could feel its putrid breath. . . . His mother was screaming in his ears. . . . She was going to be the last thing he ever heard—[53]

Remember that Harry's first encounter with death and violence was the murder of his mother. Here he hears her screams. More easily, we see that the ambitious and the violent – most all of them Death Eaters – end up in Azkaban. Indeed, the entire book *The Prisoner of Azkaban* centers on the alleged murders at the hands of Sirius Black. Harry has a chance to let the dementors win, but with the help of a friend and by calling on The Father[54], he overcomes violence and ambition – the depression and darkness in his soul.

In Phoenix, *Dolores Umbridge represents malice and fraud.* Voldemort drinking the Unicorn Blood in an unworthy manner alludes to Umbridge. It would be appropriate that the character representing the She-Wolf would be a woman. Her name means "grievous shadow".[55] If you wanted to symbolize the abstract concepts of malice and fraud into story-symbols, grief and shadows are two of the best. In fact, all of book five is a book of grief and shadows – of death itself. Harry's embrace of death, grief, and the shadows behind the veil allows him to defeat Voldemort in the end simply because he does not succumb to either, but navigates through both. It's grief to have her around; it pains the students. Umbridge maliciously cuts into Harry's

53. Rowling, J.K. *Harry Potter and the Prizoner of Azkaban* (New York: Scholastic, 1999) 384.
54. Granger *Looking,* 145-147.
55. Granger, *Looking,* 108.

hand *I must not tell lies.*[56] This is a purging scene over truth. Harry has told the truth, but has been accused of lying, of fraud. The whole writing lines scene sums up Umbridge, for it is, in itself, a malicious act of fraud. Harry is not lying, and neither does he deserve this punishment. She is the one who takes the children into the Forbidden Forest (cue Dante music), and is defeated. By grieving Sirius and overcoming the Voldemort within, Harry beats the last of the vices, and emerges a gentle (rather than malicious) and truthful (rather than fraudulent) hero.

Before we came to the She-Wolf of Malice in the story, we met Voldemort face-to-face[57]. At the climax of Crouch Jr.'s confession, we discover this:

> "You killed your father," Dumbledore said, in the same soft voice. "What did you do with the body?"

> "Carried it *into the forest*. Covered it with the Invisibility Cloak. . . . Dumbledore told me to go and look for my father. I went back

---

56. Recounting Harry's bodily injuries from *Goblet* to *Hallows*: "his leg connected with pincers and next moment he was in *excruciating* pain" (*Goblet*, 652), "and felt the searing pain on the back of his hand for a second time; once again, the words had been cut into his skin" (*Phoenix*, 267), "'[my forearm] got cut on the rock,' Harry said" (*Prince*, 578), "the hinge of his glasses, which had been knocked sideways by the fall, cutting into his temple" (*Hallows*, 724), "nails pierced him (*Hallows*, 726), "Harry Potter is dead by my hand, and no man alive can threaten me now! Watch! *Crucio!*" (*Hallows*. 726). So Harry Potter had pierced feet, hands, arms, brow, nails, was tortured, Crucio-fied, and died. By his wounds came healing.

57. We could say that *In Goblet, Barty Crouch Jr. represents malice and fraud*. Fraud is an easy case to make, but I think Crouch is there for alternate reasons. What are the points if we wanted to see Crouch as Fraud? Crouch Jr. drinks polyjuice potion in his sleep to keep up the appearance of the greatest auror to ever live. In fact, until the very end, he has us all fooled – or in classic terms – defrauded. As for malice, I find it appropriate that the cinema version of Crouch Jr. licks his lips like a serpent. He is constantly, throughout book four, referred to as Voldemort's most faithful, and until Harry touches the cup, Crouch Jr. is the presence of Voldemort on Hogwarts' campus during year four.

to my father's body. Watched the map. When everyone was gone, I Transfigured my father's body. He became a bone. . . I buried it, while wearing the Invisibility Cloak, in the freshly dug earth in front of Hagrid's cabin."[58]

This scene is interesting for many reasons. It shows the contradicting views of father-finding as opposed to murdering. The first is what is commanded of Telemachus, Odysseus' son. Oedipus – killing his father and loving his mother, commits the second. Dumbledore asks Crouch Jr. to do what Harry is doing this entire book – finding his father.[59] Instead, Crouch responds by murdering his father. This is offered to Harry, and he refuses, choosing instead to find his father in the dual wand cores.[60] It also reveals the importance of this scene on the *internal* workings of Harry. It's obvious – the only inappropriate capitalization is the word "Transfigured." Crouch is not talking about the class or the school of thought, but the act itself. Crouch transfigured his dead father, and the act of finding his father transfigured Harry. The last revelation comes at the mention of Hagrid's cabin – an unnecessary detail but for one point.

We meet Hagrid in *Stone* under the chapter title "The Keeper of the Keys." A keeper of the keys is one of three things: a custodian, an authority, or a guide. Though Hagrid is a gardener of sorts, keeping the grounds, Filch is the proper "custodian." Hagrid is not an authority on anything but animals and giants, so that rules authority out. But what about guide?

Hagrid brings Harry when he's a baby. He picks Harry up from the hut. He leads Harry through buying school supplies and the first appearance of the philosopher's stone

58. Rowling, J.K. *Harry Potter and the Goblet of Fire* (New York: Scholastic, 2000) 690-691 emphasis mine.

59. In the *Odyssey*, Odysseus' son Telemachus is commanded by Athena to find his father. Campbell, Joseph *The Power of Myth* (New York: MJF, 1988) 208.

60. Any objection to this point should take into consideration the prevalence of the word "father" in the story, and more importantly, Voldemort's use of his father's bone *"bone of the father, unknowingly given, you will renew your son!"* (*Goblet*, 641). Voldemort and Crouch both "unknowingly take" their father. Harry, however, chooses to call on his father – to *find* his father.

(cue alchemist music). He introduces Harry to school and the magical world. He's the first to tell Harry his fame, the *key* to the solution of Chamber, the way for Sirius to escape in Prisoner, the one who tells Harry about the dragons, the owner of the cabin near the philosophical death of the father, the *noticeably absent character* in *Order of the Phoenix*, the linchpin in the breakdown of Slughorn, Harry's escort in the start of book seven, and the pallbearer at Harry's funeral.

If Harry resembles Dante, the Hagrid resembles Virgil. There is one other way one can keep the keys: to the gates of hell. As Virgil escorted Dante through hell, so Hagrid escorts Harry; and in the *Order of the Phoenix*, we go into the wood one last time to seal the deal. Hagrid cannot be there, but who can escort Harry? Hagrid's brother, of course – who has but one word on his mouth, "Hagger." This is Rowling's way of echoing Dante:

> "Thy words have moved my heart to its first purpose. My Guide! My Lord! My Master! Now lead on: One will shall serve the two of us in this."
>
> He turned when I had spoken, and at his back   I entered on that hard and perilous track.[61]

What hard and perilous track? The death of Sirius Black (*nigredo),* Albus Dumbledore (*albedo*), and his own death (*rubedo*). Having been escorted past three monsters of sin, and come out clean, Harry is ready to face the ultimate task, and to have the ultimate victory. It is no surprise we enter, "The Forest Again."

The Perfect Easter

John Ciardi notes in his translation and commentary on Dante's *Inferno* that Dante's use of the astronomical lights set the tone for his perfect Easter:

The medieval tradition had it that the sun was in Aries at the time of the Creation. The significance of the astronomical

---

61. *Inferno*, 39.

and religious conjunction is an important part of Dante's intended allegory. It is just before dawn of Good Friday 1300 A.D. when he awakens in the Dark Wood. Thus his new life begins with Aries, the sign of creation, at dawn (rebirth) and in the Easter season (resurrection). Moreover, the moon is full and the sun is in equinox, conditions that did not fall together on any Friday of 1300. Dante is obviously constructing poetically the perfect Easter as a symbol of his new awakening.[62]

If we look once more at lines 37-39 in the first canto, we can feel the language:

> This fell at the first widening of the dawn
> as the sun was climbing Aries with those stars
> that rode with him to light the new creation.[63]

Thus, Dante is making a triple-entendre. "New Creation" is the meaning of the symbol Aries – that the earth was in chaos before creation, the last in a series of three celestial markers for his perfect Easter – the "new creation," and Dante's own personal awakening since the forest itself represents the sin Dante must repent from.

We now have a neat little framework: (1) Forest = Dante reference, (2) Monster = Corresponding issue to be purged. "Forest" in *Stone* refers to Dante, introducing the three monstrous sins. "Forest" in Chamber refers to Dante, using Aragog as incontinence. "Forest" in *Prisoner* refers to Dante, using Dementors as violence and ambition. "Forest" in Goblet comes after a reaffirmation of the three trials, and is an aside (like the forest scene itself) referring to Harry's method of victory – finding his father, or "didn't you know that I'd be about my Father's business?" "Forest" in *Phoenix* refers to Dante, bringing Umbridge as malice and fraud. "Forest" in Hallows, therefore, brings us into "The Forest Again," where Harry, having defeated the three trials is able to embrace his cross without hesitation. Or you could say, *I open at the close.*

The novels dealing with introversion on any level (one,

62. *Inferno,* 32
63. *Inferno,* 29.

three, five, and the start of seven) represent the four conditions
of Dante's perfect Easter. They are initiators. The novels dealing
with extroversion on any level (two, four, six, and the end of
seven) represent the four results of the actions of the initiators.

One (*Stone*), Mars is bright. Many have wondered
about Harry being the Heir of Gryffindor. Though I have heard
convincing arguments concerning "Godric's Hollow" being his
place of birth, and his ability to summon the sword of Gryffindor,
none convinces me as much as his personal initiation into the
war of life under the sign of a bright Mars – the sign of creation.
This alone makes him heir to the throne:

Astronomically speaking, and without any reference to
controversy, there can be no doubt that the most remarkable
conjunction of planets—that of Jupiter and Saturn in the
constellation of Pisces, which occurs only once in 800 years—
did take place no less than three times in the year 747 AUC,
or two years before the birth of Christ (in May, October, and
December). This conjunction is admitted by all astronomers.
It was not only extraordinary, but presented the most brilliant
spectacle in the night-sky, such as could not but attract the
attention of all who watched the sidereal heavens, *but especially
of those who busied themselves with astrology. In the year
following,* that is, in 748 AUC, *another planet, Mars, joined this
conjunction.* [64]

Jupiter (the Lord of Heaven) converged with his father
Saturn (the Lord of Creation) for a bright star, and Mars joined
them. There was a bright Mars around the time of the birth of
Christ as well. New life begins under Mars, the sign of creation,
and at dawn. This is the rebirth – *the boy who lived*, so, one
(*Stone*), Mars is Bright. Three (*Prisoner*), the moon is full. The
moon, being the first of the heavenly bodies and the symbol
of Diana – goddess of the hunt, the moon, and, alchemically,
silver. A full moon means the most illuminated night, and the
best conditions for an *albedo*. What better way to show that
in fantasy than with two canines, one of which is a werewolf?
Five (*Phoenix*), the Sun is in equinox. The sun, coming in-

---

64. Edersheim, Alfred *The Life and Times of Jesus the Messiah* (Hendrickson,
2002) 148.

between Venus and Mars after Mercury on the Ptolemaic list of planet-order, takes the role of Apollo – god of music, prophecy, the sun, and, alchemically, gold. The bright sun means prime conditions for awakening, good conditions for an *albedo*, and prophesying, appropriately, of the coming *rubedo*. Seven *(Hallows)*, it's the Easter season. This seasonal celebration is the new birth, new creation, and resurrection. In the creation novel, the Saturn novel, we learned about the boy who lived at dawn. In the resurrection stage, we learn about the boy who *lived* at dawn. Each book starts with a birthday and book seven ends in August, the month after July 31st - Harry's birthday. In the story, though not so much in reality, August is our hero's "birth month" and so we end the story with a "birth month."

Each action – two, four, six, and the climax and end of seven - follows after the appropriate initiator. Mars is bright *(Stone)*; therefore the heir of Gryffindor must battle the heir of Slytherin *(Chamber)*; for this is why he was born; he was the boy who lived. The Moon is full *(Prisoner)*; therefore the patron of the wood must out-hunt the hunter *(Goblet)*, for he is the true champion. The Sun is brightest *(Phoenix)*; therefore the son of the prophecy – and music by association - must out-soul the split-soul. The season is Easter *(Deathly* or *Deadly)*; therefore Dante's echo must both die and rise to defeat those who eat Death once and for all *(Hallows)*, for he is the boy who lives. Why would the planet of war be bright? Because the planet of *chaos* is right there, ushering in the new creation.

A parallel, then, of Ms. Sweeney's observations and my Dante framework looks like this:

		"Mars is Bright" *(god of chaos forced to order)*
Philosopher's Stone	Saturn (lead)	
Chamber of Secrets		Therefore Heir of Gryffindor beats the Heir of Slytherin
	Jupiter (tin)	

Prizoner of Azkaban	Moon (silver)	"Moon is Full" (as in *Diana goddess of the hunt*)
Goblet of Fire	Mercury (quicksilver)	Therefore Hunted ties Hunter, and begins his active work
Order of the Phoenix	Sun (gold)	"Sun is in Equinox" (as in end of winter's death)
Half-Blood Prince	Venus (copper)	Therefore whole-soul (or spring soul) beats divided-soul
Deathly Hallows	Mars (iron)	"Season is Easter" Therefore Mars is Bright – i.e. "New Creation"

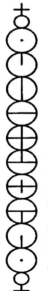

If you look at the bottom of the *Catena aurea Homeri*, you'll notice that the sun has been put over Mars. God, in the spirit, is supreme. "When *matter* is finally placed under *God*, the *spirit*, and the *divine consciousness*, perfection has been reached – Man has returned to God. This is humankind's divine condition, closely related to *Quinta essentia*, or the *fifth element, conjunctio*, the *merging with God*."[65] In other words, the way to say "perfect Easter" in Rowling's words by the end of the Harry Potter series, when God is put over matter, is to say, "Mars is Bright tonight, *unusually* bright." In scriptural language, this Easter has been finished "since the creation of the Harry Potter world." Here's the same chart, now with the Genesis account and the appropriate theology beside each day

---

65. Liungman, 57

"Mars is Bright"	**Saturn** Creation& Innocence	Day 1 – Light separated from darkness (*Harry & Voldemort meet for the first time*)
Therefore the Heir of GODric Gryffindor (Heir' y Pater) beats the Heir of Slytherin	**Jupiter** Heavens & Father	Day 2 –Expanse 'tween waters (*Chamber*) to separate deep from heavens (*duel of Heirs*)
"Moon is Full" (as in *Diana goddess of the hunt*)	**Moon** Hunt & Control of Tides	Day 3 – Gathering of land (island of *Azkaban*) for bearing of fruit (*end of passive descent*)
Therefore the Hunted ties the Hunter, and begins his active work	**Mercury** The Message	Day 4 – Creation of moon (*passive*) & sun (*active*) to govern the seasons (*crucible scene in graveyard that ends tone of first three & sets tone for last three books*)

"Sun is in Equinox"	**Sun** Song, Sun & Prophecy	Day 5 – Creation of Birds (*Order of Phoenix*) so that song birds will multiply & increase on earth (*Dumbledore's Army*)
Therefore the whole-soul (or spring soul) beats the divided-soul	**Venus** Love & Relationships	Day 6 – Creation of Beasts (*Horcruxes*) & Man in image of God (*Love*) to crush evil (*snake*)
"Season is Easter" Therefore Mars is Bright – i.e. "New Creation"	**Mars** War & Peace	Day 7 – Sabbath Rest of God. (*Conquering Death by Love in Harry's resurrection to give rest to the wizarding world.*

Concerning Day 7 – the Sabbath Rest of God, and "Day 8", the New Creation in a Perfect Easter:

> We also have had the gospel preached to us, just as they did; but the message they heard was of no value to them, because those who heard did not combine it with faith. Now we who have believed enter that rest, just as God has said, 'So I declared on oath in my anger, they shall never enter my rest.' And yet his work has been finished *since the creation of the world.* For somewhere he has spoken about the seventh day in these words: 'And on the seventh day God rested from all his work.' - [*Hebrews 4:2-4* (emphasis mine)]

It is perfect, then, that Ms. Sweeney finds good reason for the Mars book to be at the end, explaining it all through her alchemical/astrological drama. Neither does it surprise me that they split book seven into two movies. Some say this was a capitalistic ploy to grab more money. Maybe that. Or maybe book seven is actually book seven (the book of death and rest) *and* book eight (the book of life and new creation). Certainly enough major events go down in *Hallows* to justify a second book, or as the movie will say, "*Deathly Hallows*: Part 2".[66] I think it perfect that Director David Yates wants to make Part One of the seventh movie more about the realism of the series (death and rest) and Part Two more about the fantasy of the series (life and new creation).

Deathly Hallows is a book about war as any reader can see. But Harry doesn't fight using death as a weapon or via *Avada Kedavra*. He fights using life. He fights using peace. His work has been finished since the day Voldemort tried to kill him, from even the moment Hagrid placed him on the Dursley's doorstep under the stars. Harry was there for the re-creation, or as our English word for rest says, the recreation of the wizarding world. He was there to make it new. The Centaurs were prophesying the entire Harry Potter series just by looking up at the heavens, which is why they finally found fate forcing them into the Battle of Hogwarts. *Deathly Hallows'* message, and Rowling's message, comes to us in one simple phrase: "Mars is Bright tonight, *unusually* bright."

---

66. i.e. Voldemort's appearance in chapter *two*, Moody's death, destroying the first horcrux, breaking out of Malfoy Manor, Dobby's death, breaking and entering the Ministry of Magic, breaking and entering Gringott's for crying out loud, breaking back into Hogwarts, destroying *five* more horcruxes (technically six), the sacking of Snape, the Battle of Hogwart's, Harry's Death, Harry's Holy Saturday, Harry's Resurrection, etc. etc. etc.

Horcruxes in Faerie Land:
Edmund Spenser's Influence on Voldemort's Efforts to Elude Death

Elizabeth Baird Hardy

E DMUND SPENSER'S POETIC COMPLIMENT to Elizabeth I, *The Faerie Queene*, six books of the chivalric adventures of knights who each represent a different virtue, has everything that a sweeping Christian High Fantasy needs: quests, knights, ladies, monsters, and endless camping trips. However, its complex language, far less accessible than that of Spencer's contemporary Shakespeare, as well as its sometimes stiff religious and political allegories, seldom entrances modern readers. C.S. Lewis always called the epic "everyone's poem," (132) but apparently, "everyone" doesn't share that enthusiastic opinion. Despite this obstacle, Spenser still stands as one of the most important and essential early voices of fantasy, an influence on nearly all who have followed him, including J.K. Rowling. In telling Harry Potter's story, Rowling uses a number of Spenser's conventions, but few so intriguing as the connection between

Voldemort's Horcruxes and the experiences of the questing Elfin Knights (hardly any of whom are actually elves, strangely enough). In a concerted reminder a la Dumbledore, that death is not the great bogeyman we should all fear above all else, both Spenser and Rowling show us that far scarier than death is our individual potential for evil, and they often teach this lesson using very similar tools.

Spenser does not appear on any list of Rowling's favorite authors, though she undoubtedly was exposed to him during her thorough educational grounding in the great works of Western literature.. Considering *The Faerie Queene's* unkind political and religious jabs directed at the enemies of Elizabeth I and of Spenser himself, it is even likely Rowling has considerable issues with the poem. Certainly J.R.R. Tolkien made no secret of his dislike for Spenser's vilifying of Catholics, and yet, both Rowling and Tolkien, part of the fantasy tradition family tree at whose root Spenser lies, are intricately connected to *The Faerie Queene*. Rowling's characters are far more realistic than Spenser's necessarily symbol-laden knights, ladies, and villains; yet, just as Spenser uses allegorical characters and events to describe the development of Christian virtues, Rowling uses symbol, word play, and metaphor in the emotional and spiritual journey of her protagonist. Several specific associations are apparent. Spenser features an uncouth but loyal wild man who, like Grawp, uses an uprooted tree as a weapon, and the elaborate wedding of fabulously gorgeous Florimell, whose name means flower, to Marinell, son of a sea nymph, finds echo in the nuptials of Fleur (the flower) Delacour and Bill Weasley who set up housekeeping in Shell Cottage. Though Harry's adventures are page turners, and readers of Spenser are usually turning pages to find the glossary, both Spenser and Rowling use description that is "fantastic" in every sense of the word, employing their own created words to most effectively convey the story they are writing, including "portmanteau words" like his "craples"—"claws" and "grapples" (V.viii.10.4)—and her bevy of mutant words, like "vertitaserum," "remembrall," and the resonant and evocative "Horcrux." Rowling invented both the word and the definition of Horcrux, but four hundred years earlier, Spenser used some very similar magical objects in his own story of the power of virtue over the fear of death.

Ravenclaw's Diadem

Rowling frequently echoes Spenser both through the individual objects in which Voldemort invests his soul-fragments, as well as in the items' behavior. The diadem of Ravenclaw, seemingly discarded amongst the generations of detritus in the Room of Requirement, is one of the least developed of the Horcruxes. Though there are hints of its existence, including its brief cameo appearance when Harry desperately needs to stash his suddenly dangerous potions book and the odd reproduction fashioned by Xenophilius Lovegood, the diadem is the last of the intentionally made Horcruxes to be identified, and the last non-living one to be destroyed. But its provenance, revealed by a ghost, makes it far more interesting than the clunky piece of costume jewelry that Harry actually lays his hands on in *Half-Blood Prince* as he marks the hiding place of his inconvenient book. As Ravenclaw's symbol, it is representative of her storied intelligence, believed to have the power to convey brilliance upon all who wear it. As such, it becomes the object of envy for Ravenclaw's daughter, who steals it to gain her mother's power and is subsequently murdered by her ardent but impetuous admirer, the Bloody Baron. This trail of envy, pride, deceit, and murder is much like the paths followed by some of Spenser's less-than-savory female characters, in particular, the incomparable villainess Duessa and her patroness, Lucifera, mistress of the House of Pride, where entertainment includes a parade of the Seven Deadly Sins.

Though she crops up throughout Spenser's epic, the typical bad girlfriend who won't stay gone, Duessa's real starring moments appear in Book I of *The Faerie Queene* in which she stands in stark contrast to the virtuous Una. Just as her name implies, Duessa is duplicitous, dual in nature. Like Helena Ravenclaw, she wears a crown that is not rightfully hers "like a Persian mitre on her hed/...with crowns and owches garnished" (I.ii.13.4-5). This false crown, along with her fancy clothes and stolen name—Fidessa—is later stripped away to reveal her true, monstrous, and deformed nature. In addition to the crown, Duessa's mount, a many-headed beast, aligns her with the Whore of Babylon from the book of Revelation, but her constant representation of herself as something other than she is—innocent lady, victim of male perfidy, princess—is clearly echoed in the character of The Gray Lady. Helena Ravenclaw, not content with her own gifts, steals her mother's diadem, which may, after all, have been no more than a symbol and not truly capable of providing wisdom any more than Xenophilius Lovegood's contraption with its wrackspurt siphons. Her jealousy of another's state in life suits a person named Helena, like *A Midsummer Night's Dream's* statuesque Athenian maid whose object of affection has left her to become obsessed with her best friend. Yet, the crown also ties Helena Ravenclaw to the far less sympathetic Duessa, who, unlike the Gray Lady, never repents.

This is not to say crowns are only worn by negative characters in Spenser's Faerie Land, as they are often sported by rightful rulers or positive allegorical figures like Charissa (Charity) in the House of Holiness. Like Ravenclaw's diadem, the image of the crown in Spenser is not inherently a negative one, but its appropriation by the envious and the wicked turns a symbol of power and wisdom to a tool that both provokes violence and aids the fallen in the attempt to elude death.

Hufflepuff's Cup

Just as Spenser's use of diadems varies throughout the poem, the golden cups that appear frequently are also presented with different attributes, but are often dangerous, rather like Helga Hufflepuff's two-handled one. The virtuous ladies Fidelia of Book I and Cambina of Book IV both carry golden cups, each of which appears in conjunction with a snake. Fidelia, symbolizing Faith, as her name implies, actually has a snake inside the cup, representing the faith of those impervious to serpents and poison, while peacemaker Cambina's cup contains nepenthe, the mythological anti-depressant, and is accompanied by a snake-festooned caduceus, symbol of

Mercury. Hufflepuff's lost cup is at once a lovely object formerly owned by a good person and later linked with the snakey fellow himself to become more like the vessel that wily Duessa carries: "Then tooke the angrie witch her golden cup/which still she bore, replete with magick artes/Death and despeyre did many thereof sup/ and secret poison through their inner partes" (I.viii.14.1-4). The appropriately named Mordant dies by means of this cup before Duessa loses it, along with her crown.

Duessa's leige, Lucifera, even looks much like the Hufflepuff cup's longtime and ill-fated owner, the ridiculous Hepzibah Smith. Like Lucifera, Hepzibah sits enthroned, gazing at herself in a mirror, while she is waited upon by her servants. The character of Excess also bears a golden cup, into which she squeezes wine until Guyon, the knight of temperance, destroys it. Certainly, the well-fed, well-dressed, and well-made-up Hepzibah is well acquainted with excess. The cup, to the greedy Hepzibah merely a pretty treasure and part of her impressive collection of valuables, becomes, with her death, another of Voldemort's links to the physical life.

Riddle's Diary

In the *Chamber of Secrets*, long before Harry even knows of the existence of Horcruxes which include Riddle's poisonous diary, he is exposed to the dangers of the written word: "'You'd be surprised,' said Ron....' Some of the books the Ministry's confiscated...there was one that burned your eyes out... everyone who read *Sonnets of a Sorcerer* spoke in limericks for the rest of their lives. And some old witch in Bath had a book you could *never stop reading!* You just had to wander around with your nose in it, trying to do everything one-handed" (*Chamber of Secrets* 230-231). In Spenser's Faerie Land, the quaint realm of knights and castles also seems to have no shortage of printing presses, as books, particularly dangerous ones, are everywhere. Spenser was writing religious allegory, so his poem warns frequently against dangerous texts that can lead the unwary astray. A number of these are actually written in blood, a link to Riddle's diary that "bleeds" ink when it "dies" as well as to the vicious detention quill used by the repugnant Delores

Umbridge. *The Faerie Queene*'s evil sorcerer Buisarane, in his torture of the lovely Amoret, who will not yield her affections to his lascivious desires, writes "straunge characters of his art" (III.xii.31.2) in her blood, physically weakening her as he does so. Another of Buisarane's ilk, the treacherous Archimago, also relies upon books of dark magic that most definitely belong in the restricted section.

Some of most dangerous books in the poem are actually used as weapons by the first serious foe confronted by Book I's Redcrosse knight, the knight of Holiness, later St. George. When he corners Errour, the half-snake, half-woman monster, in her den, she tries to strangle him, then attacks him with her vomit, which contains, among other revolting things, "bookes and papers" (I.i.20.6). Like Riddle's diary, these books present both psychological and physical dangers, and are connected with a formidable serpentine monster.

Nagini

On the subject of snakes, the Wizarding World and Faerie Land are in complete agreement. Snakes are not always evil in these texts. The boa constrictor Harry frees from the zoo is a perfectly normal, and fairly friendly, reptile that just doesn't like being caged, and Cambina's caduceus, recognized emblem of the god Mercury, is a positive symbol. In both Harry's world and Spenser's, though, snakes that are not just regular old snakes or time-honored symbols bear careful watching. Errour, she of the appalling book-filled vomit, is a snake/woman, or a variation on the Lamia type. The Lamia, as conflation of Eve and the serpent who beguiled her, is nearly always negative, though Spenser does muddy the waters with a statue of Venus in Book IV, whose feet and legs "together twyned were with a snake" (IV.x. 40.8-9). This snake, however, is devouring its tail, and is thus the Ouroboros, ancient symbol of infinity, not a snake with unnaturally human features, which is always depicted negatively by both authors. Certainly, the Lamia is not unique to Spenser; two of the more well-known literary incarnations are Milton's Sin and Lewis's Green Witch. Errour, though, in contrast to both Milton's and Lewis's snake-ladies, is more snake or monster than human, and there is nothing alluring about her, a reminder that ordinary snakes are far less worrisome than those that have human capabilities, such as talking to humans and persuading them to eat of forbidden fruit. Voldemort's Nagini is just such a snake, far more complex, intelligent, and dangerous than the regular little adders nailed to the door of the Gaunt cottage by Morphin, product of multigenerational inbreeding. Importantly, she is also distinctly female. Gender is not always easily discernible in serpents, but Nagini's sex is clear, making her resemble the Lamia and Errour more than if she had been a mere "it." Femininity also comes into play in her sustaining of Voldemort with her venom, a process specifically referred to as "milking" the snake. The vile Errour also nourishes her noxious offspring with her poison.

Nagini's resemblance to Errour is even more clear when Voldemort's pet takes on the body of Bathilda Bagshot; in one of the most nightmarish moments in all Harry's travails, the massive serpent pours out of the old woman's neck to attack Harry in just the same fashion as Errour attacks Redcrosse, primarily through strangling. Like Errour, Nagini's "words" are dangerous, as she uses Parseltongue in Bathilda's parlor to lure Harry away from Hermione and to communicate with Voldemort. Errour and Nagini also die in exactly the same manner: by having their heads lopped off by untried young men armed with swords. The inexperienced, in-over-his-head, and nearly immobilized Redcrosse, finally freeing one arm, "raft her hatefull heade without remorse" (I.i.24.8). Neville Longbottom, also seemingly frozen by Voldemort's Body Bind spell, breaks free to draw the sword of Gryffindor from the flaming Sorting Hat and beheads Nagini in one fell swoop. Infested by Voldemort, Nagini is enough human to be far more dangerous than a mere snake. Harry, in his innate revulsion toward his "inner snake" that is the Horcrux within him, knows instinctively that there is something perverse about the human/snake blend.

The other truly terrible snake of the Hogwarts adventures, the Basilisk, though not a Horcrux itself, is

summoned via the Horcrux diary. Just as Errour regurgitates
dangerous books, the diary, a very dangerous book, brings forth
the king of serpents, which, like Spenser's villain Geryoneo's
hideous monster in Book V, lives under a statue to a revered
forerunner. Geryoneo's creature is a fearsome combination of
dog, lion, dragon, and eagle, rather than just a really big snake,
but its perverse nature is much like that of a basilisk, supposedly
created from a chicken's egg hatched by a toad. Spenser makes
the comparison between Geryoneo's strange mutant and the
Sphinx: who kills herself when Oedipus, as Spenser relates, "had
red her Riddle" (capital R in the original Spenser) (V.xi.27.5).
Riddle's snake, the basilisk, also preys upon children, as does
Geryoneo's monster, and the two creatures both appear from
hidden chambers under great idols: Geryoneo's to his ancestor,
and Slytherin's to himself. Both these creatures are killed by a
sword-wielding champion, though Rowling's description of
the basilisk's undoing is far less graphic than Spenser's, for the
benefit of younger readers (and their parents).

Peverell Ring

One of the items in Spenser's massive poem that shows
the strongest connection to the Horcruxes is actually not original
to Spenser. Just like later writers, Spenser drew upon earlier
texts in the creation of his own secondary world. One writer
whom Spenser credits frequently is "Dan Geoffery" or Chaucer,
who, in his Squire's Tale, features a remarkable ring that allows
the princess Canacee to understand the language of birds. In
Spenser's hands, Canacee is a far more complex character and
her ring has much more interesting powers than serving as an
avian universal translator. It can heal any wound, to the point
of bringing the wearer back from the dead with its "power
to staunch al wounds, that mortally did bleed" (IV.ii.39.9).
Canacee bestows this wondrous ring upon her brother Cambell
who subsequently stymies all his opponents by recovering from
the most grievous of injuries in hand-to-hand combat with the
many contenders for the hand of Canacee. It is, specifically, the
stone in this ring that holds the miraculous power, so that when

Cambell is actually dead on the field, he pops up again to fight just as his sister begins to bewail his death. There is a clear parallel with the stone in the Peverell family ring, treasured by the repugnant Marvolo Gaunt and turned by his grandson, Tom Riddle, into one of his Horcruxes. Neither of them realizes that the stone is the second of the Deathly Hallows, the Resurrection Stone which Harry uses to summon his parents, Sirius Black, and Remus Lupin to accompany him on his fateful walk into the Forbidden Forest to confront Voldemort. Though Harry uses the Stone for a good purpose, to strengthen him as he willingly goes to his presumed death, the original owner of the stone learned, to his grief, that the dead do not truly come back. Even Dumbledore, in his haste to see and apologize to his lost family, falls prey to the curse that lies on the ring after it has become a Horcrux.

Cambell also discovers that his powerful ring is not the answer to all his problems. He is only stopped in his wholesale slaughter of his sister's would-be-suitors by the youngest of three brothers whose mother has made a deal with the Fates so that as each one of them dies, his strength and spirit travel to the next brother still living. After the first two brothers fall to Cambell and his unstoppable ability to resurrect via the magical stone in his ring, the third brother, Triamond, with "two lives to spare" thanks to his fallen brethren, fights Cambell to a draw. The two are finally separated by the arrival of Triamond's healing sister Cambina and her cup of nepenthe; this "happy juice" makes the two mortal foes suddenly best friends, and sets up a nice double wedding arrangement: Triamond and Canacee live happily ever after, as do Cambell and Cambina. The Three Brothers motif is certainly one that crops up in hundreds of folk and fairy tales from around the world, almost universally making the youngest brother the one who comes out on top. Yet it is interesting to see it linked up with the Resurrection Stone that, like the one Harry drops in the forest, is pretty much dropped from the story by Spenser; it doesn't come up again in the poem.

Slytherin's Locket

The most fascinating link between the Horcruxes and Spenser is undoubtedly found in the contents of Slytherin's locket. Although there are no prominent lockets in Faerie Land, the torturous vision endured by Ron Weasley in his quest to destroy the Horcrux is almost identical to the experiences of the Redcrosse Knight in Book I of *The Faerie Queene*. When Ron, just returned from his self-imposed separation from Harry and Hermione, pulls Harry and the sword of Gryffindor from the bottom of the forest pool, Harry knows that Ron is the one who should use the sword to destroy the locket containing one fragment of Lord Voldemort's shattered soul. It is thus Ron who is attacked by the piece of the Dark Lord living in the heirloom of Slytherin.

Just as the chain of the locket has tried to strangle Harry and destroy him physically, the contents of the locket try to prevent the destruction threatened by Ron and that very big sword by attacking him psychologically. After mentioning some of Ron's deepest anxieties, including the fear that he was unwanted by a mother trying for a daughter after five boys, the spirit in the Horcrux produces distorted shapes of Harry and Hermione who scoff at Ron, claiming both that Ron's mother would prefer Harry as a son and that Hermione desires Harry sexually : "Riddle-Hermione…stretched like a snake and entwined herself around Riddle-Harry, wrapping him in a close embrace. Their lips met" (*Deathly Hallows* 377). It is a critical moment for Ron. For just a moment, "a trace of scarlet" glimmers in his eyes, but, just as it seems he will give in to the croon of temptation, he strikes with the sword of Gryffindor and destroys the Horcrux that has been the hardest sought. In this moment of transformation, Ron takes shape as a far more developed and strong individual, playing the leader much more frequently over the subsequent months. One of the most memorable scenes of the entire series, this moment is nearly identical to the agonizing experience of the Redcrosse Knight at the cottage of the devious wizard Archimago, and shows that, in this instance, Ron succeeds where the paragon of Holiness and knight of Queen Gloriana fails.

Fresh from his defeat of the monster Errour, Redcrosse and Una, the lady who has sought his aid to destroy the dragon plaguing her parents' kingdom, seek shelter with an old man who seems to be a harmless hermit. In fact, he is a wicked sorcerer who calls up legions of sprites and tempting dreams to beguile, distract, and ultimately separate his "guests" from each other and derail the noble quest upon which Redcrosse is embarked. The hermit's cottage, set in a maze-like forest, like the winding chase Harry is led by the silver doe, is beside a "christall streame" (I.i.34.8) just as the clearing in the Forest of Dean includes the critical frozen pond with its icy surface over the crystal-clear water that contains the sword of Gryffindor.

While one sprite inflicts upon Redcrosse lustful dreams sent straight from Morpheus, the dream god himself, another sprite, which Archimago has fashioned into a twin of the white-garbed and black–veiled Una, cuddles up to Redcrosse and attempts to seduce him. This coy behavior, so completely out of character for the Lady who represents purity and unity, alarms Redcrosse, despite his wanton dreams. Rather than realizing that mischief is afoot, he assumes Una is what Ron would call a "scarlet woman"; though he nearly kills her, he finally gets her to leave, still assuming that she is the real Una.

Archimago then puts the second part of his plan in action. Since he cannot tempt Redcrosse to dally with Una's double and defile the Holiness he represents, the meddling sorcerer shapes another sprite into a "young Squire, in loues and lusty hed/His wanton daies that euer loosely led" (I.ii.3.4-5), then cozies this creation up with the false lady and runs to Redcrosse to give him the bad news that "wicked wights/Haue knit themselves in Venus shameful chaine" (I.ii.4.7-8). When Redcrosse awakens, he is subjected to a vision almost identical to that endured by Ron: the image of the girl he loves in someone else's arms while he stands there stunned "with sword in hand" (I.ii.5.2). Interestingly, both Ron and Redcrosse have been set up for these external scenes by internal prodding. Ron recognizes that the locket affects him more than it does the others, bringing out the worst in him as it ticks away near his heart; Redcrosse, his head full of naughty dreams, is doubly damaged by what he sees with his waking eye, though perhaps slightly less devastating, as he sees "Una" "In wanton lust and leud embracement"(I.ii.5.5) not with his best mate, but with a stranger.

Then again, as Ron appears to have long worried that Hermione's heart is with Harry and Redcrosse is completely blind-sided by the sight of the "false couple" (I.ii.5.4), perhaps the two young men are equally hurt by their excruciating visions, each created by a Dark wizard from nothingness but wielding complete power over these two unlikely champions. Though destined to be St. George, Redcrosse, wearing old armor whose dents he has not earned, is a barely tested knight with little more experience and power than Ron, the wandering friend who carries a noble sword that is not his own. In his moment of redemption, Ron strikes the locket, and the vision he has suffered vanishes, but Redcrosse, who has not yet completed his journey toward Holiness, is wholeheartedly immersed in the terrible vision of the false Una. After barely being restrained by Archimago from visiting violence upon the seeming lovers, the troubled knight flees from his quest and his true lady, who lies slumbering unawares; he subsequently falls in with the real femme fatale, Duessa, nearly gets clobbered in a tourney at the House of Pride, has a run-in with the giant Orgoglio, and even continues to flounder after the ever-loyal Una brings in the cavalry to save the day, in the person of Prince Arthur. Ron, who succeeds against the same kind of vision that stymies Redcrosse, is reunited with his best friend. After she finishes glowering at him, he gains the girl of his dreams as well, who, like Una, is truly faithful, having been destined for Ron practically since the day she dusted off his nose on the *Hogwarts Express* six years earlier.

Though Ron's painful vision is drawn straight from his deepest fears, he defeats the false image cast up by the Horcrux, setting off a chain of Horcrux smashings and slashings, in which Harry's colleagues, like the bevy of Spenser's knights with their individual victories, each take on the task of annihilating the links Voldemort has created to his mortal existence. While Harry destroys the diary when he is only thirteen and Dumbledore's eradication of the spell on the Resurrection Stone took place before Harry even knew about the Horcruxes, Ron's destruction of the locket leads, in fairly rapid succession, to the elimination of the other Horcruxes, each by a different person: Hermione takes the cup of Helga Hufflepuff; Neville dispatches Nagini; and the credit for the diadem's melting could go to Luna, who leads Harry to the diadem as the possible relic of Ravenclaw's; or the Gray Lady, who gives Harry vital information that takes him back to the piles of lost items in the Room of Requirement; or even to Draco Malfoy's crony Crabbe, who sets off the Fiendfyre that actually defeats the diadem Horcrux. Harry then destroys the final Horcrux by offering himself up for the slaughter and taking the Avada Kedavra curse that effectively separates the bit of Voldemort's soul from his own.

Facing Death

It is in fearlessly facing death that Harry embraces a truth central to both Rowling's seven-book story and Spenser's six books and spare cantos. In all these connections between the Horcruxes and the knights of Gloriana, Spenser and Rowling are not merely overlapping in a few interesting objects and a very compelling vision. These stories also overlap in their concerted reminder that taking unnatural means to avoid death is a sure path to spiritual destruction. The pagan warrior Sansjoy (part of a set, including Sansloy and Sansfoy, perhaps a distant ancestor of Draco's) is felled by Redcrosse in single combat for the favor of the devious Duessa and for the prize of the slain Sansfoy's shield. As part of her scheme, Duessa appears to be elated at Redcrosse's victory but conceals the swooning Sarazin Sanjoy, and after getting Redcrosse off to recover from his injuries, travels, with the help of the personified old hag Night, to the Underworld to beg legendary healer Aesculapius for Sansjoy's restoration. Aesculapius has actually been condemned to Hades by Jove for violating the laws of life and death by bringing back the dead. Since Duessa convinces him that things can't get any worse for him, Aesculapius works his magic on Sansjoy and brings him back to life.

Clearly, this sort of behavior is depicted in Spenser as negative. Though his virtuous knights do sometimes recover from grievous wounds, as Redcrosse does twice during his epic battle with the dragon that is the grand finale of Book I, these knights are restored through positive means, not by consorting with the powers of darkness, and they are restored not to continue mortal existence at any cost, but to do the jobs they have been assigned. The well of life, which saves Redcrosse after his first round with the dragon, has the power to both spiritually and physically revive the knight, while Una prays fervently for him. After round two, he falls in the shade of the tree of life, the balm of which also restores him to health while Una once again keeps prayerful vigil over him, and then he rises to complete his destined defeat of the monstrous dragon. Redcrosse's reprieves from death are in stark contrast to the selfish and negative death evasion ploys Duessa uses for Sansjoy. In like fashion, positive means are used to achieve Harry's return from the dead. Harry does not die from the fatal curse, but returns, both physically and spiritually renewed, to continue the work only he can do. In contrast, Voldemort seeks to prolong his mortal existence by any means, regardless of the terrible price he must pay to do so; for him, committing murder and tearing his soul is no more troubling than is Duessa's trip to Hell for her.

Sansjoy is just one of many negative characters tinkering with death throughout the poem. Positive characters, knowing their own mortality, are not distressed to know they will someday die, so they can face visions of their futures and their descendants with resolution rather than dread. Some negative creatures like Malegar "cold and drery as a Snake" (II.xi.22.4) are spiritually dead but cannot be killed by normal means, reminding the readers that the abstract concepts represented by these individuals (in Malegar's case, melancholy) cannot always be defeated by physical means. Like Rowling's dementors, these figures are terrifying because they are a real threat, not just to the body, but to the mind. The very formidable person of Despaire uses a variety of ploys to make individuals kill themselves. Like the dementors who suck all the happiness out of a room, Despaire plays on the weaknesses of those who come within his sphere, and provides them with the necessary weapons for self-murder, including a rusty knife that, along with his long tangled hair, makes Despaire look very much like the figure of Morphin Gaunt. Despaire tries to convince Redcrosse that all his failings should make him want to die, or, as Voldemort would say "bow to death " (*Goblet of Fire* 660), but Redcrosse makes an important reply, attesting that humans should not use unholy means to either evade or seek death: "The terme of life is limited/Ne may a man prolong, nor shorten it" (I.ix.41.2-3). Redcrosse is still nearly lost in Despaire's labyrinthine arguments until Una brings him to his senses, reminding him that instead of wallowing in his own failings, he must seek to accomplish the task set before him. Having lost his victim, Despaire actually destroys himself.

Both Rowling and Spenser make clear that one should not fear life and its inherent failings so much that one leaves the stage of mortal existence prematurely like Merope Gaunt Riddle, nor should one prolong physical life at the cost of one's soul, as her son does. These reminders appear repeatedly through Spenser's epic and Rowling's; Redcrosse undergoes physical discipline to strengthen his spiritual man in the House of Holiness, while the Pagan knights like Sansjoy have only physical existence, and the giant Orgoglio actually vanishes in a puff of wind when his mortal form is struck a fatal blow. In like manner, Harry, having suffered mightily, to the point of giving up his physical existence, appears whole, even without the need for his glasses, in the place that seems to him to be King's Cross Station. The spiritually strong gain the strength to face death, to even return from it as stronger individuals, but the weak of soul cannot survive without the body, and therefore lose both body and soul in the attempt to gain immortality. Thus, Rowling and Spenser echo the words of Christ in Matthew 10: "Do not be afraid of those who kill the body but cannot kill the soul…" and "Whoever finds his life will lose it, but whoever loses his life for my sake will find it" (28, 39, NIV). In their knowledge that who they are is more than body, and that life is more than a pulse, both Harry and Spenser's protagonists have invested their very selves in something far more durable than a book, a pet, or a piece of jewelry.

It is unlikely that everyone who has been enchanted by Harry's trials and victories will immediately turn to Spenser for the next item in the reading queue, yet seeing these two authors, very different in tone, style, and readability, present the same warning, often using the same tools, is intriguing. Rowling has not only woven a tale that brings together the same sorts of crowns, cups, books, snakes, rings, and visions of jealousy as Spenser uses; she does it for the same reason, to tell us what Dumbledore tells Harry in that critical "King's Cross" chapter of *Deathly Hallows*. [T]he true master [of death] does not seek to run away from Death. He accepts that he must die, and understands that there are far, far worse things in the living world than dying" (721). That truth apparently applies to the world of Faerie Land just as it does to ours.

Works Cited

Lewis, C.S. *Studies in Medieval and Renaissance Literature*. Cambridge: Cambridge University Press, 2000.

Rowling, J.K. *Harry Potter and the Chamber of Secrets*. New York: Scholastic, 1999.

___. *Harry Potter and the Deathly Hallows*. New York: Scholastic, 2007.

—. *Harry Potter and the Goblet of Fire*. New York: Scholastic, 2000.

—. *Harry Potter and the Half-Blood Prince*. New York: Scholastic, 2005.

—. *Harry Potter and the Order of the Phoenix*. New York: Scholastic, 2003.

—. *Harry Potter and the Prisoner of Azkaban*. New York: Scholastic, 1999.

—. *Harry Potter and the Sorcerer's Stone*. New York: Scholastic, 1999.

Spenser, Edmund. *The Faerie Queene*. A.C. Hamilton, ed. London, Pearson: 2001.

'Just Behind the Veil'
Death in Harry Potter and in the Fairytales of George MacDonald

John Patrick Pazdziora

It was only when he had attained a great age that the youngest brother finally took off the Cloak of Invisibility and gave it to his son. And then he greeted Death as an old friend, and went with him gladly, and, as equals, they departed this life.[1]

I was dead, and right content.[2]

T HE DEFINING ENCOUNTER OF Harry Potter's life is with a fairy tale. Throughout *Harry Potter and the Deathly Hallow* (2007), Harry circles round the tale of 'The Three Brothers and Death.' It is the story of an uncrossable river and the three clever wizards who conjure a bridge to cross it. But Death waits on the other side, pretending to be amused.[3]

---

1. J. K. Rowling, *Harry Potter and the Deathly Hallows* (London: Bloomsbury, 2007), 332. Referenced as DH hereafter.

2. George MacDonald, *Phantastes*, 1852 (Grand Rapids: Eerdmans, 1994), 143.

3. DH, 330-332.

The tale tells of the marvellous gifts Death gives the brothers—the Deathly Hallows. These gifts can be read as a reflection of the ways people in Harry's life relate to death and mortality. Some, like Voldemort and Fudge, choose the way of the Elder Wand, seeking the power to destroy and enslave death. Others, like Dumbledore and Snape, choose the way of the Resurrection Stone, living life constantly facing their bereavement, haunted by the echoes of loved ones who have died. And a few—a very few—Hermione, maybe, and Dobby—live under the Invisibility Cloak, choosing life and living each moment as it arrives, even though they know that someday death will find them.

But, really, most of the characters, including Harry, are torn between the tensions and temptations of each option. The tale itself hints that the one who possesses all three Hallows will be 'Master of Death.'[4] It's the balance between all three ways that creates a truly liveable death.

J. K. Rowling, of course, is not the first children's writer to discuss questions of death and mortality in her stories. A reading of the *Harry Potter* series alongside the fantasies of George MacDonald (1824–1905) reveals startling thematic convergences. Both were unafraid to address difficult, even painful, elements of life in their stories. Rowling and MacDonald present a contemplative depiction of death that draws the reader's gaze through itself into a creative space to confront the struggle and the reconciliation of death.

This essay will examine that description, using the three Hallows as a framework. I will first discuss immortality as temptation, the escape from death as a denial of humanity that leads ultimately to inhumanity. I will give particular consideration to Lord Voldemort and Watho, the witch-werewolf in MacDonald's "The History of Photogen and Nycertis" (1878). Second, I will discuss mortality as a quest, a . estination rather than a destiny. I will examine in some detail the peregrine nature of mortality revealed in Harry Potter's return to Godric's Hollow, and in "The Wow o' Rivven" (1864), assessing how these contemplations of a church graveyard lead the characters into harmony with mortality. Lastly, I will discuss

---

4   DH, 332-333.

death as heroism, a chivalric act of liberation. A comparison of the heroic deaths of Dobby and Anodos (*Phantastes*, 1852) will lead to a discussion of Harry's own death, and differing presentations of afterlife.[5]

The Elder Wand: Immortality as Temptation

Professor Tolkien wrote that escape from death is one of the chief aims of the fairy tale. These tales, he argued, encompass an innate human longing for immortality.[6] A quick glance at misreading of this idea may suggest that whoever pursues immortality is thus the hero of the fairy tale. If, after all, these tales help us cope with death, shouldn't the hero be someone who escapes it? Yet MacDonald and Rowling alike realised the guile of that suggestion.

The first of the Deathly Hallows, the Elder Wand, had the distinction of being the most powerful and deadly wand ever wielded by witch or wizard. The first brother, on asking for the wand, thought that through its unrivalled power, he would be stronger than Death itself. But he didn't have the Elder Wand for more than a day before an envious wizard cut his throat and stole the wand.[7] Posturing yourself as stronger than death and trying to claim immortality by force, the tale cautions, is no escape. It's just another way to die.

That 'escape from death'—immortality—is the aim of the fairy tale is quite true. But the laws of the Perilous Realm are subtle and more powerful. The elixir that should bring eternal youth may instead bring eternal old age if pursued wrongly. The most dangerous and evil characters are those who pursue immortality by running straight at it.

---

5. Any such study, looking at a significant theme across two sprawling bodies of work, must necessarily be selective. Many fans of Rowling and MacDonald—myself included—may be disappointed at finding I have not addressed their favourite bits in the stories. But I have tried to address the most important moments, leaping from one mountaintop to the other, and hopefully any omissions I make will encourage further study.
6. J. R. R. Tolkien, "On Fairy-stories," in *The Tolkien Reader* (New York: Ballantine, 1966), 85.
7. DH, 330-333. So for all further references to the tale.

Voldemort

Lord Voldemort has spent his life escaping death. As a young man, he was willing to murder and invoke the darkest of dark magic if it might make it harder for him to die. Rowling describes his longing for knowledge about Horcruxes as 'hunger'; when he manages to flatter that knowledge out of the indulgent Professor Slughorn, his face is 'full of [...] wild happiness [...] that did not enhance his handsome features, but made them, somehow, less human...'[8] His desire to attain immortality through his own means begins a process of dehumanization. As he makes the Horcruxes, tearing his soul into fragments, he recedes from the dashing, beautiful body of Tom Riddle into the skeletal, snake-like body of Lord Voldemort.[9]

When Voldemort reincarnates from his death-like state, he boasts, 'I have never died.'[10] His body was destroyed, but the fragment of soul within retained a sort of existence. He admits, 'What I was, I do not know...I, who have gone further than anybody along the path that leads to immortality,' but insists vehemently that 'I was alive.'[11] It was, he claims, the success of his dark experiments that saved him from the rebounded killing curse. He seems unconcerned that he did not have any sort of human life. At most, he was a disembodied malevolence, capable of petty dark magic and memory. 'But,' he adds, 'I was willing to embrace mortal life again, before chasing immortal,' to resume, as it were, his journey at a closer point along the

---

8.   J. K. Rowling, *Harry Potter and the Half-Blood Prince* (London: Bloomsbury, 1995), 466. Referenced as HBP hereafter.

9.   To this extent, the Horcruxes appear to be somewhat symbiotic. The fragment of Voldemort's soul they house gives these non-human, nonorganic objects a degree of life—heartbeat, sentience, individuality (DH, 227, 305-307, et al.). But in turn, they imbue the human Voldemort with their non-humanity. The act of putting part of his human soul into a nonhuman container makes him less human. Cf. Travis Prinzi, *Harry Potter and Imagination* (Allenton, PA: Zossima Press, 2008), 74.

10.   J. K. Rowling, *Harry Potter and the Goblet of Fire* (London: Bloomsbury, 2000), 575. Referenced as GoF hereafter.

11.   GoF, 566.

path.[12]

On a personal level, it is true that Voldemort fears death—as Dumbledore repeatedly insists—and that much of his thinking is shaped through a phobic loathing of physical pain.[13] But this does little to explain his lifelong success as a charismatic leader and a skilled manipulator. Voldemort was no academic studying anti-death potions in libraries, but rather the most powerful political leader of his time. How did his pursuit of immortality transform itself into dictatorship? Why does a highly individualized, self-centred wizard in pursuit of personal survival even bother with the bureaucracy of totalitarian domination?

In a scene evoking Dickens's *Oliver Twist*, Voldemort's mother dies just hours after giving birth.[14] Voldemort's earliest awareness of personal relationship was grief and loss. Markell and Markell have discussed how the death of a loved one creates a sense of alienation in children. The grieving process—or lack thereof—becomes one of the most significant influences on their developing personalities.[15] Voldemort's overriding memory of his mother, shaped through his repressed grief, was one of weakness. She was weak enough to die, to leave him.[16] At the same time, he was discovering his own exceptional power as a wizard, in particular the power to inflict pain on people who hurt him.[17] These two deeply formative processes joined with his fear of death to both fuel and legitimize his pursuit of immortality. His struggle to reconcile the relationship of his powerful, living self with his weak, dead mother forged his view of the world.

It seems that in an attempt to rationalize loss without grief, Voldemort developed an ideology that would guide the

---

12. GoF, 569.

13. Prinzi, 158.

14. HBP, 249.

15. Kathryn A. Markell and Marc A. Markell, *The Children Who Lived: Using Harry Potter and Other Fictional Characters to Help Grieving Children and Adolescents* (New York: Routledge, 2008), 2, 6.

16. HBP, 257.

17. HBP, 254.

course of his life. It is stated most succinctly in the words of his slave, the half-possessed Professor Quirrell. 'There is no good and evil, there is only power, and those too weak to seek it.'[18] Voldemort embraced an ethic of power. He viewed life as a continuum of striving. On the bottom cluttered the weak, the powerless. On the top, there was room for one individual with absolute strength, utter power. But no matter how much an individual fought to reach the top, death reduced him to the lowest point of weakness. The greatest, most coveted power, then, was power over death. Death is weakness. Immortality is power.

This understanding also explains Voldemort's use of a pure-blood agenda with Nazi-like race laws, and his alliances with giants, dementors, and powerful half-blood wizards like Severus Snape. Voldemort seems to have quickly realized that pure-blood propaganda was an effective way to gather supporters, giving him power over them, and terrify opponents, giving him a different but equally effective form of power. It is doubtful whether the half-blooded Voldemort even believed the myths of pure-blood superiority he relentlessly propagated. Under his ideology, the central question would not have been bloodedness, but weakness. Non-magic users were weak. Segregated societies were weak. Devoted slaves were, in another fashion, weak. Weakness was easily manipulated. By inserting the fury of racial hatred into the wizarding community, Voldemort weakened everyone around him and increased his own power.

His experimentation with immortality and his political reign of terror stemmed from the same ideology. They were equal expressions of his search for power. He used both to prove to himself that he was not like his distorted lack of memory of his mother. He was not weak. He would not die. According to his ethic of power, he—and he only—was right.

---

18.   J. K. Rowling, *Harry Potter and the Philosopher's Stone* (London: Bloomsbury, 1997), 211.

Watho

Before Rowling created this evil wizard, however, MacDonald had created an evil witch. Watho's characterization is complex and in some ways surprising for a fairy tale villain. As Rowling does with Voldemort, MacDonald tells portions of the tale from Watho's perspective. From the beginning of the tale, the narrator is clear about the source of Watho's evil:

> There once was a witch who desired to know everything. But the wiser a witch is, the harder she knocks her head against the wall when she comes to it. Her name was Watho, and she had a wolf in her mind. She cared for nothing in itself—only the knowing of it. She was not naturally cruel, but the wolf had made her cruel.[19]

It is tempting at this point to rush out the proverb that 'Knowledge is Power,' and declare Watho and Voldemort partners in the same pursuit. But there is no support of such a conclusion in the text itself. Monika Hilder is correct in saying that Watho 'represents the rationalistic, scientific quest for knowledge as the ultimate good.'[20] Where Voldemort is an ideologue, Watho is a scientist, pure and simple. She is not interested in power, or even directly in immortality *per se*. She wants 'to know everything'; her pursuit is knowledge for its own sake.

This desire starts in her a process of beastward mobility. There is 'a wolf in her mind' that makes her cruel. MacDonald is overtly invoking the Red Riding Hood tale and the archetype of the Big Bad Wolf. William Raeper reports that, in an early draft, Watho 'slits open a pregnant woman while she is asleep in order to peer at the workings of the growing embryo.'[21] In a

---

19. George MacDonald, "The History of Photogen and Nycteris: A Day and Night Märchen," in *Stephen Archer and Other Tales*, 1883 (Whitehorn, CA: Johanessen, 2003), 77.

20. Monika B. Hilder, "Educating the Moral Imagination: The Fantasy Literature of George MacDonald, C. S. Lewis, and Madeline L'Engle" (PhD, Simon Fraser University, 2003), 49.

21. William Raeper, *George MacDonald* (Tring, UK: Lion, 1987), 316.

grotesque inversion of the Riding Hood tale, the wolf cuts open the belly of the mother to devour the child.[22] What should have been a salvific act of violence—the woodsman disembowelling the wolf—becomes instead rapacious, destructive. Watho's lust for knowledge is such that she will dissect a living person to pursue it.

Wolf-like, Watho preys on children. Her experiment in this tale is a clinical attempt at mothering. Stealing two children—a boy and a girl—from their mothers, she has them raised in highly specialized environments. The boy, Photogen, is never permitted to see darkness, and spends his days hunting in sunlight. The girl, Nycertis, is never permitted to see light, spending her childhood in a dim-lit mausoleum. Watho's goal, apparently, is to create two idealized gender-types—the strong, capable male and the weak, shrinking female.[23]

The tale centres on the conflict of reason and imagination, and deals with subjects such as gender relations, sexuality, mystical knowledge, and puberty. When the children—now teenagers—begin to express individuality, each discovering dark, light, and each other, Watho's clinical maternity turns to loathing. Photogen in particular was meant to embody near-transcendent virility. When, in a boyish attempt to show off for Nycertis, he braves the night to prove his manhood, the terror he encounters destroys his health. Watho is furious.

And because he was *her* failure, she was annoyed with him, began to dislike him, grew to hate him. She looked on him as

---

22. This also echoes the biblical depiction of Satan's war against the Kingdom of God; see Revelation 12.

23. Cf. Björn Sundmark, "Travelling Beastward: An Ecocritical Reading of George MacDonald's Fairy Tales," *North Wind* 27 (2008), 12. Sundmark, however, seems to miss this distinct gendering process in his analysis. The subjects he correctly lists as being severed seem to be subcategories of the greater polarization of masculinity and femininity. It is the pursuit of these Platonic ideals—informed by very Victorian gender stereotypes, particularly the patriarchal attitude denying girls good education—that inspires Watho's experiment.

a painter might upon a picture, or a poet upon a poem, which he had only succeeded in getting into an irrecoverable mess.[24]

Watho has lost the ability to see people. She sees only subjects. She is the ideal objectivist, utterly detached from the world, broken in complete dichotomy with everything she observes. Parker J. Palmer has cautioned that this sort of dichotomy between knower and known can lead to an obsession with knowledge that victimizes and destroys both.[25] It is precisely into this peril that Watho has fallen.

With her initial experiment ruined, she sets out upon another—the exploration of pain. She locks Photogen in total darkness, and tortures him with one of his own arrows. It is at this point, when Watho condemns her subject for weakness, that her resemblance to Voldemort becomes uncanny. 'She told [Photogen] she hated him like a serpent, and hissed like one as she said it, looking very sharp in the nose and chin, and flat in the forehead.'[26] Earlier, she is described as having 'white skin,' and eyes that 'had a red fire in them.'[27] Even before her gratuitous cruelty, her scientific detachment had begun dehumanizing her. Her humanity, like Voldemort's, vanishes the further she separates herself from others.

What about immortality, the great lust of Voldemort? How does that factor in Watho's scientific quest? Hilder suggests that Watho's 'dehumanizing wolf' is 'science,' a system of thought that severs intellectual and imaginative knowing.[28] But this explanation is by itself unsatisfactory. Even in the opening paragraph, MacDonald has distinguished between Watho's desire 'to know everything' and the 'wolf in her mind.'[29] The desire for knowledge, it seems, is not evil in itself: 'she was not naturally cruel,' just curious. But 'the wolf had made her cruel.' She was willing to separate herself from the rest of humanity—

24. MacDonald, "History", 129; emphasis in original.
25. Parker J. Palmer, *To Know as we are Known* (New York: Harper Collins, 1993), 6-8.
26. MacDonald, "History", 129.
27. MacDonald, "History", 79.
28. Hilder, 49.
29. MacDonald, "History", 77.

witches or otherwise—to test her curiosity.

In a telling passage, Watho performs her only use of magic in the tale, becoming a werewolf to pursue Photogen and Nycertis, who have understandably run away. MacDonald writes, 'The foolish witch had made herself invulnerable, as she supposed.' That is, through invoking the wolf she has separated herself from the deepest facet of human identity: mortality. In order to seek pure knowledge, she has attempted to make herself invulnerable to death and pain, accomplishing the very goal of Voldemort. It is not too far-fetched to describe Watho's inner wolf as a sort of Horcrux, a severing of her soul from her humanity, a willingness to inhabit some other form to enable her own survival.[30] Her destruction suggests Voldemort's; she has unwittingly connected herself to another person: 'to torment Photogen therewith, she had handled one of his arrows.'[31] This arrow—her only physical connection to anyone else—kills both her and her wolf.

The temptation of immortality is to pursue it as an object to be mastered and use it as a means to an end. Voldemort's ethic of power drove him to seek immortality as the highest state of power. Watho's warped scientific enquiry made her seize immortality as the ultimate objective detachment from a degenerating world. Succumbing to this temptation cost them their humanity and their existence.

In the end, both Watho and Voldemort appear as broken individuals. MacDonald says of Watho that 'she was straight and strong, but now and then would fall bent together, shudder, and sit for a moment with her head turned over her shoulder, as if the wolf had got out of her mind on to her back.'[32] And, in one of the most haunting moments of the Harry Potter series, 'Tom Riddle hit the floor with a mundane finality, his body feeble and shrunken, the white hands empty, the snake-like face

---

30. Note that MacDonald is quite clear that Watho volitionally transforms herself into a werewolf through a combination of magic and science; in this tale, at least, MacDonald's werewolves, unlike Rowling's, are not victims and do not deserve pity. "History," 143.

31. MacDonald, "History," 145.

32. MacDonald, "History," 77.

vacant and unknowing.'[33] Voldemort and Watho are left broken, wounded people—as needy for love and relationship as they are arrogant of their abilities. In succumbing to the temptation of immortality, in rejecting the deathly union with all other living things to attain otherwise unattainable knowledge, they become empty.

The Resurrection Stone: Mortality as Quest

If the Elder Wand cannot overmaster Death, then perhaps the Resurrection Stone can reverse it. So thought the second brother, at any rate. His Hallow brings the dead back to the living—but not to life. He brings up the shade of a girl he loved, but even with the presence of her shade, they are still separated by death. The unceasing grief drives him mad, and he takes his own life. [34] Even if we can recall the dead, the tale says, we cannot cease from weeping. The struggle is not one of conquering death but learning how to live with it.

The power and peril of the Resurrection Stone is the immediacy of its confrontation with grief. If it is used to deny loss, as the second brother and Dumbledore do, its power is destructive. But if it is used to accept and understand loss, as Harry does when facing his own death, then it truly becomes a resurrection, restoring life and hope not just to the shades of those already dead, but to the living—or dying—as well. This hallow can destroy, true, but it can also effect a reconciliation with death.

Although direct pursuit of immortality is a temptation that leads to self-destruction, the fact remains that the greatest impetus of the fairy story is escape from death; the greatest hope of the human heart is survival. Yet if immortality cannot be pursued directly, how can it be found at all?

A cryptic answer to this question appears in MacDonald's tale-within-a-tale of Cosmo von Werhstahl, as Anodos, the ostensible protagonist of *Phantastes*, reads it in the enchanted

33. DH, 596.

34. A fascinating study could be done comparing this account of the Resurrection Stone with MacDonald's ballad, "Sir Aglovaile through the churchyard rode," *Phantastes*, 130-134.

library: 'Who live, he dies; who dies, he is alive.'[35] It is unclear who speaks these words. There is a suggestion that they may have been sung, or they may signify a chapter break in the tale-within-a-tale.[36] Anodos gives the most probable explanation as he describes his reading of the tale: 'I seemed to have a kind of double consciousness, and the story a double meaning.'[37] The overt meaning, he says with deceptive simplicity, is a story about true love. Yet the second meaning—the mirrored message of the tale, if you will—seems to be this cryptic statement. The heart of the fairy tale, then, is that one can only discover life by embracing death.

Stephen Prickett has addressed some of the unsettling aspects of MacDonald's handling of death. 'Death for MacDonald,' he writes, '[...] is not the end of thing, but, as it were, a misplaced beginning.'[38] Death in these stories is a sort of 'reversed sacrament', he argues.[39] Death itself becomes merely 'the symbol for the greater reality of human dependence on God'—it is reduced to transcendent metaphor.[40]

If death is a sacrament, then mortality—the gradual process of approaching death—becomes a sort of liturgy, a preparation to encounter the sacred symbol correctly. Travis

---

35. MacDonald, *Phantastes*, 95.

36. The words are formatted on the page in the same way as Cosmo's song, 'I shall die for the love of the maiden' (94). Yet, even aside from the words' seeming irrelevance to everything that's gone before, it seems utterly out of character for Cosmo to be expressing these concepts at this point in the story. MacDonald begins each chapter in *Phantastes* with a series of quotations, so this supposed song lyric could be serving that function within the tale. Whatever the case, these words change the tenor of the tale remarkably, shifting the reader's awareness of story-within-story and speaking in the metafictional voice of the storyteller. Further elaboration of this singularly disturbing storytelling technique is regrettably beyond the scope of this study.

37. MacDonald, *Phantastes*, 84.

38. Stephen Prickett, *Victorian Fantasy*, Second Edition (Waco, TX: Baylor University Press, 2005), 200.

39. Prickett, 201.

40. Prickett, 201.

Prinzi has demonstrated at some length the significance the liturgical church calendar plays in the Harry Potter series.[41] But in pursuing the 'double meaning' of these stories, we will look not just as the calendar year as sacred time, but mortality itself as a sacred space, looking first at MacDonald to help us better understand Rowling..To revert to fairy tale parlance, mortality is a quest, with death as its Grail.

The Wow

MacDonald explores this quest in a haunting, troubling, and under-researched story, "The Wow o' Rivven."[42] It is the tale of 'an old man, whose strange appearance and dress showed that he had little capacity either for good or evil,' and the young woman, Elsie, who grows to understand him.[43] The old man is mentally disabled; the villagers give him the mock-respectful title of 'the colonel.'[44] He is a constant target for harassment and mockery, wandering through the village muttering in incoherent Scots, 'Come hame, come hame' and 'The wow o' Rivven—the wow o' Rivven'—his response to Elsie's kindnesses and charity.[45]

The colonel's origins are mysterious. A peat-cutter happened to find him 'on as lonely a hillside as any in Scotland,' an abandoned infant, 'as if the earth herself had just given birth—that desert moor, wide and dismal, broken and water, the only bosom for him to lie upon, and the cold, clear night-heaven the only covering.'[46] The villagers soon discover the child's mental disability, and he becomes an object of both scorn and pity. These origins, born incomprehensibly as if out

41. Prinzi, 103ff.

42. George MacDonald, "The Wow o' Rivven," in *The Portent and Other Stories*, 1909 (Whitehorn, CA: Johannesen, 1999).

43. MacDonald, "Wow," 237. The village idiot in the story was drawn off a real person from MacDonald's childhood; the church ruin is likewise an actual place. The events of the story, however, and the character of Elsie, are fictional. See Raeper, 360-361.

44. MacDonald, "Wow",,238.

45. MacDonald, "Wow," 239, 244.

46 . MacDonald, "Wow," 240.

of the earth, suggest the nature-births found in some versions of the Arthur legends.[47] Is this found child an heir for Usher? Or is he—born of earth and wind where Arthur was born of water and fire—called to another, yet no less great, destiny?

When Elsie, as a child, first met the colonel, she was frightened of his strange appearance and demeanour.[48] Her fear turns to wonder when she overhears a conversation between the disabled man and a street child.

> "Weel, cornel [*sic*]!" "Weel, laddie!" was the reply. "Fat dis the wow say, cornel?" "Come hame, come hame!" answered the colonel, with both accent and quantity heaped on the word *hame*. What the wow could be, [Elsie] had no idea; only, as the years passed on, the strange word became in her mind indescribably associated with the strange shape in yellow cloth on his sleeves.[49]

Elsie herself is often bullied and made fun of; this heightens her sense of homelessness and her affinity with the colonel.[50] Always hypersensitive in nature, she suffers deep emotional wounding when the man she loves deserts her without explanation. The strain this puts on her brings back a resurgence of the epilepsy she suffered as a child, and her health deteriorates. 'But now, help came to her from a strange quarter; though many might not be willing to accord the name of help to that which hastened rather than retarded the progress of her decline.'[51]

During a ramble through the Scottish countryside near her village, Elsie discovers 'the ruins of an old church which was taking centuries to crumble.'[52] At first, she finds it nothing

47. Notably MacDonald's friend Tennyson's *Idylls of the King*.
48. Here MacDonald strikes a particularly touching note, as children will often react with fear the first time they encounter disability. Indeed, "The Wow o' Rivven" could easily be read as an exploration of disability, its promise and strength, and various reactions to it.
49. MacDonald, "Wow," 244.
50. MacDonald, "Wow," 240-242.
51. MacDonald, "Wow," 248.
52. MacDonald, "Wow," 248.

more than a pleasant vantage point for watching the sunset. As night closes in however, a cold wind rushes through the church yard, 'and to Elsie's ear came a low faint sound, as from a far-off bell. But close beside her—and she started and shivered at the sound—rose a deep, monotonous, almost sepulchral voice, *"Come hame, come hame! The wow, the wow!"*[53] There is still a bell in the tower, and the colonel stands in the churchyard looking up at it; the yellow cloth on his sleeves, MacDonald says, are bell-shapes. The ruin is 'the ancient parish church of Ruthven,' and 'the wow o' Rivven' is the colonel's name for the bell. It is the bell in the churchyard that calls to him, 'Come hame, come hame!'[54] And with that knowledge, MacDonald says, Elsie realizes, 'Ah, what did she want in the whole universe of God but a home?'[55] Elsie has had an apotheosis; the longing for a home becomes her overriding thought.

> From that hour Elsie was furnished with a visual image of the rest she sought; an image which, mingling with deeper and holier thoughts, became, like the bow set in the cloud, the earthly pledge and singe of the fulfilment of heavenly hopes.[56]

The bell becomes a reversed sacrament—a physical symbol that mingles with 'holier thoughts' to touch spiritual reality, namely, the longing for place and home. The bell, simply put, is death. Elsie's sighting of the bell, her recognition that the wow was calling her 'Come hame!' is her Grail vision, drawing her irrevocably on her quest.

From this point in the story, she becomes serene, even transcendent, detached from physical life as her body fails and her spirit grows; she approaches the climax of her life's liturgy. A series of traumas, including further victimizing of the colonel, breaks Elsie's health still further. The colonel, too, is dying from weakness and old age. He is, MacDonald significantly explains, waiting for the bell, 'friendly death', to wake him from 'the long

---

53. MacDonald, "Wow," 249; emphasis in original
54. MacDonald, "Wow," 249-250.
55. MacDonald, "Wow," 249.
56. MacDonald, "Wow," 251.

sleep of this world's night.'[57] He dies mumbling, 'I'm gaein' to the wow, nae to come back again.'[58] Elsie, who was with him when he died, suffers longer, dying painfully but peacefully over the course of several months. As she dies, she repeats the words of the colonel, 'I'm gaein' hame to the wow, nae to come back.'[59]

In the hands of a lesser artist—in the hands of any other Victorian and most of the Romantics, in fact—"The Wow o' Rivven" would degenerate into a maudlin squash of sentiment. In MacDonald's hands, the story has a reverse horror, slowly building through suggestion and illusion a sense of wonder, transcendence and beauty acting in weird harmony with the progress of sickness and death. Elsie is clearly a mystic heroine, enduring mortification of her body as her spirit enters into deep communion with God through the reversed sacrament of death. It is important to an understanding of MacDonald to note that he viewed Death as an awakening. This life is dreams and shadows; dying is waking up into true morning. For MacDonald, real life, lived before God, does not actually begin in this life. The quest of mortality then, leading as it does through death, is a quest for life. The embracing of death is the escape from death; dying means going home.

Godric's Hollow

It should come as no surprise, then, that Harry Potter's quest takes him to another churchyard, one that also calls him home. Throughout the series, Harry struggles to accept his parents' deaths. His struggle is worsened in that—by fluke of Horcrux—he has Lord Voldemort's own memory of the killings. His grief, as Markell and Markell note, is not simply loss but a longing to really know his parents. Their deaths robbed him of the chance to know them as individuals. This inability to receive the parents' explanation of themselves, Markell and Markell say, accentuates the process of grieving.[60] Looking at Harry's development and the pain of his questions through

57. MacDonald, "Wow," 255.

58. MacDonald, "Wow," 255.

59. MacDonald, "Wow," 256.

60. Markell and Markell, 44-45.

the seven years of the series, it seems almost inevitable that he would return to Godric's Hollow, the site of his parents' murder and graves.

The ostensible reason for his visit is an attempt to find the Sword of Gryffindor; that there is a 'double meaning' to his visit is apparent even to him. He arrives in Godric's Hollow with Hermione, unwittingly on Christmas Eve, polyjuiced to appear as a middle-aged couple.[61] Already, the incident reflects MacDonald's imagery; the old-but-young character—'an old lady with young eyes'—is a recurring motif throughout his literature, often, significantly, as a personification of death.[62] Harry, as a young man, must face death in a body much nearer to it than his own—a body older than his parents at the time of their death. In one sense, it makes the past deaths more immediate. In another, it makes the present visit extend beyond time. Godric's Hollow is atemporal; Harry's moment at his parents' grave is eternal.

Harry's wander through the snowy graveyard with Hermione, seeking and finding his parents' gravesite, is one of Rowling's finest moments as a storyteller. She imbues the scene with cold and weariness. The organic silence of a graveyard heightens and consoles grief; it is that atmosphere that Rowling captures perfectly. Harry has been drawn not just to the memorial in the town centre, which depresses him, or even to the ruins of his parents' house, where notes from supporters cheer him, but to the churchyard itself, where his parents' snow-covered grave sits under the shadow of the bell tower. It is, in a way, a homecoming—a reunion.

His view of the headstone releases his first full sense of grief for his parents. Up till now, he has felt loss, remorse, even guilt. When he views their grave, the tragedy strikes him as if

---

61. DH, 264-265.

62. Cf. MacDonald, *Phantastes*, ch. XIX. Raeper's Jungian analysis of this motif is characteristically inadequate; the old-but-young characterization is too poignant and complex to be reduced simply to a manifestation of anima (151); Marilyn Pemberton, "The Ultimate Rite of Passage: Death and Beyond in 'The Golden Key' and *At the Back of the North Wind*," *North Wind* 27 (2008): 42.

for the first time. He felt 'as if something heavy were pressing on his chest, the same sensation he had had right after Dumbledore had died, a grief that actually weighed on his heart and lungs.'[63] At this moment, this confrontation with the actual, physical presence of his parents, Harry is no longer the 'Boy Who Lived' or the 'Chosen One.' He is simply a boy whose parents have died, and he is knotted with tangled emotions and a grief he does not understand.

> And tears came before he could stop them, boiling hot and then instantly freezing on his face, and what was the point of wiping them off, or pretending? He let them fall, his lips pressed hard together, looking down at the thick snow hiding from his eyes the place where the last of Lily and James lay, bones now, surely, or dust, not knowing or caring that their living son stood so near, his heart still beating, alive because of their sacrifice and close to wishing, at this moment, that he was sleeping under the snow with them.[64]

This is Rowling at the height of her craft. In two rushing, nearly unbroken sentences—in fact the passage reads like one sentence—she captures the choking despair of Harry's grief. Anyone passing by would have only seen a middle-aged man with a bald spot, crying beside a somewhat new grave. But Harry is a boy, old-but-young, and through his grief he is a boy metamorphosing into a man. The wow is calling him home.

At every previous encounter with the shades of his parents, they have given Harry some form of assistance. Their reflections taught him how to use the Mirror of Erised and prevent Voldemort's theft of the Philosopher's Stone. His father's patronus saved him and Sirius from the dementor attack. During his duel with the reincarnated Voldemort, the released shades of his parents instructed him and give him time to escape. His parents, who have travelled this weeping road before him, serve as his guides on his quest. But it is only here, when all his boyish—human, really—pretence is gone, when he embraces not denial of death, as he did when Sirius died, but

63. DH, 268.
64. DH, 269.

longing for it, willingness to die, that they leave him their last and greatest message. The inscription on their grave is a quote from St. Paul: 'The last enemy that shall be destroyed is death.'[65]

His quest for mortality has led him here. In the same way Galahad and the other knights saw visions of the Grail far off that spurred them to follow it, Harry unknowingly sees the vision of his own death, his own sacrifice, that will draw him in the end to dig Dobby's grave by hand, to walk unrelenting into the forest and sacrifice his own life. He will not see his parents again until he is walking to greet his own death.

The Invisibility Cloak: Death as Heroism

The third brother, the tale tells us, was the wisest of the three. He asks Death for an Invisibility Cloak, and then lives his life as life, not overshadowed by the gloom of his mortality. When he is ready to die, he removes the cloak so Death can find him. 'And then,' the tale says, 'he greeted Death as an old friend, and went with him gladly, and, as equals, they departed this life.'[66] The way of the Invisibility Cloak is to live knowing you will die—not obsessed, but not afraid. It is not a question of mastery, but familiarity of shared travel.

Marilyn Pemberton might as well have been writing about the Harry Potter books as MacDonald's stories when she wrote that 'life and death are but a journey towards spiritual perfection':

> Each individual's journey is unique and personal; some of the journey can be shared but some of it must be travelled alone. The route is different for each person and there are different obstacles, but ultimately the goal is the same: not the traditional fairy tale goal of the pot of gold at the end of the rainbow, but rather becoming part of the rainbow itself, becoming one of the "beautiful beings of all ages" climbing to "the country whence the shadows fall."[67]

---

65. 1 Corinthians 15:26.
66. DH, 332.
67. Pemberton, 44.

Both MacDonald and Rowling infuse their stories with deep spiritual imagery. Their characters pursue their unique but often shared quests, reenacting a Passion play in the liturgical drama of their lives. Neither Rowling nor MacDonald celebrates death for death's sake; the end is not obliteration. Nor do they portray dying—that most human of acts—as spiritually powerful of necessity. After all, to receive the sacrament incorrectly is blasphemy.[68] The manner of dying is as important as death itself. Rowling and MacDonald both present sacramental deaths that have the power to give life to others. In their stories, death can be an act of heroism.

Dobby

The world is divided into two groups of people: those who cried when they read about Dobby's death, and those who never read the book. Because of his love for Harry Potter, who freed him from slavery with the Malfoys, Dobby returns to Malfoy Manor to free Harry from captivity, torture, and death. The return to the place of his former slavery terrifies him; when he arrives he is trembling and can hardly speak.[69] But he quickly proves himself as resourceful and witty—even mischievous—as ever. Surely he had any number of magical interventions at his disposal, but he chose the most chaotic and explosive and unscrewed the chandelier from the ceiling. He goes from being terrified to barking orders, even scolding his former oppressors: 'You must not hurt Harry Potter!'[70]

It is not clear whether Dobby intentionally put himself between Harry and Bellatrix Lestrange's flung knife, or whether it was a freak accident. He reacts to pain and death as a child might, with bewilderment, uncertainty, raising 'his thin arms to Harry with a look of supplication.'[71] He speaks the name of his hero, 'Harry...Potter...' and dies, his eyes 'sprinkled with light

---

68. See 1 Cor. 15; St Paul's views have been widely agreed with throughout Church history.
69. DH, 379.
70. DH, 384.
71. DH, 385.

from the stars they could not see.'[72]

Dobby's final act is his greatest, an act of naming. Throughout the books, he has believed Harry to be great and just and good, the noblest and most chivalrous of wizards, terrible in battle and tender in mercy. As he dies, he looks at the flawed, frightened teenager beside him, sees instead the Grail Knight the teenager will become, and speaks the knightly name. The same way Harry liberated Dobby, Dobby liberates Harry to accept his quest, and to embrace Death as an old friend.[73]

Anodos

Unlike the liberated Dobby, Anodos's journey to sacrifice in *Phantastes* takes him into servitude; he needs to be liberated not from social structures but from his shadow-self. Once he learns to accept beauty and wonder through the aid of others, and his shadow-self is vanquished, he discovers joy though serving as a squire to a noble knight.[74] On their travels together, they come to a temple of nature, 'a great space, bare of trees, and enclosed by four walls of yew.'[75] There is a ritual under way, watched by a cheerful but reverent crowd of 'men and women and children, in holiday attire,' and rows of white-robed priests.

The knight, deeply impressed with the aura of sacredness surrounding the proceedings, is convinced that they must be waiting to hear the words of a holy prophet; Anodos is uneasy. When, to the accompaniment of worshipful music, the proper constellation rises above the yew hedge, the priests unveil a dignified idol, and present it with first a young woman and then a young man, leading them into a hidden chamber beneath the idol's throne.[76]

'More convinced than before,' Anodos says, 'that there was evil here, I could not endure that my master should be deceived, that one like him, so pure and noble, should

---

72. DH, 385.
73. Prinzi, 256.
74. MacDonald, *Phantastes*, 174.
75. MacDonald, *Phantastes*, 175.
76. MacDonald, *Phantastes*, 176-177.

respect what, if my suspicions were true, was worse than the ordinary deceptions of priestcraft.'[77] He breaks through the rows of worshippers, and pulls down the idol, 'with a noise as of cracking, and breaking, and tearing of rotten wood.'[78] An enormous wolf leaps slavering from beneath the idol; Anodos fights it, strangling it, 'with my hand upon its throat, and knee upon its heart.' [79] The worshippers turn violent, and attack him. He clings to the wolf in the hope that they will not be able to pry away his hand before the monster is dead. 'I remember no blow,' Anodos says simply. 'A faintness came over me, and my consciousness departed.'[80]

Anodos acts out of service and love. Because he has lost his shadow, he can sense purity and nobility, so he is drawn to serve the knight. But because he once had a shadow—unlike the knight—he has a greater suspicion of evil, a heightened awareness to its presence. The ritual he interrupts seems to have everything right—a beautiful natural setting, rhythm, music, diversity. But the fairer the surface, Anodos thinks, the fouler the core. Although he is unable to save the child sacrifices, he achieves his aim of exposing the horror for what it is. Beowulf-like, he throttles the monster that has been savaging the people beneath a mask of benign rule and patronage.[81] He is willing to give his life to reveal truth; by letting evil destroy him, he reveals it for what it is. Afterward, the knight's lady—Anodos's Platonic ideal of womanhood and virtue—commends him: 'He died well.'[82]

Harry Potter

Harry's quest ends with his own act of heroism: his surrender of himself to Lord Voldemort in ransom for his friend's lives. He has learned—through his Grail vision in the churchyard, and his champion's naming of him—that 'he was

77. MacDonald, *Phantastes*, 177.
78. MacDonald, *Phantastes*, 178.
79. MacDonald, *Phantastes*, 178.
80. MacDonald, *Phantastes*, 179.
81. MacDonald, *Phantastes*, 176-177.
82. MacDonald, *Phantastes*, 180.

not supposed to survive. His job was to walk calmly into Death's welcoming arms.'[83] Having surrendered 'his will to live,' his 'fear of death' nearly overwhelms him. Hero that he is, he approaches death the way Dobby did, like a child. 'Would it hurt to die?' he wonders. He allows himself a child's honesty, a frank lack of pretence that lets him to face his death with curiosity instead of defiance: 'it did not occur to him to escape.'[84] He has embraced his quest as his own, and walks forth boldly to fulfil it, greeting it 'like an old friend.'

It is no coincidence that Harry makes this journey shrouded under the Invisibility Cloak. In walking into the forest, not only, as Prinzi observes, is he pursuing a *via dolorosa*, he is literally walking into the shadow of death.[85] The Forbidden Forest is imagination, creativity, subversion, in contrast to the ordered, academic world of Hogwarts. By entering imagination, Harry faces down his own fear of death. He crosses a threshold into another atemporal moment where past, present, and future are suspended together. He is able to use the Resurrection Stone to meet his parents, Sirius, and Lupin.[86] They meet him not as guides but companions. They no longer need to show him the way his quest should take. They only need to comfort and console him as he nears the end. The killing curse will rebound a second time, and Harry will face Voldemort in the Great Hall of Hogwarts with 'mundane finality.'

But that confrontation will happen only after a meeting at King's Cross Station. Markell and Markell observe that 'even in the wizarding world [...], people are unsure about what happens to someone after they die.' Death, they say, 'remains very much a mystery in the books.'[87] The only reliable witness—a ghost— admits to never experiencing true death, despite having been beheaded, or nearly.[88] But there is Harry's half-death reunion

83. DH, 554.
84. DH, 554.
85. Prinzi, 112
86. DH, 560-561.
87. Markell and Markell, 37-38.
88. Nearly Headless Nick tells Harry, 'I know nothing of the secrets of death, Harry, for I chose my feeble imitation of life instead.' OP, 759.

with Dumbledore—or dream about Dumbledore—that seems
to give some ideas of an afterlife.

After the green blast of the killing curse, Harry's
consciousness continues.

> He lay face down, listening to the silence. He was perfect-
> ly alone. Nobody was watching. Nobody else was there.
> He was not perfectly sure that he was there himself.[89]

The world forms around Harry only as he becomes
aware of it. As he has needs or desires, things appear. 'Was he in
some great Room of Requirement?' he wonders.[90] He is, in fact,
in a spectral, empty version of King's Cross Station, London, the
main station for the Hogwarts Express.[91] Presently, to his great
surprise, Dumbledore joins him, and they are able to discuss
the events of the past year. Harry, having completed his quest, is
older now, and wiser, so his questions are more perceptive and
Dumbledore's answers more powerful than in previous years.

Excellent analysis has already explored the questions of
knowing and reality they discuss.[92] What concerns us here is
that, having attained his quest and embraced mortality, Harry
is left with a choice: to go on, presumably into true death, or to
go back to normal life at the moment he lost it.[93] He is given,
in other words, the hope of a fairy tale: escape from death. He
chooses to return to normal life—escaping death like his fabled
ancestors, the Three Brothers. Having escaped, he returns to
help restore the world.

As parting advice, Dumbledore tells him, 'Do not pity the
dead, Harry. Pity the living, and, above all, those without love.'[94] It is,
in other words, the Voldemorts of the world, loveless and undying,
who need pity, not those who have answered the wow and gone home.

89. DH, 565.

90. DH, 566.

91. It is not at all clear whether there is any connection between Rowling's
use of this location and Douglas Adams's positing of a derelict Valhalla here
in *The Long Dark Tea Time of the Soul* (New York: Simon & Schuster, 1988).

92. Cf. Prinzi, 35-41.

93. DH, 578.

94. DH, 578.

Conclusion

'I was dead,' Anodos declares, 'and right content.'[95] His sacrificial death has opened him to transcendent spiritual joy, described in an ecstatic outpouring:

> My soul was like a summer evening, after a heavy fall of rain, when the drops are yet glistening on the trees in the last rays of the down-going sun, and the wind of the twilight has begun to blow. The hot fever of life had gone by, and I breathed the clear mountain-air of the land of Death. I had never dreamed of such blessedness.[96]

Death, Anodos discovers, is life: 'who dies, he is alive.' It is life wholly poured out in love. He can delight the knight and his lady through dwelling in a flower, the earth, or the sunset. They are unaware that they are encountering him, yet his expression of himself through nature still enriches their lives.[97] He finds a world to understand and know—not rapaciously and greedily, with wolf-knowledge, but through delight and wonder, through love. 'All true love will, one day, behold its own image in the eyes of the beloved, and be humbly glad. This is possible in the realms of lofty death.'[98] Dead in fairyland, Anodos determines that he will use the perfection of love he has discovered to heal the world. Even as he thinks so, he dies back to life in his own world, but still with the same resolve.[99]

Both Rowling and MacDonald portray the escape from death as a heroic quest. The quest leads to and through death, not away from it. It embraces imagination and courage, allowing room for fear but not letting fear drive it. Although they acknowledge the devastating anguish of grief, through their contemplative art they encourage their readers to see death not as escape from life, but escape into life. The journey of death, they say, is crossing from one life into another, a homecoming.

---

95. MacDonald, *Phantastes*, 179.
96. MacDonald, *Phantastes*, 180.
97. MacDonald, *Phantastes*, 180-181.
98. MacDonald, *Phantastes*, 181.
99. MacDonald, *Phantastes*, 182ff.

This is the central paradox their works uncover. Death is escape from death. The mystery of the Hallows is how to hold all three in tension.

The walls between life and death are very thin. This numinous border is the place of fairytale, of darkness and uncertainty, of wonder and hope. Luna Lovegood, who lost her mother when she was nine, is the most bizarrely fanciful character in the books. She, like Harry, has walked into the woods of shadow and imagination. She uses her creativity to cope with her grief and understand the world.

Despite her apparent battiness, she assesses people and situations directly and shrewdly. She is the only person who can comfort Harry after Sirius's death. 'You heard them, just behind the veil, didn't you?' she asks. 'In the room with the archway. They were lurking just out of sight, that's all. You heard them.'[100] Tellingly, Luna's words echo Anodos's reflection after receiving comfort from the unseen ghosts of his ancestors as he visits their graves: 'The veil between, though dark, is very thin.'[101] If Luna has not actually read *Phantastes*, then perhaps she's had a similar journey of her own through the Perilous Realm. Her willingness to imagine, to encounter mystery and wonder, has enabled her to approach grief with hope. She can catch a whisper of life 'behind the veil,' the rich, healing love poured out from the happy dead.

These stories of imagination help children and grown-ups alike listen at that veil. By following the characters on their own quests, learning with them to welcome death as a friend, to heal the world, to live with hope and wonder even in face of maltreatment and despair, we learn to face our own quests, find our own journeys.

We may never understand why Dobby died. We may always grieve for the brave, free elf. But we know he died with his eyes toward the stars. Even in our grief, that gives us the courage to look up.

---

100. J. K. Rowling, *Harry Potter and the Order of the Phoenix* (London: Bloomsbury, 2003), 761.
101. MacDonald, *Phantastes*, 142.

Works Cited

Hilder, Monika B. "Educating the Moral Imagination: The Fantasy Literature of George MacDonald, C. S. Lewis, and Madeline L'Engle." PhD, Simon Fraser University, 2003.

MacDonald, George. *Phantastes: A Faerie Romance.* 1852. Grand Rapids: Eerdmans, 1994.

—. "The History of Photogen and Nycertis: A Day and Night Märchen." In *Stephen Archer and Other Tales*, 76–147. 1883. Whitehorn, CA: Johanessen, 2003.

—. "The Wow o' Rivven." In *The Portent and Other Stories*, 235–258. 1909. Whitehorn, CA: Johannesen, 1999.

Markell, Kathryn A., and Marc A. Markell. *The Children Who Lived: Using Harry Potter and Other Fictional Characters to Help Grieving Children and Adolescents.* New York: Routledge, 2008.

Palmer, Parker J. *To Know as we are Known.* New York: Harper Collins, 1993.

Pemberton, Marilyn. "The Ultimate Rite of Passage: Death and Beyond in 'The Golden Key' and At the Back of the North Wind." *North Wind* 27 (2008): 35–50.

Prickett, Stephen. *Victorian Fantasy.* Second Edition. Waco, TX: Baylor University Press, 2005.

Prinzi, Travis. *Harry Potter and Imagination.* Allenton, PA: Zossima Press, 2008.

Raeper, William. *George MacDonald.* Tring, UK: Lion, 1987.

Rowling, J. K. *Harry Potter and the Deathly Hallows.* London: Bloomsbury, 2007.

—. *Harry Potter and the Goblet of Fire.* London: Bloomsbury, 2000.

—. *Harry Potter and the Half-Blood Prince.* London: Bloomsbury, 1995.

—. *Harry Potter and the Order of the Phoenix.* London: Bloomsbury, 2003.

—. *Harry Potter and the Philosopher's Stone.* London: Bloomsbury, 1997.

Sundmark, Björn. "Travelling Beastward: An Ecocritical Reading of George MacDonald's Fairy Tales." *North Wind* 27

(2008): 1–15.

Tolkien, J. R. R. "On Fairy-stories." In *The Tolkien Reader*, 33–99. New York: Ballantine, 1966.

Harry Potter and the Greatest Virtue

Jenna St. Hilaire

In the end it mattered not that you could not close your mind. It was your heart that saved you. (Order 844)

The Mysterious Force

O F THE MAJOR IDEAS and themes in the *Harry Potter* novels, one supports the rest: Love, the power which Harry "possess[es] in such quantities and which Voldemort has not at all" (*Order* 843-44). Love is the homing point of the story, giving mastery over death, providing direction to courage, and driving the quest for justice.

Love, however, is a word used to cover a lot of emotional and active territory. Its indefinable aspects and variety of meanings, its gray areas and graces would have offered a wide range of possible studies behind the locked door in the Department of Mysteries. J.K. Rowling opens the great mystery to us by magical means, allowing her protagonist to explore many ways of loving and being loved, including friendship, parental and filial affection, romance, and charity.

For Harry, whose participation in religion is vague at best, love is mostly a human term. He has little association with the Anglican Christianity in which he was presumably baptized (the existence of a godfather implies christening, or baptism) and in which the concept of love is considered sacred. What Harry does not know, however, his author apparently understands.

Before undertaking the study of Harry's relationship to the sacred concept of love, a brief and somewhat weighty trip behind the locked door is in order. Love may resist definition, but like any good mystery it offers clues for the sake of knowledge.

Love Divine, All Loves Excelling

The greatest theological virtue, charity—as in "And now abideth faith, hope, charity, these three, but the greatest of these is charity" (King James Version, 1 Cor. 13.13)—is, according to Christian thought, meant to participate in all other loves and even to exist where no natural love is possible. A brief explanation in the Catechism of the Catholic Church shows the primary way in which charity is set off from the other forms of love:

> Charity is the theological virtue by which we love God above all things for his own sake, and our neighbor as ourselves for the love of God. (par. 1822)

The word *charity*, used here merely for purposes of distinction, is an older translation of the koine Greek word *agape*, which in more recent translations of the Bible is simply rendered *love*. The Greek language was perhaps a more precise vehicle for thought and contained several words for the varying concepts described as Love by English speakers; the word agape has no clear translation to differentiate it, yet as the ideal for which Christianity strives, it needs distinction.

As a term, charity itself is problematic, since by modern definition it refers almost entirely to donations or work for the less fortunate members of society. This is not a bad place to start when thinking about the meaning of this form of love, but it is only part of the great circle which passes from God through humanity and back to God again.

There are a number of sources which provide some explanation of the concept, beginning with Christ, the Son of God, whose incarnation, death, and resurrection form the Christian's ultimate example of love and its power.

Christ speaks of love a great deal. "If you love me, you will obey what I command" (English Standard Version, John 14.15) and "My command is this: Love each other as I have loved you. Greater love has no one than this, that someone lay down his life for his friends" (John 15.12-13). Elsewhere, he says "Love your enemies and pray for those who persecute you" (Matt 5:44). He gives the two greatest commandments, the fulfillment of the entire Jewish law, as "Love the Lord your God with all your heart and with all your soul and with all your mind" and "Love your neighbor as yourself" (Matt 22:37-40). These quotations form only part of what he has to say on the subject, but they provide much of the foundation for the *Catholic Encyclopedia's* paean to Christian charity:

Its excellence appears in the following points: love of the neighbour is akin to love of God; the neighbour is to [be] beloved even as the self; men are brothers, members of the same family; the law of charity extends to the whole human race, thus making all persons equal; men are obliged to love even their enemies; the neighbour is not merely a rational creature made in the image and likeness of God, but also the supernaturally adopted son of the Father, and the brother of the Father's Only-Begotten Son; finally, the Gospel presents the supreme exemplification of brotherly love in the death of Christ on the Cross (Ryan).

The Scriptures contain numerous other references to love, of which St. Paul the Apostle wrote what is probably the most famous. The opening lines make increasingly bold claims about the necessity of love, ending with "If I give all I possess to the poor and surrender my body to the flames, but have not love, I gain nothing" (1 Cor 13:3). He then goes on to describe the love of which he speaks:

Love is patient, love is kind. It does not envy, it does not boast, it is not proud. It is not rude, it is not self-seeking, it is not easily angered, it keeps no record of wrongs. Love does not delight in evil but rejoices with the truth. It always protects, always trusts, always hopes, always perseveres.

Love never fails. (1 Cor. 13.4-8)

The chapter ends with the statement quoted much earlier, which in the English Standard Version reads, "And now these three remain: faith, hope and love. But the greatest of these is love."

These ideas, read by humans, naturally make a certain sense within the circle of human concern. In the context of Scripture and the Judeo-Christian tradition, however, the loop is much larger. C.S. Lewis, working from the New Testament, describes love as originating from God:

God is love. Again, "Herein is love, not that we loved God but that He loved us" (I John IV, 10).... We begin at the real beginning, with love as the Divine energy. This primal love is Gift-love. In God there is no hunger that needs to be filled, only plenteousness that desires to give (126).

St. Thomas Aquinas reaches further back in Scripture and carries the circle to its completion:

> Now the Divine Law contains precepts about the acts of faith, hope, and charity: for it is written (*Ecclus*. ii. 8, *seqq*.): *Ye that fear the Lord believe Him*, and again, *hope in Him*, and again, *love Him*. Therefore faith, hope, and charity are virtues directing us to God. Therefore they are theological virtues (*Summa Theologica*, 1a 2ae, Question 62, art. 1).

To summarize the indefinable in a few simplistic words: In Christian belief, *agape* love, or charity, comes from God to humanity, works between people, and is given in return from humans to God. As Christ explained in John chapters 14 and 15, those who love him will obey his command, which is to love one another as he loved us. This love entails an attitude of giving toward others that culminates—figuratively, if not literally—in the laying down of one's own life.

In the popular realm at least, even secular thoughts of ultimate love usually contain an ideal of self-giving not unlike Christ's. Determining the relation of that common thesis to Christianity and other possible origins would require another essay, or perhaps a book. For this study, it is enough to know that charity, as propounded by Christianity, includes the sacrifice of Christ as its central example and the crux of its definition.

Love, God, and Harry

If the distinction between natural love and divine charity is ultimately the focus of the virtue on God, what does charity have to do with the *Harry Potter* books, in which religion receives only vague mention and next to no shown practice? The Dursleys did not, apparently, provide Harry with any religious instruction, Hogwarts is a multi-faith school at which the students sleep in on Sunday, and when Harry reads a Scripture verse off his own parents' gravestone, he thinks it is a Death Eater idea. It is reasonable to assume that Harry's love is not motivated by a conscious direction of heart or will to God.

Because of this, reading strictly on the surface level, the love in Harry's story will appear merely natural and not theological. Further, Rowling makes no clear distinction between the various forms of love, and every one that Harry exemplifies is valuable in the fight against evil.

Taking theological love as a subject for consideration in the *Potter* series thus means accepting two challenges from the outset. First, a concept dependent upon the existence and impetus of God will be manifested, if at all, in reading beneath the surface. Second, it will be nearly impossible at times to distinguish between true charity and a perfectly natural love.

There are, however, ways of tracing that virtue throughout the tale: symbolism and subtle references, placed deliberately or otherwise by an author who almost certainly understands the Christian tradition in which she wrote, provide numerous examples. Among these, Rowling has drawn a stark image of divine love's opposite.

I. The Antithesis of Charity

"Power the Dark Lord Knows Not"

> And if I … understand all mysteries and all knowledge … but have not love, I am nothing. (1 Cor. 13.2)

Voldemort stands in such clear antagonism to all forms of love that his rebellion against charity hardly needs stating. His creator spoke openly of his lovelessness in an interview:

> *Audience question:* Has Voldemort or Tom Riddle ever cared for or loved anyone?
>
> *J.K. Rowling:* Now, that's a cracking question to end with—very good. No, never. [Laughter.] If he had, he couldn't possibly be what he is." (Rowling, Interview with Fraser)

Perhaps the most obvious expression of that rebellion is this: while charity in its highest and truest form devotes itself to God, Tom Riddle renounces the possibility of any superior. Instead, he sets himself up as a form of deity: immortal, all-demanding, the power over all power. He may never have considered the existence or rights of God, but his actions demonstrate his utter rejection of any such being. Another comment from Rowling, this time from the Anelli/Spartz interview of 2005, illustrates this:

> *Emerson Spartz:* [W]hat would [Voldemort] see if he were in front of the mirror of Erised?
>
> *J.K. Rowling:* Himself, all-powerful and eternal. That's what he wants.

Another, more subtle example of Voldemort's lack of charity is in his actions toward himself. In the Christian tradition, charity is the redemptive force in a human soul; grave or mortal sins are considered such because they are believed to effectively destroy charity in the heart.

Murder, by its offense against the God-given life of another human being, is an active and thoroughly destructive sin against charity. As Hermione explains to Harry and Ron in *Deathly Hallows*, injury and destruction of the body cannot harm the soul; Voldemort, uninterested in the health of his soul, murders in order to tear it into pieces, hoping only to avoid physical death. Had there been any charity in him to begin with, it would have been long gone before he went to kill Harry the first time.

Interestingly, Hermione's explanation does not work in reverse, and as Voldemort destroys his soul, his body slowly reflects the horror within. Even his own natural beauty is annihilated in his quest for self-preservation. These direct acts of Voldemort against himself are contrary to the self-love of charity. Christ's command to love our neighbor as ourselves implies that a love of self is a necessary part of human existence[1], and Voldemort shows himself incapable of both.

By divine orchestration, charity makes us more human; Voldemort's actions against charity remove him further from his humanity, to the point where his appearance is more often compared to that of a snake than of a man.[2]

It is worth noting also that charity has been no part of Voldemort's ancestry. The Tom Riddle who fathered him gave no thought to the care of his child, which true charity ought to have done no matter how the child came into existence. Marvolo and Morfin Gaunt exist in a selfish and inhuman squalor, untouched by charity from without or within. Even Merope, who as Dumbledore said ought not be harshly judged, acts against charity in her bewitching of Voldemort's father.

---

1. As per the *Catholic Encyclopedia*: [T]he precept of supernatural love of self is not only possible or needed, but also clearly implied in Christ's command to love our neighbour as ourselves. Its obligation, however, bears in a vague manner on the salvation of our soul (Matthew 16:26), the acquisition of merits (Matthew 6:19 sqq.), the Christian use of our body (Romans 6:13; 1 Corinthians 6:19; Colossians 3:5), and can hardly be brought down to practical points not already covered by more specific precepts. (Sollier)
2. Thanks to Katrina Hansen for this point.

Voldemort, born from an utter lack of true love, refuses from the beginning to accept charity. He lives in the orphan asylum as a child, for the sake of self-preservation, but he rejects Dumbledore's every charitable offer unless he has no other choice. He must rely on financial aid, but he will have nothing to do with personal assistance. While not above giving the appearance of humility and gratitude on occasion, it is contrived, and he drops it as soon as the cover is unnecessary to him.

Number 4, Privet Drive

The Dursleys, in a different way from Voldemort, show an almost complete lack of the virtue. Rather than thorough detachment, they display affection, emotional love, untouched by charity. Affection can be selfishly motivated, and as Dumbledore points out early in *Half-Blood Prince,* such a thing can be immensely destructive even to its object:

> "You have never treated Harry as a son.... The best that can be said is that he has at least escaped the appalling damage you have inflicted upon the unfortunate boy sitting between you."
>
> Both Aunt Petunia and Uncle Vernon looked around instinctively, as though expecting to see someone other than Dudley squeezed between them. (*Prince* 55)

Charity and selfishness work contrary to each other. Divine love could have conquered Petunia's resentment toward Lily and given Harry compassionate treatment; the best that can be said for her, however, is that she never went quite so far as to turn her nephew out of the house, knowing that it would cost him his life.

The Dursleys' "love" for their son is hardly worthy of the name, as Dudley is given everything he wants instead of what is best for him; their open animosity toward Harry and his family is something of a spiritual hatred. The Potters are part of a supernatural world, the existence of which the Dursleys would gladly disbelieve; Harry's obvious participation in that world drives their dislike of him even more than their pride and self-aggrandizement.

As Dante says:

The soul's love strays if it desires what's wrong

or loves with too much strength, or not enough….

One fears the rising of another man,

fears to lose favor, honor, power and fame,

and gloomily learns to love to see him fail.

(*Purgatorio* canto 17)

Of course, the one young man that Vernon and Petunia would have preferred their son never, ever meet is the one who proves to be Dudley's salvation. Despite Harry's emotional hatred toward Dudley, despite the bitterness and competition between them, he acts without hesitation to protect Dudley's soul, sending his own Patronus to drive the dementor away at the beginning of *Order of the Phoenix*.

Dudley, alone of all the Dursleys, finds redemption within the tale: He knows Harry has saved him, and something changes in him. The last time we see him, he expresses a thorough reversal of attitude and shakes hands with Harry, eliciting the first kind words Harry ever speaks to him.

Cowards and the Coldhearted

There are other examples of failed charity in the books: Peter Pettigrew, who for lack of moral courage betrayed his friends; Zacharias Smith and Cormac McLaggen, both of them utterly self-absorbed; the cruelty of Lucius Malfoy, the Carrows, and other Death Eaters; Bellatrix Lestrange's weird obsessive worship of her psychopathic leader; Dolores Umbridge's relentless injustice. None of these are willing to lay down their lives, even in the smallest ways.

The heartlessness toward other lives—the inability to show kindness or mercy, the choice to dominate instead of respect and to take instead of give, is the evil that Harry and his friends fight against. That evil is in all ways contrary to charity. There is no God among these people, only a perverse and self-gratifying submission to a power that allows and encourages their inhumanity. There is no brotherly love even amongst themselves, only competition and mutual disrespect.

Harry Potter's life, however, begins in charity. His heart, like his eyes, is an inheritance from his mother, and she gives him his first lesson in Christ-like love.

II. Lily and the Cross

> But in fact Christ has been raised from the dead ... For as in Adam all die, so also in Christ shall all be made alive.... For he must reign until he has put all his enemies under his feet. The last enemy to be destroyed is death. (1 Cor. 15.20-21, 25-26)

The white lily's association with Easter—the rising of Christ from the dead—is one of numerous reasons that the name Lily works in beautiful symbolism for Harry's mother. Her association with death and resurrection closely parallels Christ's great act of charity in several ways, the first being her form. Standing upright, arms outstretched, she is the image of a cross placed between her son and death:

> He forced the door open, cast aside the chair and boxes hastily piled against it with one lazy wave of his wand ... and there she stood, the child in her arms. At the sight of him, she dropped her son into the crib behind her and *threw her arms wide...* (*Hallows* 344, emphasis mine)

Second, her selflessness:

> "Not Harry, please no, take me, kill me instead –" (*Hallows* 344)

The third way is, of course, the result of her act. Her blood forms a protection over Harry that thwarts Voldemort over and over again, most of all when Voldemort attempts to appropriate that power. Lily's death saves Harry not only at the first Avada Kedavra, but as Quirrell and Voldemort attack him for the philosopher's stone, and as he grows up calling the house of Lily's sister his home; her blood even participates in Harry's return from his own self-sacrifice.

It is Lily's love as victor over Harry's death that draws the closest association with ultimate charity. The verse quoted above from 1 Corinthians, "The last enemy that shall be destroyed is death," is written on her tombstone; her love, natural though it may be—what mother would stand aside and watch her child killed?—bears too near a resemblance to Christ's to be overlooked. "[T]o have been loved so deeply, even though the person who loved us is gone, will give us some protection forever. (*Stone* 299).

Dumbledore explains that he used Lily's sacrifice to provide as much safety for Harry as possible: "You would be protected by an ancient magic of which [Voldemort] knows, which he despises, and which he has always, therefore, underestimated—to his cost. I am speaking, of course, of the fact that your mother died to save you. She gave you a lingering protection he never expected ... While you can still call home the place where your mother's blood dwells, there you cannot be touched or harmed by Voldemort" (*Order* 835-36).

Finally, in Harry's King's Cross, Dumbledore points out the ultimate result of her act. "He took your blood believing it would strengthen him. He took into his body a tiny part of the enchantment your mother laid upon you when she died for you. His body keeps her sacrifice alive, and while that enchantment survives, so do you and so does Voldemort's one last hope for himself" (*Hallows* 710).

Voldemort's attempt to appropriate Lily's sacrifice becomes his undoing and Harry's resurrection. The power of her act could have saved Voldemort, too, if only he had been willing to repent (as Harry puts it, "try for some remorse" [*Hallows* 741]). Harry, having followed his mother's self-sacrificial example, survives the killing curse again, and Voldemort, having refused the offer of salvation, is struck dead by his own ricocheting spell.

As victorious and powerful as is Harry's return to life, the legacy Lily passed on to him gives him another protection, one far more important than that from death. Dumbledore says in *Half-Blood Prince*:

> "Harry, despite your privileged insight into Voldemort's world ... you have never been seduced by the Dark Arts, never, even for a second, shown the slightest desire to become one of Voldemort's followers!"

> "Of course I haven't!" said Harry indignantly. "He killed my mum and dad!"

> "You are protected, in short, by your ability to love!" said Dumbledore loudly. "The only protection that can possibly work against the lure of power like Voldemort's!" (*Prince* 511)

As Christ's self-sacrificing love offers protection to the Christian from spiritual death and the lures of selfish ambition (working with the free choice of the recipient, of course), Lily's protects her son. Her enchantment completes what it set out to do. That work lines up, point for point, with Christ's great work of charity, and gives Harry the very thing he needs to become the Christ-like victor over evil and death: her heart.

III. Harry's Friends and Enemies

"Love Your Enemy"

> But I say to you, love your enemies, and pray for those who persecute you. (Matt. 5.44)

In *Deathly Hallows*, Griphook the goblin looks at Harry with curiosity and surprise after Harry saves his life and—having been unable to save Dobby's—buries the house-elf without the help of magic. Goblins and house-elves are not used to such consideration from wizards, Griphook says.

Whether owing to the attitudes of his race or his own personality, Griphook proves someone that Harry is not able to like. Griphook is bloodthirsty and self-serving and carries a lot of bitterness towards wizardkind. That does not stop Harry from plunging his hand into burning gold to save Griphook's life yet again in the Lestranges' Gringotts vault.

Harry's life-saving tendencies extend over and over to those he does not personally like. His protection over Dudley during the dementor attack is a greater example than the goblin's rescue, and by the end of the series, his kindness extends even to his most outright adversaries.

Among all the many expressions of charity in the *Harry Potter* books, Harry's own progression towards loving his enemies is arguably the most beautiful and difficult. Eleven-year-old Harry does a lot of open hating: his cousin, Draco Malfoy, Snape. Fifteen-year-old Harry, going through some of his darkest moments in the series, is not much better—but it is in his fifteenth year that Harry saves Dudley, and from there the changes continue.

In his sixteenth year, Harry spends much of his time trying to figure out what Draco Malfoy is planning to accomplish for Voldemort. The rivalry between the two boys has reached its peak, and their battle in Moaning Myrtle's bathroom is fierce. Because Harry is, ultimately, a loving person, he is acting primarily from self-defense; still, it is hatred that draws him to use a spell about which he knows nothing except that it is meant "for enemies" (*Prince* 518). Of course, he nearly kills Draco, much to both of their surprise. Rather than triumph, his immediate response is remorse. That moment sets the stage for another, when he will watch Draco approach Dumbledore with the intent, but not the will, to kill. After that, most of his responses to young Mr. Malfoy are compassionate, ending in his risking his own life to save Draco's in the final book and living thereafter without particular animosity.

Severus Snape is a harder case, and it takes a trip through the man's memories before Harry understands how thoroughly he has misunderstood Snape's motives throughout his life. The sheer emotional dislike between the two of them is extremely powerful right up to the last minute of Snape's life—and then Harry's last act toward a living Snape is in some way a charitable one. He approaches the dying man, not with a Malfoyish gloating or a Voldemortish detached regret, but with horror and implied compassion. Snape makes a final request: "Take it" (his memories) and Harry, with a little help from the always compassionate Hermione, obeys.

What Harry sees in those memories totally undoes his hatred. He could have allowed himself to hold onto the hundreds of times in which Snape was unfair and cruel toward him; Snape's passion for Harry's mother would not necessarily, in and of itself, be enough to bring about understanding and forgiveness for years of willful personal mistreatment. Harry forgives so completely, however, that he gives the dead man's name to his own son—a gift of life. That is a decided shift from his being prepared, at the end of his sixteenth year, to kill Snape on sight. "You were named for two headmasters of Hogwarts," Harry tells young Albus Severus. "One of them was a Slytherin, and he was probably the bravest man I ever knew" (*Hallows* 758).

Regarding the boy's name: if it hadn't been for King's Cross, Dumbledore might not have been on the top of Harry's name-my-kids-for-these-people list either. Dumbledore spent years getting to know Harry, watching and guiding him, giving him information while keeping important secrets that Harry felt he had a right to know, and in the end he asks Harry to be willing to walk up to Voldemort and die. Walking the path of the Christ, however, and talking with Dumbledore afterward, changes Harry permanently.

"Love one another as I have loved you," Jesus says (John 15.12). For Harry to do just that—even to the point of giving his life for his friends—and follow it up by spending a little time in a place called "King's Cross" is unmistakable symbolism. The Christ-like Harry of King's Cross, the Harry who would offer assistance even to the repulsive creature struggling under a bench, is made so perfect in charity that he shows it to the most unlovable being in the story.

While Dolores Umbridge may be the easiest character to hate, with her unfair and evil nature covered in the personality equivalent of lard frosting, Voldemort, by the time Harry meets him, is simply unable to attract natural love (Bellatrix's love being unnatural, hellish rather than human or divine). He excites no warmth of emotion from any healthy soul, only terror and cold rage and disgust. As Harry's archenemy, the murderer of his parents, Voldemort has as little reason to expect care from Harry as from anyone.

King's Cross Harry, however, looks at Tom Riddle as a redeemable soul, breaking past the self-created "Lord Voldemort" identity, forcing him to see his own weaknesses, things no one (since Dumbledore's setting fire to the wardrobe) has ever shown him. "This is you as you really are," Harry's responses basically say. "You've got one last hope. Repent!" Or, in Harry's actual words: "It's your one last chance, it's all you've got left … I've seen what you'll be otherwise … Be a man … try … Try for some remorse" (Hallows 741).

The fully purified Harry could find the last redeemable part of his worst enemy and offer hope. This is charity. As Lewis says:

> natural Gift-love is always directed to objects which the lover finds in some way intrinsically lovable … But Divine Gift-love in the man enables him to love what is not naturally lovable; lepers, criminals, enemies, morons, the sulky, the superior and the sneering. (128)

Besides Dudley, there is at least one other case where Harry's charity is effectively redemptive. The elf Kreacher, a despicable character in *Order of the Phoenix* and *Half-Blood Prince*, complicit in the murder of Sirius, winds up under Harry's direct control. Harry hears the story of Regulus Black's death and—with a little help from Hermione—understands that his unwilling servant may be redeemable. A little kindness, a small gift, and Kreacher becomes loyal.

Of course, Regulus' sacrificial death plays a part in Kreacher's change as well. Regulus died in the elf's place, and it is the name of Regulus Black in which Kreacher joins the final

battle against Voldemort and the Death Eaters. For a former
Death Eater to offer his own life in the place of a house-elf's is
remarkable love indeed, and the young Slytherin well deserves
mention in the roll of souls who, in Harry's story, connected
themselves to charity.

"For His Friends"

> By embracing in his human heart the Father's love for
> men, Jesus "loved them to the end," for "greater love has
> no man than this, that a man lay down his life for his
> friends." Jn 13:1, 15:13.

> In suffering and death his humanity became the free
> and perfect instrument of his divine love which desires
> the salvation of men. (*The Catechism of the Catholic
> Church* par. 609)

Part of the importance of Harry's great sacrifice in the
Forbidden Forest is its innate willfulness, as is explained in
Deathly Hallows: "I meant to let him kill me!" Harry says, and
Dumbledore responds "And that will, I think, have made all the
difference" (Hallows 708). Like Lily's, Harry's act is obviously
drawn in parallel with Christ's: "The thief comes only to steal
and kill and destroy. I came that they may have life and have it
abundantly..... I lay down my life that I may take it up again. No
one takes it from me, but I lay it down of my own accord" (John
10.10, 17-18).

Voldemort doesn't merely manage to aim a successful
AK in a fight; he asks Harry to surrender and then performs
his curse, only to find that Dumbledore, Lily, Harry, and magic
itself have played a real trick on him. This tricking of evil in
sacrificial ransom is not a new idea, as will be explained in a
later section. It is enough, now, to know that the sly exchange
works and Harry has the opportunity to take his own life up
again.

Harry's choice to continue living is made at least in part
for the sake of others, just as was his choice to give up his life.
Dumbledore tells him the following:

I think … if you return now, there is a chance that he may be finished for good. I cannot promise it…. By returning, you may ensure that fewer souls are maimed, fewer families are torn apart. If that seems a worthy goal, then we say goodbye for the present. (Hallows 722)

Without further hesitation, Harry acquiesces. For those he attempted to die for and many others, he again surrenders himself to a will greater than his own. He returns to consciousness on the forest floor and embraces the rest of his calling, fulfilling the prophecy and completing his own great act of love. The word "savior", which Rowling applies to Harry a few pages later (Hallows 744), is fairly given. If Christ says "Greater love has no one than this" (John 15.13) it hardly need be doubted that Harry acts with charity.

This, of course, does not resolve the fact that he apparently knows little of Christianity and has no conscious thought of the divine sacrifice he emulates or that God incarnate would call such an act the greatest of all loves. According to Lewis, however, it is possible to love God even unconsciously:

And as all Christians know there is another way of giving to God; every stranger whom we feed or clothe is Christ. And this apparently is Gift-love to God whether we know it or not. Love Himself can work in those who know nothing of Him. (128-29)

Lewis is referring to Matthew 25.35ff: " 'I was hungry and you gave me food, I was thirsty and you gave me drink, I was a stranger and you welcomed me, I was naked and you clothed me, I was sick and you visited me, I was in prison and you came to me.' Then the righteous will answer him, saying 'Lord, when …?' "

If giving his life were not enough, Harry's "saving-people thing" never long withstands watching a fellow creature suffer; he consistently offers assistance, help and hope to friends and strangers and the unlovable and even his enemies. As the King answers the righteous, "'Truly, I say to you, as you did it to one of the least of these my brothers, you did it to me.'" (Matt 25.39)

IV. Dobby and Christian Love

> Now it is by faith that the intellect apprehends the object
> of hope and love. Hence in the order of generation,
> faith precedes hope and charity.... Now from the very
> fact that a man hopes to be able to obtain some good
> through someone, he looks on the man in whom he
> hopes as a good of his own. Hence for the very reason
> that a man hopes in someone, he proceeds to love him:
> so that in the order of generation, hope precedes charity
> as regards their respective acts. (Summa Theologica 1a
> 2ae, Question 62, art. 4)

While none of the characters in the Potter books admit
onstage to a love for God himself, for Dobby the house-elf,
Harry Potter might as well be God.

Dobby's first noisy and humorous appearance in Harry's
story shows an alternately determined and terrified creature,
unused to any sort of kind treatment, who knows he is bound
to serve the wicked Malfoy family for life. Despite feeling the
need to inflict terrible punishments on himself, Dobby keeps
trying to save Harry's life, and Harry manages to see past the
elf's misguided deeds to his motives. Eventually, Harry tricks
Lucius Malfoy into freeing Dobby, saving the elf from Malfoy's
brutality as well as his unfair terms of service. Dobby becomes
to Harry a servant more loyal in his freedom than he ever was
to the Malfoys in slavery.

A servant bound in the power of evil turns to a
personification of Love and is set free, becoming the loyal and
willing servant of Good. This is clear symbolism, and though
Harry does not sacrifice himself for Dobby, the fact that he frees
the elf by means of practicing deception on Lucius Malfoy—
whose first name draws a connection to Lucifer and whose last
is basically French (mal foi) for bad faith—works parallel to an
ancient theological idea that considered Christ's redemptive
work as tricking the devil out of his rights over humanity. The
fourth-century bishop Gregory of Nyssa treats Christ's divinity,

hidden under the guise of a human nature, as bait and hook:

> For since, as has been said before, it was not in the nature of the opposing power to come in contact with the undiluted presence of God, and to undergo His unclouded manifestation, therefore, in order to secure that the ransom in our behalf might be easily accepted by him who required it, the Deity was hidden under the veil of our nature, that so, as with ravenous fish, the hook of the Deity might be gulped down along with the bait of flesh, and thus, life being introduced into the house of death, and light shining in darkness, that which is diametrically opposed to light and life might vanish; for it is not in the nature of darkness to remain when light is present, or of death to exist when life is active. (Great Catechism Chapter XXIV)

Lewis makes use of the same basic idea in The Lion, The Witch and The Wardrobe, accomplishing Aslan's redemption of Edmund through the White Witch's limited knowledge: she knows magic only as far back as the dawn of Time. Aslan puts his life in the power of a magic set in motion before the dawn of Time; he resurrects, Edmund is free, and another evil slave-master is tricked out of her prey. Rowling has stated on numerous occasions that she admires at least the first Narnia books[3]; it is not surprising that she would use a similar idea in her own work.

Dobby's entire way of relating to Harry is worshipful. "Dobby has heard of your greatness, sir, but of your goodness, Dobby never knew" (Chamber 15). He looks at Harry adoringly, grateful for the slightest kindness, even before Harry achieves his freedom; when he returns as a free elf in Goblet of Fire and later books, he throws himself into helping Harry with utter

---

3   For example, in an interview "The Golden Fairytale" with Sally Blakeney, *The Australian*, 7 November 1998; with Helena de Bertodano, "Harry Potter Charms a Nation", *The Electronic Telegraph*, 25 July 1998. Sources courtesy of www. accio-quote.org.

joy. But perhaps the most poignant sign of this comes as he dies after rescuing Harry and the other captives from Malfoy Manor, the site of his own former captivity: his last words, looking into the eyes of his savior, are simply "Harry Potter."

From the moment of Dobby's original freedom, his life is oriented toward Harry. The dirty sock Harry tricked Lucius into throwing to Dobby becomes a symbol to the elf, and "Socks are Dobby's favorite, favorite clothes!" (Goblet 409) In life and in death, his greatest joy is doing anything for Harry, his greatest pride in having that service asked of him. He values the gift of freedom Harry gave and refuses to submit again to slavery, hunting two years for paid work until finding it at last from Dumbledore and Hogwarts.

These are the responses of a devout to his god, and as such provide a beautiful symbolic portrayal of charity in its full theological sense.

V. Snape, Dumbledore, and Redeeming Love

[E]very day I expect to discover fresh flaws in myself.…

I remember that 'charity covereth a multitude of sins' and … I cry with David: "I have run the way of Thy commandments when Thou didst enlarge my heart." Charity alone can enlarge my heart. (Thérèse of Lisieux 129)

As sin, in Christian thought, works against charity in the heart of a person, charity works consistently toward the redemption and transformation of those who find and attempt it. *The Catechism of the Catholic Church* puts it thus:

The practice of all the virtues is animated and inspired by charity… Charity upholds and purifies our human ability to love, and raises it to the supernatural perfection of divine love. (par. 1827)

Two conflicted and enigmatic characters in Harry's world, each having failed dramatically in the area of human love, face the necessity of changing who they are by making a choice to reach for a higher love than either has yet achieved at their crux moment. Fans, divided by adoration and condemnation, have long been fascinated by Snape and Dumbledore.

VI. The Redemption of Severus Snape

Almost until the moment of his death, Snape could present an image of what charity is not. His long-lived passion for Lily Evans neither turns him from the Death Eaters when his beloved begins to question the nature of his friendships, nor gives him forgiveness toward James (charity, and only charity, could have done that), nor provides him with the fortitude to be kind to Lily's son even as he protects Harry's life. He has a strong natural love for her, but it is not charity.

Not, at least, at first. Under the influence of Albus Dumbledore, and faced with the test of showing love toward what he hates, he begins to re-learn what it means to love and be loved. He is torn between despising Harry—the son of his enemy with his loved one—and the will to care for him for Lily's sake; the latter, with Dumbledore's guidance, brings him to act in charity. He does so inconsistently, imperfectly, and sometimes only when it matters most, but he does so.

Snape essayist Logospilgrim writes extensively on the topic of the Potions Master's goodness:

> I would suggest that Snape's sanctity resides in his steadfastness, in his dutifully standing firm to the end and in his self-denial: therein lies his love. It is not perfect, but it is still love. ("What is Despised, God has Chosen")

Again:

> Snape is not good, in the same sense that no one is good. Yet everyone is capable of imitating Christ. Everyone can be like Christ. Everyone can be worthy in Christ. Everyone is called to be part of the royal priesthood. We simply must make the right choice. ("Professor Snape and the Eucharist")

The end of Professor Snape's life seems odd and ambiguous; he dies expecting Harry to join him any time, obeying Dumbledore's orders despite their strange and seemingly wrong nature, having only the strength to look into Harry's eyes one last time. Those eyes gave him a look into the heart of the woman he loved, and from that last act, John Granger makes the argument that Severus found redemption. After discussing the parallels between Snape and Dante, who found both human and divine love through a green-eyed girl, Granger says:

> Dante's love for Beatrice was a beginning love that grew into a spiritual vision of Love Himself.... Severus' childhood love for Lily, a marker of which lives in the eyes of her son, has grown, through courageous self-sacrifice and love of his enemy, to become his encounter with Christ in the figure of Harry and Lily's eyes, at his death. Seemingly destroyed by the serpent of his Slytherin nature, he embraces and sees at his death his Golden Griffin reward for his heroic life. (*Lectures* 145)

Logospilgrim has another interesting point about the Potions master's role in Harry's life:

> Harry will defeat Voldemort with the power that the Dark Lord knows not. But love requires trust. As long as Harry cannot bring himself to trust the one his mentor has always trusted, he does not completely possess that power stronger than fear and death. Snape's role in the books is to teach Harry about the nature of trust. The moment Harry begins to consider the possibility that Snape may in fact be good, when the one thing he has always been sure of suddenly becomes doubtful, when he experiences metanoia, "changes his mind and turns around," then he will be ready to trust Dumbledore... Trust Snape, despite his flaws... And not be surprised that "only love" will destroy Voldemort, who cannot trust anyone. Trust is the key to the power of Love. Hence Snape is the key to Voldemort's defeat. ("Snape is Not Ambiguous")

The presence of Severus Snape at Hogwarts forces Harry to learn to trust; much like Harry, however, even Snape apparently found it difficult to trust Dumbledore in the last two years of his own life. Give over the hope of protecting Harry for Lily's sake? Allow Harry to sacrifice himself to Voldemort? Protect Draco Malfoy by committing an act of murder for him? While that last is certainly morally questionable for both Snape and Dumbledore, in Snape's memories we see him acting over and over again in faithfulness to Dumbledore's plan, against his own feelings, even submitting his judgment to the knowledge of a greater understanding than his own. Snape lives and dies a difficult, harsh man, but his final choices are clear, and he dies firmly on the side of good.

If love is the only way to defeat Voldemort, Snape may have little to offer in comparison with Harry, Hermione, the Weasleys, Dobby, and many others from Hogwarts and the Order of the Phoenix. He offers, however, all the love he has, and it is enough.

The Transformation of Albus Dumbledore

Jesus answered him, "Simon, I have something to tell you."

"Tell me, teacher," he said.

"Two men owed money to a certain moneylender. One owed him five hundred denarii, and the other fifty. Neither of them had the money to pay him back, so he canceled the debts of both. Now which of them will love him more?"

Simon replied, "I suppose the one who had the bigger debt canceled."

"You have judged correctly," Jesus said. (Luke 7.40-43)

"[Dumbledore] changed, Harry, he changed! It's as simple as that!" (*Hallows* 361)

In Harry Potter and Imagination, Travis Prinzi devotes a chapter to the explanation of Dumbledore's commitment to the principles of love, a commitment that would have required no defense to anyone until the release of Rita Skeeter's The Life and Lies of Albus Dumbledore. Despite many post-Rita detractors, both fictional and real, it is arguable that though Harry's example was the purest, no one in the series understood love better than Harry's mentor.

> Voldemort thought it was a magical device he needed— Lily's blood. Instead, it was love itself. Dumbledore knew this, and it was his highest priority to teach Harry that. Ultimately, he taught Harry this by example… (Prinzi 181)

For both Harry Potter and Severus Snape, Professor Dumbledore acts as something of a spiritual leader. He guides each of them in the direction of love, trust, and what might even be called salvation, teaching them to surrender their faulty wills to a higher law.

His ability to teach this well comes not because he has lived out the ways of love perfectly himself, but because he has made a great failure. His own misplaced, even idolatrous confidence in Gellert Grindelwald and supremacist ideology led to the loss of his sister's life. No one in the Harry Potter series learns love the hard way more shockingly and terribly than Albus Dumbledore.

Throughout his lifetime and even in his own death he continues to learn, sometimes through mistakes; as he says to Harry after Sirius' death, "I cared about you too much … I cared more for your happiness than your knowing the truth … more for your life than the lives that might be lost" (Order 838). Later, he asks a service of Snape that would certainly be considered by all orthodox Christianity as an act outside of God-inspired charity. The trajectory of his life, however, moves toward love.

The Dumbledore who saw the remnant of his own family go to pieces because of his selfishness is the Dumbledore who stands over a grieving Death Eater and gives him the one choice that might possibly lead to his redemption. "If you loved

Lily Evans, if you truly loved her, then your way forward is clear" he says (Hallows 678), and Severus takes the offered task.

The Dumbledore whose failure to love cost his sister's life and his brother's respect is the Dumbledore who recognizes the effective strength of Lily's sacrifice and acts upon it for Harry's safety, who teaches Harry very carefully of the "power the Dark Lord knows not" and encourages him over and over again in the exercise of that power.

The Dumbledore repentant of the ideas and associations which would have led him to the destruction of many lives is the Dumbledore who gave wages and holidays and free speech to a house-elf, who could be compassionate to a Muggle child wanting entrance to Hogwarts (and welcomed to the school a werewolf both as student and teacher). He also saw the lack of charity when the young Tom Riddle's charisma blinded nearly everyone else, and through kind firmness offered him the chance to change. Prinzi again:

> [H]e does not shun the "diseased others." Who but Dumbledore would have the mercy to forgive Severus Snape and take him on as a confidante?... would have actually clapped, out of courtesy and respect, at the end of Dolores Umbridge's speech in Order, and then after all she did throughout the year, march into the forest to rescue her from the centaurs? Who but Dumbledore would think it appropriate to show manners to Death Eaters, standing before him on the tower, mocking him? (Prinzi 187)

Dumbledore has often been accused of Machiavellian behavior toward Harry, but in the spiritual sense, his plan is charitable. He knows love, and he knows what love will require of Harry Potter. Harry may die at the hands of Voldemort and Dumbledore has to take that risk, but Harry's soul is at stake, with part of Voldemort's soul attached and growing in the ability to manipulate Harry's emotions and actions. While love took Harry to save Sirius (Order 844), Harry's misinterpretation of his dream cost Sirius' life; who is to say that years of continuing under the influence of the evil wizard, even if the rest of Tom

Riddle were destroyed, would not have eventually warped and perverted Harry's ability to love? Dumbledore knew that influence had strengthened with time, as he explains to Snape:

> Part of Lord Voldemort lives inside Harry, and it is that which gives him the power of speech with snakes, and a connection with Lord Voldemort's mind that he has never understood.... Meanwhile, the connection between them grows ever stronger, a parasitic growth (*Hallows* 686-7)

A little later, in the King's Cross chapter, Harry asks if that part of Voldemort's soul is gone. Dumbledore says "Yes, he destroyed it. Your soul is whole, and completely your own, Harry." (Hallows 708) The act of self-sacrifice that Dumbledore eventually asked of Harry, far from being the surety of death, is Harry's only hope for spiritual freedom.

Albus' own repentance and journey into charity began with the biblical words he placed on his mother's and sister's tombstone. That verse appears in its Scriptural context as shown:

> Do not lay up for yourselves treasures on earth, where moth and rust destroy and where thieves break in and steal, but lay up for yourselves treasures in heaven, where neither moth nor rust destroys and where thieves do not break in and steal. For where your treasure is, there your heart will be also. (*Matt* 6.19-21)

The treasures Albus sought with Gellert were not so much matters of wealth as of fame and accolade, but he sought the Hallows to provide him with the freedom to pursue earthly glory. His choice of that verse as a sign of his remorse toward Ariana is an expression of a major shift in his values. The grandeur of the world will no longer be his goal. Henceforth, what he loves most is hidden in the life beyond death.

This, combined with his intimate understanding of the power of life-offering love, is highly suggestive of some level of faith in Christ. Dumbledore never preaches an overt sermon, never even mentions God in our hearing; the great alchemist, though, the wise old man who understood his own strengths and weaknesses as well as others', the coach to Harry and Severus in matters of pure and faithful love, may yet have held a measure of belief in his heart. He may be a universalist; he may be something of an agnostic; we're given no outright information, just the subtle words and actions of a man familiar with Scripture, repentant of his past sins, transformed by and devoted to love—and the human expressions of that love appear very much like that which results from true charity.

He has learned, as St. Thérèse says, that though the great deeds he once dreamed of are forbidden him, "even all the most perfect gifts are nothing without love" and quite possibly that "charity is the most excellent way of going safely to God." (Thérèse of Lisieux 161)

His worship, if he makes any, is accomplished offstage; his pursuit of love, however, is not unlike that of the woman whose guilt led her to lavish her repentance in perfume on the feet of Love Himself:

> Then [Jesus] turned toward the woman and said to Simon, "Do you see this woman? I came into your house. You did not give me any water for my feet, but she wet my feet with her tears and wiped them with her hair. You did not give me a kiss, but this woman, from the time I entered, has not stopped kissing my feet. You did not put oil on my head, but she has poured perfume on my feet. Therefore, I tell you, her many sins have been forgiven—for she loved much." (*Luke* 7.44-47)

Conclusion: Rowling, Her Characters, and Charity

> The unbreakable bond between love of God and love of neighbour is emphasized. One is so closely connected to the other that to say that we love God becomes a lie if we are closed to our neighbour or hate him altogether… [L]ove of neighbour is a path that leads to the encounter with God, and … closing our eyes to our neighbour also blinds us to God. (Benedict XVI, *Deus Caritas Est* 16)

The issue of author intent is always raised in a study of this sort. Did Rowling think of love in the theological sense when she wrote the tale? To that sort of question, another usually responds "Does that really matter?" and the conversation proceeds to the affirmatives, the negatives and the maybes.

While Rowling alone can answer for her own choices, John Granger defends the likelihood of her conscious or subconscious weaving of her stories upon a warp of traditional philosophical and theological ideas: "Her books reflect an understanding of the truths of Plato, Aristotle, Augustine, and Aquinas because she has read these greats—and read them as attentively as reading them in the original languages requires." (*Looking* xvi)

While the thought that her knowledge and probable assent to at least some parts of historical Christian understanding would support the case, either way, in Western culture it is impossible that English-language books written so obviously in the tradition of Shakespeare, Austen, Dickens and the Inklings should not be interpreted in relation to Christian thought.

Through the concept of sacrifice and the emphasis on loving the outcasts and the unlovable, even the enemy, Rowling's work provides an ideal of love at least parallel to the human display of charity. Through characters acting in Christlike self-giving, her story exemplifies an orientation toward the ultimate act of charity shown by God incarnate. Finally, through the symbolism provided by Dobby's relationship to Harry and through a possible faith held by Albus Dumbledore, charity makes its final connection in a God-inspired, God-directed love.

In the end, of course, as Travis Prinzi says, "Love remains a mystery, and that's as it should be.... Love is a room in the Department of Mysteries. But in everyday life, it is worked out through grief, pain, suffering, tears, turning to hope, joy, faith, and courage" (180). Love resists the attempt to define and formulate, expressing itself in a number o actions and ideas that all point in the same direction. God, too, is a Mystery. Love points to God, and God is Love.

Works Cited

Unless otherwise indicated, Scripture quotations are from The Holy Bible, English Standard Version®, copyright © 2001 by Crossway Bibles, a division of Good News Publishers. Used by permission. All rights reserved.

Alighieri, Dante. Purgatorio. Trans. Anthony Esolen. New York: Random House. 2003. Print.

Benedict XVI, encyclical, Deus Caritas Est. Vatican City: Libreria Editrice Vaticana, 2005. Web. 27 May 2010. <http://www.vatican.va/holy_father/benedict_xvi/encyc-licals/documents/hf_ben-xvi_enc_20051225_deus-cari-tas-est_en.html>.

Catechism of the Catholic Church. New York: Doubleday, 1995. Print.

Granger, John. The Deathly Hallows Lectures. Allentown, PA: Zossima Press, 2008. Print.

Granger, John. Looking for God in Harry Potter. N.p.: Tyndale, 2006. Print.

Gregory of Nyssa. The Great Catechism. Trans. William Moore and Henry Austin Wilson. Nicene and Post-Nicene Fathers, Series II. Eds. Philip Schaff and Henry Wace. Vol. 5. Christian Classics Ethereal Library. Web. 25 May 2010. <http://www.ccel.org/ccel/schaff/npnf205.xi.ii.xxvi.html>.

Lewis, C.S. The Four Loves. New York: Harcourt, Brace, 1960. Print.

Logospilgrim. "Professor Snape and the Eucharist: on the importance of Christian sacrifice in J.K. Rowling's work." Web. 18 May 2010. <http://logospilgrim.livejournal.com/222047.html>.

_____. "Snape is not ambiguous." Web. 18 May 2010. <http://logospilgrim.livejournal.com/109854.html>.

_____. "What is despised, God has chosen: Severus Snape as a divine instrument." Web. 18 May 2010. <http://logospilgrim.livejournal.com/167174.html>.

Rowling, J.K. Harry Potter and the Chamber of Secrets. New York: Scholastic, 1999. Print.

_____. Harry Potter and the Deathly Hallows. New York: Scholastic, 2007. Print.

_____. Harry Potter and the Goblet of Fire. New York: Scholastic, 2000. Print.

_____. Harry Potter and the Half-Blood Prince. New York: Scholastic, 2005. Print.

_____. Harry Potter and the Order of the Phoenix. New York: Scholastic, 2003. Print.

_____. Harry Potter and the Sorcerer's Stone. New York: Scholastic, 1998. Print.

_____. Harry Potter and the Prisoner of Azkaban. New York: Scholastic, 1999. Print.

_____. Interview with Lindsey Fraser and audience at the Edinburgh Book Festival. Web. 16 May 2010. <http://www.jkrowling.com/textonly/en/news_view.cfm?id=80>.

_____. Interview with Melissa Anelli and Emerson Spartz. Web. 16 May 2010. <http://www.accio-quote.org/articles/2005/0705-tlc_mugglenet-anelli-2.htm>.

Ryan, John Augustine. "Charity and Charities." The Catholic Encyclopedia. Vol. 3. New York: Robert Appleton Company, 1908. Web. 26 May 2010. <http://www.newadvent.org/cathen/03592a.htm>.

Sollier, Joseph. "Love (Theological Virtue)." The Catholic Encyclopedia. Vol. 9. New York: Robert Appleton Company, 1910. Web. 26 May 2010. <http://www.newadvent.org/cathen/09397a.htm>.

Thérèse of Lisieux. The Story of a Soul. Trans. John Beevers. New York: Doubleday, 1957.

Thomas Aquinas. Summa Theologica. Trans. Fathers of the English Dominican Province. New York: Benzinger Bros, 1948. Print.

Meet the Nerds

Travis Prinzi is the author of *Harry Potter and Imagination: The Way Between Two Worlds* (Zossima 2008) and editor of *Hog's Head Conversations: Essays on Harry Potter* (Zossima 2009). A regular Featured Presenter at Harry Potter conferences, he blogs at TheHogsHead.org and runs The Hog's Head PubCast on FarPoint Media. Travis holds graduate degrees in education and theology from the University of Rochester and Northeastern Seminary. He lives in Geneseo, NY with his wife Tricia, daughter Sophia, son Jack, and their dog, Moses.

Sandra Miesel holds an M.S. in biochemistry and an M.A. in medieval history from the University of Illinois at Urbana-Champaign. In 1967, she began analyzing speculative fiction for fun and soon afterwards for profit. She has also occasionally written and edited sf. Her novels are *Dreamrider* (Ace Books, 1982) and *Shaman* (Baen Books, 1989). Since 1983, she has contributed more than 400 articles to the Catholic press, often on history, hagiography, or art. She is the co-author with Carl E. Olson of *The Da Vinci Hoax* (Ignatius Press, 2004) and with Peter Vere of *Pied Piper of Atheism: Philip Pullman and Children's Fantasy* (Ignatius Press, 2008). With Paul E. Kerry, she co-edited an anthology of criticism, *Light beyond All Shadow: Religious Experience in the Work of J. R. R. Tolkien* (Fairleigh-Dickinson UP, forthcoming). Miesel has spoken at religious and academic conferences, appeared in several video documentaries, and given numerous media interviews.

J. Steve Lee - A true professor of defending against the dark arts, Steve has taught philosophy and theology at Prestonwood Christian Academy in Plano, Texas since 1998 as well as having taught philosophy and world religions at Mountain View College in Dallas, TX. With a degree in history and education from the University of North Texas, Steve continued his education at Southwestern Baptist Theological Seminary with a M.A. in philosophy of religion and is pursuing a doctorate at the University of Texas at Dallas in the history of ideas. He continues to be involved in defending divine discourse in public speaking ranging from civic groups, churches, and professioanl development as well as writing book reviews for professional philosophy journals and articles for the *Apologetics Study Bible for Students* (B&H Publishing, 2010).

John Granger, the "Dean of Harry Potter Scholars" according to TIME's Lev Grossman, is the author of *The Deathly Hallows Lectures* and *The Ultimate Unlocking Harry Potter: Seven Keys for the Serious Reader*. He blogs at HogwartsProfessor.com, speaks at universities, schools, churches, and libraries, and lives with his wife and family in Oklahoma City.

James W. Thomas is Professor of English at Pepperdine University, where he has taught since 1981. He is the author of *Repotting Harry Potter: A Professor's Book-by-Book Guide for the Serious Re-Reader*, (Zossima 2009) and *Rowling Revisited: Return Trips to Harry, Fantastic Beasts, Quidditch & Beedle the Bard* (Zossima 2010). He and his wife Kanet live in Westlake Village, California, and have three children and four grandchildren.

Joel Hunter joined the faculty of Barrett Honors College at Arizona State University in 2008. His regular teaching duties include an interdisciplinary Socratic seminar of the world's greatest literature. He is also the faculty sponsor of the university's Harry Potter Society and in 2011 is teaching the College's first seminar on Harry Potter. Joel earned his Bachelor's degree in electrical engineering from Georgia Tech and worked for several years as an environmental consultant designing and building systems to clean up polluted soil and water. He completed his PhD in philosophy from the University of Kentucky in 2008. His teaching and research interests include the philosophies of technology, science and religion. He sojourns with his wife and three children on the lands of the Akimel Au-Authm and Piipaash.

Kathleen Langr is a student of linguistics whose research focuses on insult and swearing in the English language. She recently graduated from Arizona State University with a

B.A. in English Linguistics and will be joining the University of Washington graduate theoretical linguistics program in September of 2011. Kathleen's undergraduate thesis, *You Just Got Served: A Basic Guide to Modern American Insult*, serves as a manual of American insult for foreign students of English. She presented an overview of Rowling's wizarding insult system at Infinitus 2010 and her past work with *Harry Potter* includes the creation of a vocabulary unit for high school students based on Greek and Latin roots found in the series' nomenclature.

A devoted Ravenclaw, **Priscilla Hobbs** is a doctoral student at Pacifica Graduate Institute, where she is writing her dissertation on Disneyland and American mythology. She has presented at several Harry Potter conventions over topics ranging from the Hero's Journey to the new theme park, and is - slowly but surely - writing a book about Harry Potter and mythology. In her spare time, she teaches Humanities in Austin, Texas.

Erin Sweeney is a yoga teacher and a science fantasy writer; she is also studying to become a physical therapist. She has authored five and co-authored two online Harry Potter essays at www.scribbulus.com under the pen names Caltheous, Roseanne Roseannadanna, Dr. Rip VanHinklemeyer, and Callinawkes. Erin is also an essay editor for the Scribbulus essay project. Her favorite fantasy concepts are transcendence, the chosen one, and prophecy and she likes to debate time theory into the wee hours of the night. She spends any remaining free time chasing tarot cards in the wind and wondering why all clouds look like characters out of Harry Potter. You can find out more about her by visiting her websites: www.GreenPhoenixYoga.com and www.CaltheousIsland.com.

Lancelot Schaubert graduated from Ozark Christian College in Joplin, MO with a Bachelor in Christian Ministry in 2009. He's pursuing their five-year Bachelor in Theology this year, hoping to move toward a masters in Literature or Creative Writing, and a PhD in the Bible and Literature. Lance hosts a blog titled "Literating", and writes fiction. His wand's three inches of mahogany with a Pegasus-feather core.

Elizabeth Baird Hardy, author of *Milton, Spenser, and the Chronicles of Narnia: Literary Sources for the C.S. Lewis Novels* (McFarland 2007), is a senior instructor of English at Mayland Community College, where she was the 2006 Outstanding Faculty Member, having never turned any students into ferrets. She is also a proud faculty member at the Hogwarts Professor blog and has presented at national literary conferences including the Mythopoeic Society Conference, C.S. Lewis the Man and his Work Conference, the Carolina Mountains Literary Festival, the Witching Hour, and Infinitus. A contributor to projects as diverse as *The Encyclopedia of Appalachia* and *Twilight and History* (Wiley 2010), she is an active scholar who collaborates with other writers, particularly her husband, award-winning historian Michael C. Hardy. They live with their children on a North Carolina mountain which can primarily be accessed via portkey.

John Patrick Pazdziora is a freelance writer and editor. He holds a BA from the Moody Bible Institute, Chicago, and a PGDip (Hons) in Theological Studies from Belfast Bible College. Currently, he is a doctoral candidate at the University of St Andrews, working on a dissertation provisionally entitled 'George MacDonald's Romantic Iconography of Death in his Writings for Children.' His short story "Ragabone" appeared in *New Fairy Tales* (Issue 5). He hosts the literary blog The Paradoxes of Mr Pond, serves on the editorial panel for The Hog's Head, and is the copy editor for *StreetWise Magazine*. John lives in Scotland with his wife and daughter, where he changes diapers.

Jenna St. Hilaire writes mythic fiction and songs as well as essays, various blogstuff, and the occasional poem. Her work has appeared in sundry corners of the world wide web and she is a member of the Blogengamot at The Hog's Head. She lives in the Pacific Northwest with her husband and a lot of houseplants and books.

Lightning Source UK Ltd.
Milton Keynes UK
UKOW02f2359141116
287663UK00001B/211/P

9 780982 963326